UndocuAsians

UndocuAsians

Lived Experiences and Social Movement Activism Across the Diaspora

Edited by
Kevin Escudero and
Rachel Freeman-Wong

Foreword by Ju Hong

R

RUTGERS UNIVERSITY PRESS

NEW BRUNSWICK, CAMDEN, AND NEWARK, NEW JERSEY

LONDON AND OXFORD

Rutgers University Press is a department of Rutgers, The State University of New Jersey, one of the leading public research universities in the nation. By publishing worldwide, it furthers the University's mission of dedication to excellence in teaching, scholarship, research, and clinical care.

978-1-9788-2026-5 (cloth)

978-1-9788-2025-8 (paper)

978-1-9788-2027-2 (epub)

Cataloging-in-publication data is available from the Library of Congress.
LCCN 2025019428

A British Cataloging-in-Publication record for this book is available from the British Library.

rutgersuniversitypress.org

For all those who organize to ensure a more just present and future, thank you.

CONTENTS

PART THREE

Family, Faith, and Navigating Higher
Education in the United States

PART FOUR

Mental Health, Activism, and
Community Healing

FOREWORD

JU HONG

UndocuAsians consists of narratives of research and activism by powerful
Asian undocumented immigrant leaders and allies, many of whom I have
had the honor of meeting during my involvement in the U.S. immigrant
rights movement over the past fifteen years. Each person has a unique journey and yet shares common struggles as undocumented immigrants in this
country.

Asians / Asian Americans are the fastest growing immigrant population in
the United States (Budiman and Ruiz 2021). While immigrants are often thought
of in the mainstream imaginary as primarily Latinx, of the approximately
eleven million undocumented immigrants, almost two million are Asian (Millet 2022). In fact, the federal Development, Relief, and Education for Alien
Minors (DREAM) Act was inspired by a Korean immigrant, Tereza Lee, whose
allies reached out to Senator Dick Durbin of Illinois when she was accepted to
the prestigious Juilliard University music program but could not afford to
attend because of her undocumented immigration status. When I first started
sharing my own personal immigration story in 2009, I had heard of only a
handful of Asian immigrant rights activists. For instance, I recall Tam Ngoc
Tran, Prerna Lal, and Mohammad Abdollahi, just to name a few, whom I read
about in newspapers and on social media, watched on television, and eventually met some of them in person.

Now, I have met hundreds of Asian undocumented immigrants across the
country. Some are activists who are now married and have kids, while others
have unfortunately been separated from their families and loved ones. Some
have adjusted their immigration status through various means, while others
continue to fight to adjust their status, and some have decided to leave the
United States. In *UndocuAsians*, you will read stories of some of the incredible
Asian undocumented immigrant leaders from all walks of life. These individuals are among the many people I have met through activism, and I hope these
unique stories teach you something new and inspire you to take action on
immigration.

The Ongoing Uncertainty of the Current U.S. Immigrant Rights Political Landscape

On June 15, 2024, we celebrated the twelfth anniversary of the Deferred Action for Childhood Arrivals (DACA) program and honored the undocumented immigrant youth who fought for and won this critical program that has provided relief to nearly 800,000 undocumented young people who came to the United States as children (Krogstad 2017).

The DACA program, however, also faces legal challenges, and a growing number of immigrant youth are ineligible for temporary relief from deportation and access to work permits that the program offers due to arbitrary requirements and legislative holdups. This also presents a stark reminder that DACA is a vulnerable, temporary program with limitations.

While the DACA program continues to be litigated in the courts, members of Congress have yet to fulfill their promise to secure a permanent solution for millions of undocumented immigrant community members. Anti-immigrant legislation is being introduced nationally and in various states, while anti-immigrant rhetoric and false narratives are spreading across the country, instilling fear and dehumanizing the immigrant community nationwide. As a result, the stories in this volume and the strength that they demonstrate are needed now more than ever.

My Journey

The challenges facing undocumented immigrants are not just news headlines; they reflect the daily, lived experiences for many of the contributing authors to the *UndocuAsians* edited volume and for myself.

My awareness of my immigration status came about during high school, as my single-parent immigrant mother had kept it a secret until I discovered it on my own. At first, I did not know what it meant to be undocumented, until I realized that I was not able to get a job, obtain a driver's license, or receive financial aid to attend college. Worst of all, I was at risk of being deported back to my home country of South Korea.

Knowing that I had limited opportunities in the United States due to my immigration status, I felt discouraged from continuing to pursue higher education. But I remembered how my mother sacrificed to support my education, so I reaffirmed my dream of attending college.

I was able to enroll at Laney College in Oakland, under California's Assembly Bill 540 (AB 540), which allows undocumented students and certain other qualifying individuals to attend public universities in California and pay in-state tuition rates. Once I learned more about AB 540 and the federal DREAM Act, I became hopeful and more motivated to continue to pursue higher education.

Laney College

As I learned more about the rights of undocumented immigrants in the United States, I also discovered and learned more about the stories of other undocumented students. One of the first undocumented students I heard about was Tam Ngoc Tran, an undocumented Vietnamese filmmaker and part of one of the first groups of undocumented students to graduate from college and enter graduate school. Tragically, in 2010 she, along with another undocumented organizer, Cinthya Felix, was killed in a car accident caused by a drunk driver. Tam Ngoc Tran's spirit and legacy still live on as she made a huge impact in the immigrant youth movement. I became inspired when I saw other students risking their lives to share their testimonies about their immigration status. That is when I decided that I wanted to be active in a community and to let my voice be heard.

At Laney College, I immersed myself in student government and engaged in the immigrant rights movement through work with nonprofit organizations. I was elected as the first Asian and youngest student body president, advocating for the rights of undocumented students on campus.

Around that time, I recall traveling from Oakland, CA, to Washington, D.C., by Amtrak and driving a van from Los Angeles, CA, to D.C. to participate in various immigration rallies. I also connected with fellow undocumented immigrant youth online and in person, participating in local protests and organizing events together. More and more, I felt a sense of belonging in immigrant rights organizing spaces and became comfortable, and confident, in my identity as an immigrant rights activist.

UC Berkeley

After transferring from Laney College to the University of California, Berkeley (UC Berkeley), I continued my activism, openly identifying as an undocumented immigrant. I ran for the student body senate on a platform of advocating for immigrant rights issues. I was actively involved in the Rising Immigrant Scholars Through Education (RISE) student group, connecting and collaborating with other undocumented rights activists. The RISE student organization was where I felt accepted as who I was and surrounded by people who understood my struggles and shared visions for a collective future. Despite the challenges I faced on and off campus, being in community with fellow undocumented student leaders, I found joy and made unforgettable memories, and together we left a legacy.

San Francisco State University

Upon graduating from UC Berkeley, I decided to immediately pursue a master's degree in public administration at San Francisco State University. With this degree, I aimed to become a public administrator in a nonprofit organization dedicated to immigrant rights. Yet throughout my academic journey I have remained engaged in the immigrant rights movement, transitioning from direct organizing to policy advocacy and program management. As a first-generation immigrant who grew up in a single-parent household, my completion of a master's degree was a huge milestone. Pursuing higher education was a means to inspire my family and others, showing what is possible despite one's immigration status.

Emerging Leaders

It has been fifteen years since I initially became involved in the immigrant rights movement. We have made significant strides advancing the immigrant rights agenda. At the same time, there is still much more work to be done and many challenges ahead. Despite these ongoing challenges, witnessing emerging undocumented youth organizers carrying the legacy of the immigrant rights activists who paved the way before us fills me with hope for the future of the movement.

Final Thoughts

The chapters and stories in this collection, while unable to capture the full breadth of undocumented immigrant experiences in this country, serve as an important example of the immense power of undocumented youth and, more specifically, the role of Asian undocumented youth in the immigrant rights movement. Asian undocumented immigrant stories often go unnoticed within the immigrant community, and this publication sheds light on these critical narratives. I hope that this book inspires others and contributes to the larger movement of those advocating for the rights of the immigrant community.

REFERENCES

Budiman, Abby, and Neil Ruiz. 2021. "Asian Americans Are the Fastest-Growing Racial or Ethnic Group in the U.S. Pew Research Center, April. https://www.pewresearch.org/short-reads/2021/04/09/asian-americans-are-the-fastest-growing-racial-or-ethnic-group-in-the-u-s/.

Krogstad, Jens Manuel. 2017. "DACA Has Shielded Nearly 790,000 Young Unauthorized Immigrants from Deportation." Pew Research Center, September. https://www.pewresearch.org/short-reads/2017/09/01/unauthorized-immigrants-covered-by-daca-face-uncertain-future/.

Millet, Evin. 2022. "A Demographic Profile of Undocumented Immigrants from Asia and the Pacific Islands." Center for Migration Studies, June. https://cmsny.org/undocumented-aapi-millet-061322/.

"IT'S OKAY"

BO THAI

It's okay

Even though it seems like things may have not change

It's okay

Even though you haven't made it home yet

I know you got regrets from fumbling your blessings

You couldn't be where you have not been

And you couldn't feel what you have not feel

I don't blame you

That's why it's call a journey

hurt and pain

They became your friends

They became your purpose

But life is more than just fighting and healing

more than just making it and running away from it all

It's the pause and the meanwhile too

It's the I don't know what I'm doing

and it is what it is too

Just love yourself a little more

You don't got to prove nothing

You can just be

As you are

where you at

And move at your pace

Love will come and so do blessings

You're not gonna run this time

and you'll be there

Ready to live and ready to receive

You're home now

With you and the people you love

You can stay and you can feel now

All the emotions you haven't felt

And all the things was too much to feel

It's all within you

You don't gotta be scared now

You don't gotta carry that weight no more

You can just live now

And I accept of you for everything you've been through

And I forgive you for all the things you've done

And I'll love you til the end of things

It's okay

You're okay

UndocuAsians

Introduction

KEVIN ESCUDERO
RACHEL FREEMAN-WONG

Set Hernandez is an undocumented immigrant filmmaker and community organizer with roots in Bicol in the Philippines. Set recently produced a film about an aspiring social worker who is both undocumented and blind and, in an interview with "Democracy Now," posed the following questions: "How can we reclaim the narrative [about undocumented immigrants] for ourselves instead of further uplifting the perspectives that politicians have about our community? How can we really lean on each other and amplify [our] voices and the ways that we understand our lives and the world?" Heeding Set's and others' calls for directly impacted community members to lead the development of the narratives about their own communities, *UndocuAsians: Social Movement Activism and Lived Experiences Across the Diaspora* weaves together academic research and activist narratives to shed light on the plight of Asian undocumented immigrants in the United States today.

Research on Asian undocumented immigrants has often considered the experiences of this community in relation to those of Latinx immigrants who constitute the largest group of undocumented immigrants in the United States (Cho 2019; Enriquez 2019; Escudero 2020; Patler 2014). A historically informed, comparative approach to examining undocumented immigration to the United States can shed important light on the unique experiences of Asian immigrant communities and the community's role in the development of the U.S. immigration system beginning in the mid-nineteenth century. For instance, as Asian American historians have noted, the U.S. Border Patrol was initially developed to deter Chinese undocumented immigration during the Chinese Exclusion Era (1882–1943) (Lee 2003; Lew-Williams 2018). In particular, Chinese immigrants during this period devised innovative strategies to circumvent these barriers such as transiting through Latin America and presenting documents of Chinese Americans at U.S. ports of entry (Lee 2003; Romero 2004). As a result of restrictive, but also shifting federal immigration laws, Chinese and other Asian immigrant communities have continued their arrival to the United States into the contemporary period (Buenavista and Chen 2013; Buenavista and Tran 2009; Chin 1999; Cho 2019; Chung 2021).

While this academic work has been critical to the development of a space for scholarly research on this topic, a growing number of directly impacted community members have also written about and theorized their experiences as Asian undocumented immigrants (Chan 2010; Wong et al. 2012). This shift is reflective of a broader development in the field of immigration studies, specifically research on undocumented immigrant youth activism (Abrego and Negrón-Gonzales 2020; UCLA Labor Center 2008; Valdivia and Valdivia 2014; Vienrich 2019). Additionally, over the past several years, Asian undocumented immigrants have been recognized as constituting the fastest growing segment of the U.S. undocumented immigrant population (Kim and Yellow Horse 2018; Nayak et al. 2024; Ramakrishnan and Shah 2017). At the same time, the category of Asian undocumented immigrants refers to a heterogeneous community. The largest groups of Asian undocumented immigrants currently include migrants from India, China, the Philippines, and South Korea, each with their own legacy of migration, relationship to the United States, and racialization within the category of Asian American.

UndocuAsians takes its cue from these academic and community-based conversations oriented around centering the perspectives and lived experiences of Asian undocumented community members, both research-based narratives and firsthand testimonials. In doing so, it addresses the following questions: *How do Asian undocumented immigrants experience, navigate, and contest life under a state-based system of legal violence? Relatedly, how have Asian undocumented immigrants written about their community's experiences on their own terms recognizing the similarities and differences within the category of Asian undocumented immigrant? Lastly, what does Asian immigrant joy and resilience look like, and how might we center that in discussions of undocumented immigration today?*

Chapters in this edited volume initially emerged from a conference held at Brown University in the fall of 2018 titled "Liminally Legal Asians: Consciousness Raising, Political Activism, and (Re)Articulations of Belonging," co-organized by Kevin Escudero and Daniela Pila. The book also includes chapters that were solicited from scholars and scholar-activists writing on the topic, including authors who identify as undocumented immigrants and/or members of mixed-status immigrant families. Collectively, the chapters' authors engage the book's overarching questions by exploring Asian undocumented immigrant experiences across multiple contexts including family, faith, education, and social movement participation. In the process, these contributions illustrate the distinct and overlapping ways that Asian undocumented communities experience "illegality," their ongoing efforts to contest its impact in their everyday lives, and efforts to theorize their subjectivities aside from solely being defined by their immigration status.

Contributing to a Growing Area of Academic Research and Activist Praxis

UndocuAsians contributes to and intervenes in an important set of ongoing scholarly conversations taking place across the fields of sociology, anthropology, ethnic studies, history, education, and others around the contemporary experiences of Asian undocumented immigrant communities in the United States. It also complements research and popular publications by grassroots and community-based organizations working to raise awareness about the plight of Asian and all undocumented community members. Moreover, in studies of contemporary Asian undocumented immigration, similar to previous scholarship on Asian American social movement activism, Asian American panethnicity has played an important role. While we acknowledge panethnicity's challenges, such as an emphasis on the development of a collective group identity rather than a focus on individual group histories and circumstances, we draw on its utility as a political framework for uniting related yet distinct communities. Describing the political use of panethnicity by Asian American activists, ethnic studies scholar Yen Le Espiritu (1992) writes, "Pan-Asian American ethnicity is the development of bridging organizations and solidarities among several ethnic and immigrant groups of Asian ancestry. . . . The emphasis here is on the political nature of panethnicity, that is, on the distribution and exercise of, and the struggle for, power and resources inside and outside the community. Panethnicity is political not only because it serves as a basis for interest group mobilization but also because it is linked with the expansion of the role of the polity" (14–15).

Sociological and anthropological research on immigration, in particular undocumented immigration, has resulted in the development of the framework of "migrant illegality" and the related concept of "legal violence" to discuss the role that one's immigrant legal status plays in restricting one's freedoms, opportunities, and life outcomes (De Genova 2002; Menjívar and Abrego 2012; Menjívar and Kanstroom 2013). Scholars have also examined the ways that undocumented immigrant activists have contested these multiple forms of marginalization through political protest and national and local legislative campaigns (Escudero 2020; Gleeson 2010, 2016; Gleeson and Gonzales 2012; Gleeson and Sampat 2018 Gonzales 2008; Nicholls 2013; Prieto 2018; Terriquez 2015; Terriquez, Brenes, and Lopez 2018; Voss and Bloemraad 2011). Expanding the concept of migrant illegality, scholars have also theorized the concept of "racialized illegality." Racialized illegality assists in describing the intersection between an individual's racial/ethnic identity and immigrant legal status (Enriquez, Vera, and Ramakrishnan 2019; García 2017; Joseph and Golash-Boza 2021; Patler 2014; Zamora 2018). Within this vein, researchers have begun to address the relationship between Asian racial identity and undocumented immigrant status, including as it varies among members of different Asian immigrant ethnic communities (Cho 2017; Enriquez, Vera, and Ramakrishnan 2019; Hsin and Aptekar 2022; Patler 2014).

Comparative ethnic studies and Asian American studies scholars have similarly sought to foreground an analysis of the co-constitutive nature of racial/ethnic identity and immigrant legal status. In this work, researchers have highlighted the ways that Asian undocumented immigrants have in some instances been able to "pass" as holding legal status during the post–1965 era, the role of U.S. imperialism and foreign policy in producing undocumented migration from Asia, and the capacity of Asian immigrant-serving organizations to assist undocumented immigrants—especially Asian undocumented youth in securing access to resources (Buenavista and Chen 2013; Chan 2010; Dao 2017). Describing trends in post–1965 Asian immigration, in particular the growth in Asian documented immigration that the Immigration and Nationality Act of 1965 ushered in, John S. W. Park (2018) explains, beginning in the 1970s "the United States had liberalized its immigration rules to allow for the migration of skilled workers through the employment-based preference [system and as a result] workers from Asia were coming in significant numbers through the two obvious pathways. First, college graduates were finding higher-paying jobs in the United States and they were immigrating [from Asia] with their families. . . . Second, many college graduates were continuing advanced studies in the United States, but instead of returning home to [their countries of citizenship], they petitioned to adjust their status into [U.S.] permanent residency as well" (92). The Immigration and Nationality Act thus resulted in a foundational shift in immigration patterns from Asia, leading to a situation of two extremes. On the one hand were highly educated and mobile members of the Asian immigrant elite and their family members who were granted permission by the federal government to remain in the country on a long-term basis, while on the other hand were Asian undocumented immigrants whose families fled the political instability in Asian economics due to the legacies of U.S. imperialism and neoliberal economic reforms. Yet, as the chapters in this edited volume demonstrate, the Deferred Action for Childhood Arrivals (DACA) program with its two-year reprieve from deportation and issuance of a work permit has facilitated the ability of some Asian undocumented immigrant youth to begin pursuing educational and career pathways more closely aligned with those of their post-1965 documented peers. These two groups of Asian immigrants have increasingly found themselves engaging with each other through institutions such as the K–12 public school system, religious institutions and organizations, and the workplace. Lastly, acknowledging the unique challenges facing Asian undocumented immigrant community members, scholars in the field have applied a comparative lens to explore Asian and Latinx undocumented immigrant experiences and pointed to the potential for solidarity and coalition building between Asian undocumented immigrants and other undocumented immigrant groups (Cho 2017; Escudero 2020; Rubio 2019).

A corresponding thread of research has examined the case of refugee communities. Many Asian immigrants during the second half of the twentieth century arrived to the United States as refugees with the support of various refugee resettlement programs. These refugees, however, found themselves inhabiting a precarious legal status (though they receive increased government support compared to undocumented immigrants) and remained potentially subject to the threat of deportation.[1] Refugee communities, while often discussed separately from immigrant communities in academic research, have increasingly been examined relationally. This has been due to the pathbreaking work of scholars who themselves or whose families were refugees to the United States (Critical Refugee Studies Collective). Some notable examples of this shift include the work of sociologists David Scott FitzGerald and Rawan Arar (2018), who argue that "the sociology of international migration and refugee studies can mutually enrich each other and push theorization in both directions" (388), and ethnic studies scholar Yen Le Espiritu's (2014) development of a critical refugee studies framework. According to Espiritu, critical refugee studies "conceptualizes 'the refugee' not as an object of investigation but rather as a *paradigm* 'whose function [is] to establish and make intelligible a wider set of problems" (11). By promoting the agency and perspectives of refugee subjects, Espiritu's call for a critical refugee studies provides an important space for understandings of community formation, resilience, and intergenerational processes of (re)membering (Espiritu 2014; Schlund-Vials 2012). Moreover, the legal distinction between an individual being classified as an immigrant or a refugee is highly porous. These determinations are often based on international and national legal definitions and rubrics that are often incongruent with immigrant and refugee communities' own forms of self-identification and articulations of their circumstances for their need to relocate (Hamlin 2021). In fact, some of the undocumented immigrant communities whose experiences are discussed in this edited volume at one point sought to pursue a refugee and/or asylum claim but had that claim denied and in turn became undocumented immigrants.

Historical research on Asian undocumented immigrant communities has focused on the Chinese Exclusion Era (1882–1943) and its implications for present-day undocumented immigration. As such, this work has underscored the roots of undocumented immigration in the United States and its connections to the experiences of Chinese immigrants (Lee 2003; Lew-Williams 2018;

Ngai 2004; Park 2004). Lee (2004) examines the U.S. shift toward becoming a "gatekeeping nation" predicated upon the Exclusion Era's barring the entry of Chinese immigrant laborers. As Lee (2004) aptly points out, Chinese immigrants constituted the first group of individuals to be excluded from entry into the United States on the basis of their race.[2] Lew-Williams (2018) focuses on the violence that Chinese immigrant men were subjected to in the period leading up to the enactment of the Chinese Exclusion Act of 1882 and the role of this violence in precipitating additional anti-Chinese measures, thereby transforming this racial community into an "illegalized" one. Focusing on the period between the passage of two major pieces of U.S. immigration legislation—1924 to 1965—Ngai (2004) draws readers' attention to the years at the end of the Exclusion Era and their effect on the development of the contemporary U.S. immigration system. In doing so, Ngai importantly underscores the relationship between one's racial/ethnic identity and immigrant legal status, noting how white immigrants, in contrast to nonwhite immigrants, were provided a mechanism to adjust their immigration status during this period while nonwhite immigrants were not.[3] John S. W. Park (2004) engages in an important examination of the dual principles of equality and national sovereignty in shaping the treatment of immigrant groups under U.S. law. Beginning with the treatment of Chinese immigrants during the Exclusion Era and connecting these legacies into the present-day struggles of Asian and Latinx undocumented immigrants, Park's scholarship illustrates the importance of making such connections and including Asian immigrant communities as an integral part of this narrative.

Alongside these academic writings, publications by grassroots and community-based activists documenting the history of Asian and Latinx undocumented immigrant organizing and cross-group coalition building have also emerged. A prime example of these efforts is a series of books written by activists and published by the UCLA Labor Center: *Undocumented and Unafraid: Tam Tran, Cinthya Felix, and the Immigrant Youth Movement* in 2012 and *Underground Undergrads: UCLA Undocumented Immigrant Students Speak Out* in 2008. *Undocumented and Unafraid* commemorates the legacies of two iconic undocumented immigrant activists, Tam Tran and Cinthya Felix, who tragically both passed away in a car accident caused by a drunk driver in spring 2010. Focused on commemorating Tam and Cinthya's lives as well as their ongoing legacies of activism, the book consists of a series of short essays and testimonies written by immigrant rights organizers accompanied by photographs of various movement events and protests. Powerfully written, the book underscores the potential for cross-racial/ethnic coalition building in the contemporary immigrant rights movement. *Underground Undergrads* was published at a time during which there was very little scholarship in the mainstream academic literature on undocumented immigration and the lived experiences of undocumented community members. Focusing on the narratives of self-identified undocumented activists, the edited volume provides a space for activists to tell their own stories on their own terms. While at this time there were Asian undocumented immigrants active in the U.S. immigrant rights movement, it was not until the publication of the second volume, *Undocumented and Unafraid*, that their voices became more fully represented within this discourse. Also, given the timelines of academic publications, these edited volumes have foreshadowed what has now grown into a sizable body of academic literature on the topic.

Related, several national immigrant rights organizations today, particularly those composed of and led by Asian/Asian American community members, have played critical roles in expanding the conversation around immigration to incorporate an intergenerational approach to the issue. Intergenerational activism can be seen in the activities of Tsuru for Solidarity and Nikkei Progressives.[4] The efforts of these groups, organizations composed primarily of Japanese American community members, including individuals whose families were incarcerated by the U.S. government during World War II, are evidence of an intergenerational approach that seeks to connect the historical treatment of Japanese immigrants and Japanese Americans to contemporary immigrant rights movements in the United States. By drawing on their own families' lived experiences as inspiration for their participation in organizing, activists in Tsuru for Solidarity and Nikkei Progressives have underscored the role that historical memory can play in motivating one to participate in activism (Fujino 2018). Additionally, efforts to expand which issues are seen as "Asian American" can be seen in the movement to pass the Adoptee Citizenship Act (ACA). Spearheaded by groups such as Adoptees for Justice, the ACA would provide a path to U.S. citizenship for all adoptees regardless of their previous engagement with the criminal justice system (Choy 2013).[5] Though adoptees, a significant number of which are Asian American, arrive in the United States with legal status (similar to refugee arrivals), as immigrants they too face the potential for deportation depending on whether their adoptive families complete the naturalization process on their behalf (Choy 2013).

As this overview of academic as well as grassroots and community-based publications on Asian undocumented immigration has illustrated, there is a rich, growing set of research on the topic. This work has been approached from a variety of disciplinary and activist-based perspectives and contexts. At the same time, scholarship on undocumented immigration has increasingly been written by individuals who are currently or were formerly undocumented in the United States. As these voices continue to weigh in on this important topic and scholarly as well as public interest in the issue grows, it will be exciting to see what work follows in the years after the publication of this edited volume. Taking a broad approach to the topic, *UndocuAsians* combines chapters from scholars who have conducted research on the topic of Asian undocumented immigration and reflections from authors who are currently and/or were formerly undocumented in the United States. As such, this edited volume provides a holistic approach to the experiences of these community members' lived experiences and participation in social movement activism in a manner that highlights the community's multiple perspectives.

Chapter Outline

The chapters in *UndocuAsians* are organized into four sections: (1) "Historical Context and Theorizing the Nexus of Race and 'Illegality,'" (2) "Community-Based Methodological Approaches and Reclaiming Representations of Asian Undocumented Immigrant Experiences," (3) "Family, Faith, and Navigating Higher Education in the United States," and (4) "Mental Health, Activism, and Community Healing." Bringing together academic research and personal testimonials by directly impacted community members, this volume centers both collective and individual resistance to oppressive systems.

In the first section, Rikka De Joya Venturanza's opening chapter provides a critical overview of U.S. laws and policies that have governed the lives of Asian undocumented immigrants and their U.S. citizen children, historically through to the contemporary moment. Complementing this overview, Jessica Law's chapter draws on interviews with Chicago-based organizers to theorize the interaction between an Asian racialized identity and the legal construct of "migrant illegality" as has been applied to members of the Asian diaspora. Through this work, Law reveals not only the innovative ways that Asian undocumented organizers have reflected on their own subject positioning but also how doing so might offer potential avenues for solidarity and coalition building with members of similarly situated groups.

Next is a section composed of three chapters, by Tracy Lachica Buenavista, Sara P. Lopez Amezquita, and Amritpal Kaur, Amandeep Kaur, and Jaspreet Kaur, discussing methodological approaches and considerations regarding how Asian undocumented immigrant narratives are framed in academic and activist spaces. Drawing on her own experience as a self-identified "Pinay scholar" who has worked alongside Asian undocumented immigrant communities for over a decade, Buenavista's chapter reflects on the role of *tsismis* or *chisme* as "a strategic form of information sharing among undocumented immigrant communities and their allies." Buenavista offers, for current and future scholars collaborating with directly impacted communities, strategies to reconsider what is traditionally understood and accepted as "data" in the academy as part of a process of centering community agency and knowledge. Lopez Amezquita's chapter takes a rhetoric and writing instruction approach to analyze the linguistic practices and composition strategies that Asian undocumented immigrant students in New York City have utilized as they navigate the varied forums in which they tell their stories and advocate on behalf of their fellow community members. Kaur, Kaur, and Kaur's chapter explores the importance of film as a storytelling medium and recounts the context that led to the founding of their production company, Brown Girl Joy, rooted in their Sikh heritage and family migration experiences. They underscore "the importance of representation in shaping perceptions and challenging systemic biases."

The third section focuses on the relationship between the family unit, faith, and Asian undocumented immigrant youths' journeys in their pursuit of higher education, including at the graduate and professional levels. Cynthia Maribel Alcantar, Rachel Freeman-Wong, Victoria Kim, 'Inoke Hafoka, Trisha Mazumder, and Set Hernandez's chapter centers the role of the family unit and support—from parents, siblings, and friends—on the development of civic values as part of a research project with Filipina/o and Chinese (from Taiwan) undocumented college students. Esther Yoona Cho analyzes the Korean Protestant Church's impact on Korean undocumented immigrant youths' experiences feeling support and shame within their church communities as a result of their immigrant legal status. Pratishtha Khanna's chapter reflects on her own family's challenges accessing the U.S. health care system as undocumented immigrants, her experiences caring for her immigrant parents' health while balancing life as a full-time student, and her journey pursuing medical school and training to become a physician to serve members of the immigrant community in the future. Zhelin Jeff Li discusses his own experience navigating the U.S. higher education system in the STEM field and recommendations for other undocumented peers interested in pursuing careers in science and technology.

The fourth section covers the topics of mental health, activism, and community healing. UndocuScholar and therapist Huyen "Kiki" Vo's chapter begins with an overview of her family's migration experience, followed by the ways that those experiences helped inform her decision to become a therapist and work to support the healing of other Asian undocumented immigrant individuals. Siyue Lena Wang and Madison Villanueva's chapter builds on their own experiences as former Asian undocumented individuals in the immigrant rights movement to highlight the specific needs of Asian undocumented immigrant youth today. Also, as they note, while Asian undocumented immigrants have frequently been rendered as a "minority within a minority," organizations such as UPLIFT LA, an Asian and Pacific Islander undocumented youth–led activist group in the greater Los Angeles area, have importantly sought to shift this narrative. Their chapter explores cases of intersectional organizing and strategies for addressing activist exhaustion and burnout.

The chapters constituting *UndocuAsians* highlight some of the cutting-edge topics in terms of Asian undocumented immigrant experiences in the United States. While not purporting to be an exhaustive discussion of these issues, these pieces can be understood as indicative of emergent trends in the field. Illustrating an intentional and highly unique aspect of the volume, chapters in *UndocuAsians* are situated at the convergence of overlapping interests between academic researchers and activists working to address these pressing community needs. As such, they consist of both preliminary case studies and personal testimonials about the intersection of a racialized Asian/Asian American identity and undocumented immigrant status. Wrapping up the book with a discussion of healing and activism, we underscore the point that Asian undocumented communities are already playing a pivotal role in the development of community-led strategies to envision and enact an alternative, liberatory future for themselves and their peers.

REFERENCES

Abrego, Leisy. 2006. "'I Can't Go to College Because I Don't Have Papers': Incorporation Patterns of Latino Undocumented Youth." *Latino Studies* 4 (3): 212–231.

Abrego, Leisy, and Genevieve Negrón-Gonzales, eds. 2020. *We Are Not Dreamers: Undocumented Scholars Theorize Undocumented Life in the United States.* Duke University Press.

Buenavista, Tracy Lachica, and Angela Chuan-Ru Chen. 2013. "Intersections and Crossroads: A Counter-Story of an Undocumented Asian American College Student." In *The Misrepresented Minority: New Insights on Asian Americans and Pacific Islanders, and the Implications for Higher Education*, edited by Samuel D. Museus, Dina C. Maramba, and Robert T. Teranishi, 198–212. Routledge.

Buenavista, Tracy Lachica, and Tam Tran. 2009. "Undocumented Immigrant Students." In *Encyclopedia of Asian American Issues Today*, edited by Edith Chen and Grace Yoo, 253–257. Greenwood.

Chan, Beleza. 2010. "Not Just a Latino Issue: Undocumented Students in Higher Education." *Journal of College Admission* 206: 29–31.

Chin, Ko-lin. 1999. *Smuggled Chinese: Clandestine Immigration to the United States.* Temple University Press.

Cho, Esther Yoona. 2017. "Revisiting Ethnic Niches: A Comparative Analysis of the Labor Market Experiences of Asian and Latino Undocumented Young Adults." *RSF: The Russell Sage Foundation Journal of the Social Sciences* 3 (4): 97–115.

———. 2019. "Invisible Illegality: The Double Bind of Being Asian and Undocumented." PhD diss., University of California, Berkeley.

Choy, Catherine Ceniza. 2013. *Global Families: A History of Asian International Adoption in America.* New York University Press.

Chung, Ga Young. 2021. "An Ambivalent Magic: Undocumented Asian Immigrants and Racialized 'Illegality' in the US Imperial Project." *Amerasia Journal* 47 (2): 267–282.

Coutin, Susan Bibler, Justin Richland, and Veronica Fortin. 2014. "Routine Exceptionality: The Plenary Power Doctrine, Immigrants, and the Indigenous Under US Law." *UC Irvine Law Review* 4: 97–120.

Critical Refugee Studies Collective. https://criticalrefugeestudies.com/.

Dao, Loan Thi. 2017. "Out and Asian: How Undocu/DACAmented Asian Americans and Pacific Islander Youth Navigate Dual Liminality in the Immigrant Rights Movement." *Societies* 7 (3): 17. https://doi.org/10.3390/soc7030017.

De Genova, Nicholas P. 2002. "'Migrant 'Illegality' and Deportability in Everyday Life." *Annual Review of Anthropology* 31 (1): 419–447.

Enriquez, Laura E. 2019. "Border Hopping Mexicans, Law-Abiding Asians, and Racialized Illegality: Analyzing Undocumented College Students' Experiences through a Relational Lens." In *Relational Formations of Race: Theory, Method and Practice*, edited by Natalia Molina, Daniel Martinez HoSang, and Ramón A. Gutiérrez. University of California Press.

Enriquez, Laura E., Daisy Vazquez Vera, and S. Karthick Ramakrishnan. 2019. "Driver's Licenses for All? Racialized Illegality and the Implementation of Progressive Immigration Policy in California." *Law & Policy* 41 (1): 34–58.

Escudero, Kevin. 2020. *Organizing While Undocumented: Immigrant Youth's Political Activism Under the Law.* NYU Press.

Espiritu, Yen Le. 1992. *Asian American Panethnicity: Bridging Institutions and Identities.* Temple University Press.

———. 2014. *Body Counts: The Vietnam War and Militarized Refugees.* University of California Press.

FitzGerald, David Scott, and Rawan Arar. 2018. "The Sociology of Refugee Migration." *Annual Review of Sociology* 44 (1): 387–406.

Fujino, Diane C. 2018. "The Indivisibility of Freedom: The Nisei Progressives, Deep Solidarities, and Cold War Alternatives." *Amerasia Journal* 21 (2): 171–208.

García, San Juanita. 2017. "Racializing 'Illegality': An Intersectional Approach to Understanding How Mexican-Origin Women Navigate an Anti-immigrant Climate." *Sociology of Race and Ethnicity* 3 (4): 474–490.

Gleeson, Shannon. 2010. "Labor Rights for All? The Role of Undocumented Immigrant Status for Worker Claims-Making." *Law & Social Inquiry* 35 (3): 561–602.

———. 2016. *Precarious Claims: The Promise and Failure of Workplace Protections in the United States.* University of California Press.

Gleeson, Shannon, and Roberto G. Gonzales. 2012. "When Do Papers Matter? An Institutional Analysis of Undocumented Life in the United States." *International Migration Review* 50 (4): 1–19.

Gleeson, Shannon, and Prerna Sampat. 2018. "Immigrant Resistance in the Age of Trump." *New Labor Forum* 27 (1): 86–95.

Gonzales, Roberto G. 2008. "Left Out but Not Shut Down: Political Activism and the Undocumented Student Movement." *Northwestern Journal of Law & Social Policy* 3: 219.

Hamlin, Rebecca. 2021. *Crossing: How We Label and React to People on the Move.* Stanford University Press.

Hirono, Mazie. 2024. "Hirono, Collins, Smith, Bacon Lead Bipartisan, Bicameral Legislation to Close Loophole and Grant Citizenship to International Adoptees." June 6. https://www.hirono.senate.gov/news/press-releases/hirono-collins-smith-bacon-lead-bipartisan-bicameral-legislation-to-close-loophole-and-grant-citizenship-to-international-adoptees.

Hsin, Amy, and Sofya Aptekar. 2022. "The Violence of Asylum: The Case of Undocumented Chinese Migration to the United States." *Social Forces* 100 (3): 1195–1217.

Joseph, Tiffany, and Tanya Golash-Boza. 2021. "Double Consciousness in the 21st Century: Du Boisian Theory and the Problem of Racialized Legal Status." *Social Sciences* 10 (9): 345. https://doi.org/10.3390/socsci10090345.

Kenny, Kevin. 2023. *The Problem of Immigration in a Slaveholding Republic: Policing Mobility in the Nineteenth-Century United States.* Oxford University Press.

Kim, Soo Mee, and Aggie J. Yellow Horse. 2018. "Undocumented Asians, Left in the Shadows." *Contexts* 17 (4): 70–71.

Lee, Erika. 2003. *At America's Gates: Chinese Immigration During the Exclusion Era, 1882–1943*. University of North Carolina Press.

Lew-Williams, Beth. 2018. *The Chinese Must Go: Violence, Exclusion, and the Making of the Alien in America*. Harvard University Press.

Menjívar, Cecilia, and Leisy Abrego. 2012. "Legal Violence: Immigration Law and the Lives of Central American Immigrants." *American Journal of Sociology* 117 (5). https://doi.org/10.1086/663575.

Menjívar, Cecilia, and Daniel Kanstroom, eds. 2013. *Constructing Immigrant "Illegality": Critiques, Experiences, and Responses*. Cambridge University Press.

Nayak, Sameera S., Amanda Cardone, Kina Soberano, and Meghan Dhond. 2024. "The Health Status of Undocumented Immigrants from Asian Countries in the United States: A Scoping Review and Recommendations for Future Directions." *Journal of Immigrant and Minority Health* 26: 1099–1112.

Negrón-Gonzales, Genevieve, Leisy Abrego, and Kathleen Coll. 2015. "Introduction: Immigrant Latina/o Youth and Illegality: Challenging the Politics of Deservingness." *Association of Mexican American Educators Journal* 9 (3): 7–10.

Ngai, Mae M. 2004. *Impossible Subjects: Illegal Aliens and the Making of Modern America*. Princeton University Press.

Nicholls, Walter J. 2013. *The DREAMers: How the Undocumented Youth Movement Transformed the Immigrant Rights Debate*. Stanford University Press.

Park, John S. W. 2004. *Elusive Citizenship: Immigration, Asian Americans, and the Paradox of Civil Rights*. New York University Press.

———. 2018. *Immigration Law and Society*. Polity Press.

Patler, Caitlin. 2014. "Racialized Illegality: The Convergence of Race and Legal Status Among Black, Latino and Asian-American Undocumented Young Adults." In *Scholars and Southern Californian Immigrants in Dialogue: New Conversations in Public Sociology*, edited by Victoria Carty, Rafael Luévano, and Tekle Woldemikael. Lexington Press.

Prieto, Greg. 2018. *Immigrants Under Threat: Risk and Resistance in Deportation Nation*. New York University Press.

Ramakrishnan, Karthick, and Sono Shah. 2017. "One Out of Every 7 Asian Immigrants Is Undocumented." AAPI Data. https://aapidata.com/narrative/blog/asian-undoc-1in7/.

Romero, Robert Chao. 2004. "Transnational Chinese Immigrant Smuggling to the United States via Mexico and Cuba, 1882–1916." *Amerasia Journal* 30 (3): 1–16.

Rubio, Elizabeth Hanna. 2019. "'We Need to Redefine What We Mean by Winning': NAKASEC's Immigrant Justice Activism and Thinking Citizenship Otherwise." *Amerasia Journal* 45 (2): 157–172.

Schlund-Vials, Cathy J. 2012. *War, Genocide, and Justice: Cambodian American Memory Work*. University of Minnesota Press.

Terriquez, Veronica. 2015. "Intersectional Mobilization, Social Movement Spillover, and Queer Youth Leadership in the Immigrant Rights Movement." *Social Problems* 62 (3): 343–362.

Terriquez, Veronica, Tizoc Brenes, and Abdiel Lopez. 2018. "Intersectionality as a Multipurpose Collective Action Frame: The Case of the Undocumented Youth Movement." *Ethnicities* 18 (2): 260–276.

UCLA Labor Center. 2008. *Underground Undergrads: UCLA Undocumented Immigrant Students Speak Out*. UCLA Labor Center.

Valdivia, Carolina, and Diana Valdivia. 2014. "My Un(DACA)mented Life: Experiences of Undocumented Young Adults Growing Up and Resisting Through Activism." *Journal of Transborder Studies*.

Vienrich, Alessandra Bazo. 2019. "Dreams of College: In Pursuit of Higher Education While Undocumented." PhD diss., University of Massachusetts, Boston. https://scholarworks .umb.edu/doctoral_dissertations/529/.

Voss, Kim, and Irene Bloemraad, eds. 2011. *Rallying for Immigrant Rights: The Fight for Inclusion in 21st Century America.* University of California Press.

Wong, Kent, Janna Shadduck-Hernández, Fabiola Inzunza, Julie Monroe, Victor Narr, and Abel Valenzuela, eds. 2012. *Undocumented and Unafraid: Tam Tran, Cinthya Felix, and the Immigrant Youth Movement.* UCLA Labor Center.

Zamora, Sylvia. 2018. "Mexican Illegality, Black Citizenship, and White Power: Immigrant Perceptions of the US Socioracial Hierarchy." *Journal of Ethnic and Migration Studies* 44 (11): 1897–1914.

NOTES

1. For instance, see the work of the Southeast Asian Freedom Network (www.seafn.org), seeking to halt the deportations of Southeast Asian Americans in the United States, some of whom are U.S. permanent residents, but as non-U.S. citizens who received a court conviction, found themselves placed in deportation proceedings.

2. It is important to note that during this period, while not immigrants, enslaved African people were forcibly brought to United States. The history of the United States and the transatlantic slave trade, including the "logics" employed in the process, were also closely intertwined with the nation's development of a restrictive, race-based immigration system (Kenny 2023).

3. Also at play during this period and into the present-day moment are competing sovereignties: the federal government's exertion of sovereignty over what is now known as the United States and the sovereign-to-sovereign relations between the U.S. federal government and Native nations. In fact, when the federal government did extend U.S. citizenship to Native peoples residing in these lands in 1924 under the Indian Citizenship Act, it did so as part of broader efforts to bring Native peoples further under its control. For additional discussion of these processes and the federal government's use of the plenary power doctrine to simultaneously subjugate members of these communities while treating them differently under the law, see Coutin, Richland, and Fortin (2014).

4. For more information, see Tsuru for Solidarity (https://tsuruforsolidarity.org) and Nikkei Progressives (www.nikkeiprogressives.org).

5. For more information about the Adoptee Citizenship Act, see Hirono (2024); additionally, see the work of organizations such as Adoptees for Justice (www.adopteesforjustice .org).

PART ONE

Historical Context and Theorizing the Nexus of Race and "Illegality"

Toward a Critical Understanding of the Historical and Sociopolitical Contexts for Asian American College Students in Mixed-Status Im/migrant Families

RIKKA DE JOYA VENTURANZA

> I remember at the age of nineteen first learning about your "status," [I felt] shook, taken aback, and confused . . . I was sad and heartbroken. What was I to do but to figure it out and sacrifice my sanity just so I can take care of you. . . . I had to learn to be the expert. . . . Did you try to at least [ask] people for help? Or did you know one day I would be responsible for it? I get it, I'm your daughter, I'm indebted to you. Sometimes being a daughter of a mom with no [legal] status, being Filipino, being your only child, is a burden. I'm not sure who would take care of you if I weren't here.

I begin this chapter with a memorable excerpt from a research study I conducted in 2021. The study explored the lived experiences of second-generation U.S.-born citizens who were undergraduate students and identified as Asian Americans in mixed-status im/migrant families.[1] Through this study, I examined the relationship between race, U.S. birthright citizenship, and illegality and how these factors shaped the educational journeys of this student population.[2] I offer the above excerpt, taken from an unsent handwritten letter addressed to the student's mother "with no [legal] status," to illuminate a narrative that is often overlooked in higher education discourse regarding Asian Americans. This participant shared the first time she discovered the undocumented status of a parent, reflecting upon a season of distress amid her undergraduate career, while realizing the lifelong challenges she endured as a result of seeking to protect her mother.[3] Notably, according to the preliminary findings of my study, college-bound high school Asian American students in mixed-status families were more likely than enrolled undergraduate Asian Americans in mixed-status families to experience such a confounding and life-changing discovery regarding a parent's immigration status. Typically, high school students are tasked with gathering their parents' information, including immigration status, while applying for financial aid as part of the college application process. Another process that may lead to the discovery of a parent's immigration status, at times initiated by undocumented parents, is a parental request to their U.S. citizen children to petition them for legal permanent residency upon reaching the legal age (twenty-one) to apply.[4] Through these tasks, an implicit or explicit conversation potentially unfolds regarding the precarity of at least one parent's undocumented immigration status.

Post-discovery, U.S. citizen students face fraught season(s) negotiating the illegality of their parents' immigration status and their role as a U.S.-born citizen in a mixed-status family. These seasons represents only a fraction of stressors that these students might face. Denoting a tendency to stay silent or withhold from seeking campus resources, support, or community, the following statement from the same research participant further underscores the complex positionality members of this student population must contend with: "I feel like the reason why I seldomly told people [about being a member of a mixed-status family] was because I've never really heard of Asians being undocumented." A recent system-wide survey-based report, "Advancing Equity for Undocumented Students and Students from Mixed-Status Families at the University of California," found comparable findings to this student's narrative. The report highlighted the harmful impact of U.S. immigration policy on students enrolled at UC Campuses who identified as U.S. citizens and who have at least one undocumented parent. A remarkable finding from the report demonstrates that despite holding U.S. citizenship status, this student population often had worse academic performance and mental health outcomes compared to undocumented students (Enriquez et al. 2021). These findings continue to be an object of my critical reflection, as a critical race scholar-practitioner and advocate for im/migrant justice, as I strive to increase equity advancements in serving underrepresented and underserved student populations. Moreover, they have generated more questions about the multigenerational consequences of an undocumented status among college students, both those who identify as undocumented and those who are members of mixed-status families (i.e., having an undocumented parent or sibling).

Offering a critical understanding of the complicated context this student population inhabits, this chapter is guided by the following questions: What historical and contemporary contexts have shaped the educational journeys of

Asian American students in mixed-status families? And what is the connection between the sociohistorical context of Asian im/migrants and Asian Americans in the United States and their pursuit of higher education today?[5] To address these questions, this chapter begins with a brief background of mixed-status immigrant families in the United States, followed by a literature review of contemporary U.S. immigration policies. Next, it proceeds to a review of literature on the history of illegality and im/migrant populations in the United States and an overview of Asian immigration to the United States and their experiences related to race and illegality. Literature focused on illegality and race is also examined to investigate how undocumented parents' statuses can generate challenges and barriers throughout multiple aspects of a student's educational journey. With an emphasis on higher education, this chapter offers a sociohistorical context in which these students are situated as emerging adults and full-time college students.

Background of Mixed-Status Families in the United States

Mixed-status families represent a growing demographic in the United States. These families may include any combination of U.S. citizen, documented, and/or undocumented members living in the same household (Castañeda 2019). Apart from the dichotomy of legality and "illegality," a range of im/migrant categories may also be present in a mixed-status family such as undocumented im/migrants, DACA recipients, legal permanent residents, temporary protected status holders, multiple humanitarian statuses, and U.S. citizens (Abrego 2019). With unpredictable timelines and massive backlogs, the U.S. immigration system has been shown to at times inhibit certain immigrants' adjustment of their immigrant legal status, especially many im/migrants of color, instead creating conditions where undocumented im/migrant families are forced to live in long-term precarity (Hamilton, Patler, and Hale 2019).

Children are some of the most vulnerable members of mixed-status families (Abrego 2019). This is primarily due to the dependency dynamics between children and their parents. Along with the disparate consequences of immigration status for different members of a mixed-status family, it also sets the stage for a family's likelihood of upward mobility in society (Enriquez 2015). Notably, immigration studies scholars have found low-wage employment and job insecurity to be significant factors that generate hardships for these families (Schmalzbauer and Andres 2019). On top of this, U.S. citizen children of undocumented im/migrants are likely to attend underresourced schools that typically do not offer the services needed to ensure their academic success (Suárez-Orozco and Suárez-Orozco 2009).

The growth in mixed-status families overall and their demographic characteristics have been central areas of focus within social science research over the past two decades (Fix and Zimmerman 2001; Passel 2011). Apart from key topics such as an understanding the dynamics of couples, children, parents, and/or family units within these contexts, a significant amount of research in this subfield has been dedicated to understand how U.S. laws, policies, and practices have been deployed by the state to create unique hardship conditions across an entire family unit (documented and undocumented). Predicted life outcomes have also been a central focus of mixed-status family research and how immigration policy can serve as a mechanism for stratification (Enriquez 2015; Rodriguez 2016; Romero 2008), especially amid an increasingly anti-immigrant national climate (Abrego 2019). Similarly, with a focus on U.S. citizen students who are part of these mixed-status families, educational scholars have examined pervasive ideologies of racism, xenophobia, and nativism as influential forces that promote the brutal mistreatment of this im/migrant population (Huber et al. 2008).

The differential rights and life outcomes of mixed-status families in comparison to families that hold some form of long-term legal status have served as a foundational underpinning of the U.S. immigration laws and their impact on immigrant community members' daily lives. For example, Menjívar (2006) examined Latino undocumented im/migrants experiences of illegality as "the gray area between legal categories, how this 'in-between' status or liminal legality shapes different spheres of life" (1000). From this research, the concept of *liminal legality* emerged, illuminating how all mixed-status family members—documented, undocumented, and those in-between—are impacted by immigration policy on individual and relational levels. This research has offered a more holistic way of understanding the experiences of these individuals bound by a shared positionality of a relation to the experience of illegality. It is through these pursuits in research that we may begin to understand how the intersectional social locations of race, birthright U.S. citizenship status, and illegality can hinder or propel postsecondary educational trajectories and outcomes of U.S. citizen college students in mixed-status families.

Contemporary U.S. Immigration Policy

Starting in the 1990s, the emergence of blatant anti-immigrant policies significantly increased, negatively affecting the experiences of Asian American communities alongside their Latino/a counterparts and other im/migrant communities (Massey and Sánchez 2010). Leading scholars who study this population contend that U.S. immigration policy and the anti-immigrant political climate of the country compounded experiences that insulate and delimit the day-to-day lives of *all* members of mixed-status families (Abrego 2019; Chan 2010; Enriquez 2015; Passel and Taylor 2010; Seo 2011; Suárez-Orozco and Yoshikawa 2015). Further, the quality of life for undocumented im/migrants and their family members is perpetually impacted by the federal government's inaction in passing comprehensive immigration reform, adding years of uncertainty and fear, while magnifying the anti-immigrant climate of the country (Burciaga et al. 2019). An example of this can be observed in the passage of the Illegal Immigration Reform and Immigrant Responsibility Act of 1996 (IIRIRA). According to Rodríguez (2018), the IIRIRA has been responsible for increasing the number of mixed-status families in the U.S. population. Due to this bill, a three- to ten-year bar was enacted for undocumented im/migrants who reside in the country for a certain period of time. As such, an unauthorized residence in the United States under a year resulted in a three-year bar, while a ten-year bar was enforced for more than one year of unauthorized residency.

Following the September 11, 2001, tragedy, the United States established another wave of punitive immigration policies, resulting in increased family separations (Kanstroom 2007; Suárez-Orozco and Yoshikawa 2015). In a research study on undocumented im/migrant families, Abrego (2018) found that "families are uniquely vulnerable to changes in policies because they rely on stable jobs, access to schooling, health care, and social services for the social reproduction of all their members" (194). And due to the precarity of their immigration status, undocumented loved ones are vulnerable to multiple punitive measures such as detention, deportation, and family separation.

Enriquez's (2015) concept of "multigenerational punishment" further illustrates the reproduction of harm from an undocumented status across generations within a mixed-status family. Her research specifically emphasized that "legal sanctions intended for a specific population spill over to negatively affect individuals who are not targeted by laws" (939). Enriquez also highlighted that due to the strong social ties between family members, the family was a prime site for multigenerational punishment to occur. Menjívar and Abrego (2012) framed this form of punishment "legal violence." Their scholarship demonstrates that "the suffering that results from and is made possible through the implementation of the body of laws . . . delimit and shape individuals' lives on a routine basis" (1387). It is important to note the significance of the term "legal violence" as it deems immigration policies the source of structural and symbolic violence, which in turn generates the constrained and harmful conditions mixed-status families are likely to endure.

While there have been advancements in research that examines the negative impact of U.S. immigration policy on mixed-status families, much of this research has focused on Latino/a im/migrants and students (Abrego 2019; Enriquez 2015). Leading sociology scholars who study mixed-status families attribute this focus to the racialization of Latino/a communities being disproportionately burdened as primary targets of punitive policies and practices (Menjívar 2021). Considering how race differentiates the experiences of illegality, a growing population of Asian im/migrants and Asian American similarly impacted by immigration policies must also be examined. This is critical as scholars must determine how this heterogeneous community can also be better served and supported (Buenavista 2018; Cho 2017; Gutierrez 2022; Kim and Yellow Horse 2018). While dominant and politicized stereotypes deem a monolithic Latino/a community as the primary undocumented community of the United States (Cervantes 2019), vast disparities are simultaneously hidden through pervasive racist stereotypes such as the model minority myth that characterizes Asian Americans as universally successful (Buenavista 2018; Cho 2017), thereby concealing a marginalized Asian im/migrant population—the second largest group (16 percent) of the 11.4 million undocumented population, many of whom are also part of mixed-status families (Capps et. al. 2020).[6]

Additionally, while an increasing amount of scholarship has examined the challenges and barriers experienced by undocumented im/migrants (Buenavista 2018; Gonzales 2016; Suárez-Orozco and Yoshikawa 2015), little is known about mixed-status families and their U.S.-born citizen children, specifically those who emerge into adulthood and are likely to pursue higher education. U.S. citizen college students in mixed-status families will likely add further insight as they are likely to contend with compounded intersectional hardships throughout their higher education trajectories. As such, they are less likely than students with documented family members to complete their academic goals or obtain full membership and participation in U.S. society (Gonzales and Vargas 2016). Notably, the scholarship related to this community is slowly increasing. Yet based on higher education, student affairs, and community college academic journals, there continues to be very little research that explores the experiences of Asian American college students in mixed-status families who are likely influenced and negatively affected by the undocumented status of at least one family member.

Overview of Historical Immigration Policy and Asian Immigration Patterns in the United States

Comparable to other im/migrant communities of color, Asian im/migrants have contended with European settler society since their initial migration to the United States. Native studies scholars who have significantly critiqued white-supremacist settler-colonial logic have also revealed the use of orientalist ideologies to understand the historical ostracization of Asian im/migrants. As part of these ideologies, the West was positioned "as a superior civilization by constructing itself in opposition to an 'exotic' but inferior 'Orient'" (Said 1994, as cited by Smith 2012, 69). Extending these critiques, according to Rana (2015), racist characterizations were imposed upon Asian im/migrants to ensure they would be "cast[ed] through the narratives of empire, war, and migration" (1). As such, regardless of how hard Asian im/migrants worked, how much they endured exclusionary laws and restrictions, or how long they resided in the United States, these ideologies persisted in characterizing Asian im/migrants as perpetual foreigners who threatened the safety and security of the country, especially during wartime (Rana 2015).

Historically, this logic was used to generate mechanisms of exclusion toward Asians and Asian Americans. For example, during the 1840s Asian im/migrants who migrated to the United States were ineligible for naturalization as U.S. citizens (Rodríguez 2018). As early as 1879, Chinese im/migrants were considered nonresidents. In many states, they were prohibited from holding any real estate, while white foreigners were given the right to own land as native citizens (Glenn 2015). One of the most appalling sanctions in U.S. immigration history was the enactment of one of the nation's first race-based immigration policies: the Chinese Exclusion Act of 1882. And later the Immigration Act of 1917 further restricted Chinese and other Asian im/migrants' access to and entry into the country (Rodríguez 2018). In contrast, the Gentlemen's Agreement between 1907 and 1908 exempted Japanese migrants from this law until the Immigration Act of 1924. Similarly, im/migrants from the Philippines, which was at this time under U.S. rule, were not subjected to such restrictions. Despite these steady exclusionary regulations, Asian im/migrants from India, Japan, Korea, and the Philippines arrived to work at sugar plantations located in Hawai'i (Tamura 2003). Eventually, a large number of Asian im/migrants came into the United States after the Immigration Act of 1965 that prioritized family-based migration (Tamura 2003). This significantly increased the Asian and Asian American populations in the country (Chan 1991). By the 1960s and 1970s, the United States embarked on prioritizing its economic agenda, creating immigration policies that prioritized skilled workers, including many from the Philippines, India, and countries throughout East Asia. Concurrently, the brutal conditions in Southeast Asia following U.S. intervention during the 1970s generated multiple waves of migration (e.g., Vietnamese, Cambodians, Hmong, and Lao) who arrived and resettled in various parts of the United States as refugees (Museus and Yi 2014).

Educational Access and Opportunities of U.S.-Born Asian Americans in Mixed-Status Families

Over four million U.S. citizen children live in a household with at least one undocumented family member (Enriquez et al. 2021). As noted earlier, in terms of education children of undocumented im/migrants, despite being U.S. citizens, are likely to attend underresourced schools that do not provide services or resources to ensure their academic success (Suárez-Orozco and Suárez-Orozco 2009). Considering this, the likelihood of socioemotional harm increases among these children as their rights as U.S. citizens are neglected (Abrego 2019; Enriquez et al.

2021). Though a better quality of life is associated with birthright citizenship (Aptekar 2016), U.S.-born citizen children in mixed-status families are up against multiple challenges and barriers as they continue to endure the cascading hardships generated by their parent(s)' or other loved ones' undocumented status.

Moreover, much of the research on Asians and Asian Americans in education—mainly Asian Americans—substantiates the impact of race in their lives. The concept of racialization or racism as a social process (Byng 2013) offers critical insight into how the perception or racial identity of Asian Americans is largely obscured, resulting from perpetual mischaracterizations of the community, especially in higher education (Teranishi and Kim 2017). Research examining the differential racialization of Asian Americans often identifies the model minority myth as a critical factor in this process (Chang and Kiang 2002; Yi et al. 2020). This myth is found to render and distort Asian and Asian Americans, a tremendously diverse community, as a monolithic population. What is most problematic about this myth is the misconception that they are unharmed by structural inequities, while collectively accomplishing universal success (Lee and Zhou 2015). For example, college faculty and staff may not think Asian and Asian American students can benefit from support and guidance because they are stereotyped as being high achievers in educational settings. As a consequence of this racialization, im/migrants from Asian countries and their U.S. citizen children become significantly overlooked in varied discourses, including in higher education (Buenavista 2018).

The Racialization of Immigration-Impacted Asian Americans

Within the lives of immigration-impacted Asian and Asian American communities, the roles of race and racism have been well articulated across a variety of disciplines and through empirical evidence.[7] Critical race scholars, for example, have found that Asian undocumented immigrants are keen to develop practices of nondisclosure and protective strategies to ensure their safety in the United States. Differentiating racial logics imposed upon Asian undocumented and Latino undocumented students have also been found to work alongside each other to maintain racial inequities across institutions (Gutierrez 2022). Accordingly, sociologists have found that when Asian undocumented immigrants are recognized or rendered visible, they continue to be racialized by being grouped with other hardworking im/migrants who are celebrated for their success (Kim and Yellow Horse 2018). Last, other sociological research has demonstrated how the status of being both Asian and undocumented functions as a double-edged sword, specifically serving as a racial shield or cloak that protects members of the community from immigration enforcement while being excluded or underserved by im/migrant service organizations that provide appropriate resources and support (Cho 2017).

Other research has highlighted transnational portrayals of Asians and Asian Americans that generate distinct racial characterizations, as contrasted with the lived experiences of Asian undocumented youth. Researchers in the field of psychology, in particular, have focused on the racialized portrayals of Asian im/migrants through the naming and examination of the phenomenon termed "parachute children." According to Tsong and Liu (2009), this entails a situation in which minors, mostly from Asian countries, are sent or, as the term implies, dropped off to the United States and other Western nations solely to obtain an education. Typically this phenomenon is associated with immigrant-concentrated upscale neighborhoods (Zhou 1998).

At the same time, it has been noted that "Asian Americans suffer from discrimination, much of which is quantitatively and qualitatively different from other disempowered groups" (Chang 1993, 1247). Educational scholars strongly link the model minority myth with racial microaggressions, discrimination, and harmful stereotypes experienced by Asian American college students (Chan 2017; Lewis, Chesler, and Forman 2000; Palmer and Maramba 2015). Kohli and Solórzano (2012), in a study on the racism experienced by young adults, found that Asian American students frequently internalize racism. Asian American participants in their study shared a variety of feelings that involved shame and struggle with their racial and ethnic identity and rejection of their language and culture. In a qualitative study of Asian American student experiences in higher education, Chan (2017) illustrated how Asian American students' racial identity was strongly connected to their education, specifically how their identity as an Asian American was often synonymous with their academic achievement. One participant in their study disclosed, "There was this belief that Asians are really smart. . . . I had to hold myself up to that belief . . . caring about grades . . . kind of just merged with being Asian" (1010).

Comparably, in analyzing the influence of racism on Asian American students' educational experiences, Museus and Park (2015) offer deep insight into common interactions this student population faces. One of their participants disclosed, "I don't know if it was because I'm quiet, but I've been called a '*****' and other names. . . . It's usually just when I'm walking past somebody, and they'll just scream it. . . . I don't cause conflict, so I don't know why they're causing crap with me" (557). These findings align with empirical research of previous studies that determined racial hostility in postsecondary campuses is negatively affecting Asian American students. Corresponding to these findings, Palmer and Maramba (2015) offer rich qualitative data demonstrating a variety of racialized Asian American student experiences. For example, a participant in their study expressed, "Some of my Black and White friends on campus will say things like, 'All Asians are smart in math.' So that's the first thing they say. I tell them, 'No, it's not true: not every Asian is smart,' but they think I'm . . . kidding" (714). Similarly, Lewis, Chesler, and Forman (2000) found that the model minority stereotype masks the discrimination Asian Americans experience and overlooks the variety of forms of racism they face in educational contexts. Altogether, race-based research on this student population demonstrates the contradictory ways Asian Americans experience race and racism, especially in educational settings.

It is important to note that research on the disparate experiences of race and racism among Asian Americans is critical as this growing student population continues to increase in heterogeneity. According to educational researchers, the Asian im/migrant and Asian American student population is projected to grow faster than other im/migrant populations in the United States (Kim and Yellow Horse 2018; Teranishi and Kim 2017; Zhou and Gonzales 2019). Researchers attribute the significant demographic growth to international migration rather than natural growth (i.e., births minus deaths) (Vespa, Armstrong, and Medina 2018; Yellow Horse and Vargas 2021). Alongside these trends are evolving and unabating punitive immigration policies that are unlikely to change. As such, mixed-status families and their U.S. citizen members continue to be vulnerable to family separation through deportation. Further, as Asian Americans continue to be racialized as perpetual or "forever foreigners" (Li and Nicholson 2021; Tuan 1998; Zhou 2004), they are likely to remain excluded from full participation in U.S. society. While this continues to be the case, im/migrant rights advocates forewarn "a drastic increase in targeted enforcement against long-time community members, including many long-term residents and refugees" (Asian Americans Advancing Justice 2019, para. 2). Therefore, this research and body of scholarship are critical as we continue to pursue a deeper understanding of the unique needs and forms of support for this underserved growing student population.

Conclusion

By providing a critical understanding of the historical and sociopolitical contexts for Asian American college students in mixed-status im/migrant families, this chapter offered insight into the intersectional experiences of Asian Americans in the United States. Specifically, this chapter examined what it means to be a child of Asian im/migrants, a U.S. citizen member of a mixed-status im/migrant family, and what it means to hold and carry these social identities while pursuing higher education. At the very least, a key objective of mine has been to promote a deeper understanding, across audiences and disciplines, of an underrepresented Asian / Asian American student population ongoingly underserved throughout the educational pipeline.

Based on the featured literature, it is my hope to compel educational scholars and practitioners to consider educational outcomes when examining the intersection of race and immigrant legal status. The negative impact and unique effects that these factors may have on immigrant-origin student populations must be accounted for in order to better understand how to truly serve them and enable their success in U.S. higher education today. While this chapter is only the beginning of a fuller understanding of Asian immigrant and Asian American experiences in the context of mixed-status families, I also hope that it promotes a genuine curiosity and desire to further examine the complexity and expansiveness of this student population's experiences. More importantly, I hope a critical concern about their well-being and prosperity beyond degree completion may also ground and cultivate future conversations in equity-oriented projects and initiatives. Notably, while some might consider an individual's undocumented immigrant status to impact solely certain individuals in the family unit, as this chapter and the research cited within it demonstrate, that is not necessarily the case, especially when centering the perspectives of directly impacted community members. Therefore, I consider these efforts critical first steps toward many possibilities ahead as we strive for a more just, inclusive, and equitable future for all Asian Americans and members of other racial/ethnic minority communities more broadly.

REFERENCES

Abrego, Leisy J. 2018. "Renewed Optimism and Spatial Mobility: Legal Consciousness of Latino Deferred Action for Childhood Arrivals Recipients and Their Families in Los Angeles." *Ethnicities* 18 (2): 192–207.

———. 2019. "Relational Legal Consciousness of U.S. Citizenship: Privilege, Responsibility, Guilt, and Love in Latino Mixed-Status Families." *Law and Society Review* 53 (3): 641–670.

Aptekar, Sofya. 2016. "Making Sense of Naturalization: What Citizenship Means to Naturalizing Immigrants in Canada and the USA." *Journal of International Migration and Integration* 17 (4): 1143–1161.

Asian Americans Advancing Justice. 2016. "Inside the Numbers: How Immigration Shapes Asian American and Pacific Islander Communities." https://advancingjustice-aajc .org/sites/default/files/2016-09/Immigration%20Enforcement_Why.pdf.

———. 2019. "Inside the Numbers: How Immigration Shapes Asian American and Pacific Islander Communities." https://advancingjustice-aajc.org/sites/default/files/2019-07 /1153_AAJC_Immigration_Final_0.pdf.

Assalone, Amy, and Ashley Fann. 2017. "Understanding the Influence of Model Minority Stereotypes on Asian American Community College Students." *Community College Journal of Research and Practice* 41 (7): 422–435.

Buenavista, Tracy Lachica. 2018. "Model (Undocumented) Minorities and 'Illegal' Immigrants: Centering Asian Americans and U.S. Carcerality in Undocumented Student Discourse." *Race, Ethnicity and Education* 21 (1): 78–91.

Burciaga, Edelina M., Lisa M. Martinez, Kevin Escudero, Andrea Flores, Joanna Perez, and Carolina Valdivia. 2019. "Migrant Illegality Across Uneven Legal Geographies: Introduction to the Special Issue of *Law & Policy*." *Law & Policy* 41 (1): 5–11.

Byng, Michelle D. 2013. "You Can't Get There from Here: A Social Process Theory of Racism and Race." *Critical Sociology* 39 (5): 705–715.

Capps, Randy, Julia Gelatt, Ariel G. Ruiz Soto, and Jennifer Van Hook. 2020. "Unauthorized Immigrants in the United States: Stable Numbers, Changing Origins." Migration Policy Institute.

Castañeda, Heide. 2019. *Borders of Belonging: Struggle and Solidarity in Mixed-Status Immigrant Families.* Stanford University Press.

Cervantes, Andrea Gómez. 2019. "Looking Mexican: Indigenous and Non-Indigenous Latina/o Immigrants and the Racialization of Illegality in the Midwest." *Social Problems* 68 (1): 100–117.

Chan, Beleza. 2010. "Not Just a Latino Issue." *Journal of College Admission* 206: 29–31.

Chan, Jason. 2017. "'Being Asian American Is a Lot Different Here': Influences of Geography on Racial Identity." *Journal of College Student Development* 58 (7): 1001–1017.

Chan, Sucheng. 1991. *Asian Americans: An Interpretive History.* Twayne.

Chang, Mitchell J., and Peter N. Kiang. 2002. "New Challenges of Representing Asian American Students in U.S. Higher Education." In *The Racial Crisis in American Higher Education: Continuing Challenges for the Twenty-First Century*, edited by William A. Smith, Philip G. Altbach, and Kofi Lomotey. State University of New York Press.

Chang, R. S. 1993. "Toward an Asian American Legal Scholarship: Critical Race Theory, Post-Structuralism, and Narrative Space." *California Law Review* 81 (5): 1241–1323.

Cho, Esther Yoona. 2017. "A Double Bind-Model Minority and Illegal Alien." *Asian American Law Journal* 24:123.

DeLaRosby, Hal R. 2016. "Localized Belonging, Microaggressions, and Authentic Community: Asian American-Pacific Islander Students Persisting at Predominantly White Institutions." PhD diss., Azusa Pacific University.

Eng, David L., and Shinhee Han. 2019. *Racial Melancholia, Racial Dissociation.* Duke University Press.

Enriquez, Laura. 2015. "Multigenerational Punishment: Shared Experiences of Undocumented Immigration Status Within Mixed-Status Families." *Journal of Marriage and Family* 77 (4): 939–953.

Enriquez, Laura E., Cecilia Ayón, Jennifer Nájera, Annie Ro, and Zulema Valdez. 2021. "Advancing Equity for Undocumented Students and Students from Mixed-Status Families at the University of California." University of California Collaborative to Promote Immigrant and Student Equity. https://ucpromise.uci.edu/reports/undocumented -and-mixed-status-families/

Espiritu, Yen Le. 1992. *Asian American Panethnicity: Bridging Institutions and Identities.* Temple University Press.

Fix, Michael, and Walter Zimmermann. 2001. "All Under One Roof: Mixed-Status Families in an Era of Reform." *International Migration Review* 35 (2): 397–419.

García, David G. 2018. *Strategies of Segregation: Race, Residence, and the Struggle for Educational Equality.* University of California Press.

Glenn, Evelyn Nakano. 2015. "Settler Colonialism as Structure: A Framework for Comparative Studies of U.S. Race and Gender Formation." *Sociology of Race and Ethnicity* 1 (1): 52–72.

Gómez Cervantes, Andrea. 2021. "'Looking Mexican': Indigenous and Non-Indigenous Latina/o Immigrants and the Racialization of Illegality in the Midwest." *Social Problems* 68, no. 1 (2021): 100–117.

Gonzales, Roberto G. 2016. *Lives in Limbo: Undocumented and Coming of Age in America.* University of California Press.

Gutierrez, Rose Ann Rico Eborda. 2022. "Racialized Realities at the Intersection of Race and Undocumented Status: A Critical Narrative Inquiry into the Lives of Undocumented Asian Students in Higher Education." PhD diss. University of California, Los Angeles.

Hall, Lisa Kahaleole. 2015. "Which of These Things Is Not Like the Other: Hawaiians and Other Pacific Islanders Are Not Asian Americans, and All Pacific Islanders Are Not Hawaiian." *American Quarterly* 67 (3): 727–747.

Hamilton, Erin, Caitlin C. Patler, and Jo Mhairi Hale. 2019. "Growing Up without Status: The Integration of Children in Mixed-Status Families." *Sociology Compass* 13 (6). https://doi.org/10.1111/soc4.12695.

Hofferth, Sandra L., and Ui Jeong Moon. 2016. "How Do They Do It? The Immigrant Paradox in the Transition to Adulthood." *Social Science Research* 57: 177–194.

Huber, Lindsay Perez, Corina Benavides Lopez, Maria C. Malagon, Veronica Velez, and Daniel G. Solórzano. 2008. "Getting Beyond the 'Symptom,' Acknowledging the 'Disease': Theorizing Racist Nativism." *Contemporary Justice Review* 11 (1): 39–51.

Kanstroom, Dan. 2007. *Deportation Nation: Outsiders in America's History.* Harvard University Press.

Kim, Soo Mee, and Aggie J. Yellow Horse. 2018. "Undocumented Asians, Left in the Shadows." *Contexts* 17 (4): 70–71.

Kim-Ju, Greg M., Wayne Maeda, and Cara Maffini. 2009. "A Historical and Contemporary Overview of Asian American and Pacific Islander Experiences: Immigration, Racialization, and Liminality." *Aggression and Violent Behavior* 14 (6): 437–444.

Kohli, Rita, and Daniel Solórzano. 2012. "Teachers, Please Learn Our Names: Racial Microaggressions and the K–12 Classroom." *Race Ethnicity and Education* 15 (4): 441–462.

Labrador, Roderick N., and Erin Kahunawaika'ala Wright. 2011. "Engaging Indigeneity in Pacific Islander and Asian American Studies." *Amerasia Journal* 37 (3): 134–147.

Lee, Jennifer, and Min Zhou. 2015. *The Asian American Achievement Paradox.* Russell Sage Foundation.

Lee, Jennifer C., and Samuel Kye. 2016. "Racialized Assimilation of Asian Americans." *Annual Review of Sociology* 42: 253–273.

Lewis, Amanda E., Mark Chesler, and Tyronne A. Forman. 2000. "The Impact of 'Colorblind' Ideologies on Students of Color: Intergroup Relations at a Predominantly White University." *Journal of Negro Education* 69: 74–91.

Li, Yao, and Harvey L. Nicholson Jr. 2021. "When 'Model Minorities' Become 'Yellow Peril': Othering and the Racialization of Asian Americans in the COVID-19 Pandemic." *Sociology Compass* 15 (2): e12849. https://doi.org/10.1111/soc4.12849.

Maeda, Daryl Joji. 2016. "The Asian American Movement." In *Oxford Research Encyclopedia of American History.* https://doi.org/10.1093/acrefore/9780199329175.013.21.

Massey, Douglas S., and Maria Sánchez. 2010. *Brokered Boundaries: Immigrant Identity in Anti-Immigrant Times.* Russell Sage Foundation.

Menjívar, Cecilia. 2006. "Liminal Legality: Salvadoran and Guatemalan Immigrants' Lives in the United States." *American Journal of Sociology* 111 (4): 999–1037.

———. 2021. "The Racialization of 'Illegality.'" *Daedalus* 150 (2): 91–105.

Menjívar, Cecilia, and Laura J. Abrego. 2012. "Legal Violence: Immigration Law and the Lives of Central American Immigrants." *American Journal of Sociology* 117: 1380–1421.

Merolla, Jennifer, S. Karthick Ramakrishnan, and Chris Haynes. 2013. "'Illegal,' 'Undocumented,' or 'Unauthorized': Equivalency Frames, Issue Frames, and Public Opinion on Immigration." *Perspectives on Politics* 11 (3): 789–807.

Museus, Samuel D., and Julie J. Park. 2015. "The Continuing Significance of Racism in the Lives of Asian American College Students." *Journal of College Student Development* 56 (6): 551–569.

Museus, Samuel D., Kiana Shiroma, and Jude Paul Dizon. 2016. "Cultural Community Connections and College Success: An Examination of Southeast Asian American College Students." *Journal of College Student Development* 57 (5): 485–502.

Museus, Samuel D., and Varaxy Yi. 2014. "Asian American College Students." In *Today's College Students: A Reader*, edited by Pietro A. Sasso and Joseph L. DeVitis. Peter Lang.

Nguyen, Bach Mai Dolly, Mike Hoa Nguyen, Jason Chan, and Robert T. Teranishi. 2016. "The Racialized Experiences of Asian American and Pacific Islander Students: An Examination of Campus Racial Climate at the University of California, Los Angeles." National Commission on Asian American and Pacific Islander Research in Education.

Nguyen, Mike Hoa, Jason Chan, Bach Mai Dolly Nguyen, and Robert T. Teranishi. 2018. "Beyond Compositional Diversity: Examining the Campus Climate Experiences of Asian American and Pacific Islander Students." *Journal of Diversity in Higher Education* 11 (4): 484–501.

Palmer, Robert T., and Dina C. Maramba. 2015. "A Delineation of Asian American and Latino/a Students' Experiences with Faculty at a Historically Black College and University." *Journal of College Student Development* 56 (2): 111–126.

Passel, Jeffrey S. 2011. "Demography of Immigrant Youth: Past, Present, and Future." *Future of Children* 21 (1): 19–41.

Passel, Jeffrey S., and Paul Taylor. 2010. "Unauthorized Immigrants and Their U.S.-Born Children." Pew Research Center. http://pewhispanic.org/reports/report.php?ReportID=125.

Patel, Viraj S. 2010. "Challenging the Monolithic Asian American Identity on Campus: A Context for Working with South Asian American Students." *Vermont Connection* 31 (1): 72–81.

Poon, OiYan, Dian Squire, Corinne Kodama, Ajani Byrd, Jason Chan, Lester Manzano, Sara Furr, and Devita Bishundat. 2016. "A Critical Review of the Model Minority Myth in Selected Literature on Asian Americans and Pacific Islanders in Higher Education." *Review of Educational Research* 86 (2): 469–502.

Ramakrishnan, Karthick, and Sono Shah. 2017. "One Out of Every 7 Asian Immigrants Is Undocumented." *AAPI Data*, September 8. https://aapidata.com/blog/asian-undoc-1in7/.

Rana, Junaid. 2015. "Race." In *Keywords for Asian American Studies*, edited by Cathy J. Schlund-Vials, Linda Trinh Võ, and K. Scott Wong. New York University Press.

Reed, Holly E., Sofya Aptekar, and Amy Hsin. 2022. "Managing Illegality on Campus: Undocumented Mismatch Between Students and Staff." *Harvard Educational Review* 92 (1): 32–54.

Rodriguez, Cristina. 2016. "Experiencing 'Illegality' as a Family? Immigration Enforcement, Social Policies, and Discourses Targeting Mexican Mixed-Status Families." *Sociology Compass* 10 (8): 706–717.

———. 2019. "Latino/a Citizen Children of Undocumented Parents Negotiating Illegality." *Journal of Marriage and Family* 81 (3): 713–728.

Rodríguez, Noreen Naseem. 2018. "From Margins to Center: Developing Cultural Citizenship Education Through the Teaching of Asian American History." *Theory & Research in Social Education* 46 (4): 528–573.

Romero, Mary. 2008. "The Inclusion of Citizenship Status in Intersectionality: What Immigration Raids Tell Us About Mixed-Status Families, the State and Assimilation." *International Journal of Sociology of the Family* 34: 131–152.

Schmalzbauer, Leah, and Alelí Andres. 2019. "Stratified Lives: Family, Illegality, and the Rise of a New Educational Elite." *Harvard Educational Review* 89 (4): 635–660.

Seo, Michelle J. 2011. "Uncertainty of Access: U.S. Citizen Children of Undocumented Immigrant Parents and In-State Tuition for Higher Education." *Columbia Journal of Law and Social Problems* 44 (3): 311–352.

Smith, Andrea. 2012. "Indigeneity, Settler Colonialism, White Supremacy." In *Racial Formation in the Twenty-First Century*, edited by Daniel Martinez HoSang, Oneka LaBennett, and Laura Pulido. Oxford University Press.

Suárez-Orozco, Carola, and Marcelo M. Suárez-Orozco. 2009. *Children of Immigration*. Harvard University Press.

Suárez-Orozco, Carola, and Hirokazu Yoshikawa. 2015. "The Shadow of Undocumented Status." In *Transitions: The Development of Children of Immigrants*, edited by Carola Suárez-Orozco, Mona M. Abo-Zena, and Amy K. Marks. New York University Press.

Suárez-Orozco, Carola, Hirokazu Yoshikawa, Robert T. Teranishi, and Marcelo M. Suárez-Orozco. 2011. "Growing Up in the Shadows: The Developmental Implications of Unauthorized Status." *Harvard Educational Review* 81 (3): 438–473.

Surla, Kristen, and Oiyan A. Poon. 2015. "Visualizing Social Influences on Filipino Americans and Southeast Asian American College Choice." *Journal of Southeast Asian American Education and Advancement* 10 (2): 1–23.

Tamura, Eileen H. 2003. "Introduction: Asian Americans and Educational History." *History of Education Quarterly* 43 (1): 1–9.

Tang, Jennifer, Simon Kim, and Don Haviland. 2013. "Role of Family, Culture, and Peers in the Success of First-Generation Cambodian American College Students." *Journal of Southeast Asian American Education and Advancement* 8 (1): 1–19.

Teranishi, Robert T., and Victoria Kim. 2017. "The Changing Demographic Landscape of the Nation: Perspectives on College Opportunities for Asian Americans and Pacific Islanders." *Educational Forum* 81 (2): 204–216.

Tsong, Yuying, and Yuli Liu. 2009. "Parachute Kids and Astronaut Families." In *Asian American Psychology: Current Perspectives*, edited by Nita Tewari and Alvin N. Alvarez. Routledge.

Tuan, Mia. 1998. *Forever Foreigners or Honorary Whites? The Asian Ethnic Experience Today.* Rutgers University Press.

Vespa, Jonathan, David M. Armstrong, and Lauren Medina. 2018. "Demographic Turning Points for the United States: Population Projections for 2020 to 2060." U.S. Department of Commerce, Economics and Statistics Administration, U.S. Census Bureau.

Willen, Sarah S. 2012. "How Is Health-Related 'Deservingness' Reckoned? Perspectives from Unauthorized Im/migrants in Tel Aviv." *Social Science & Medicine* 74 (6): 812–821.

Yellow Horse, Aggie J., and Edward D. Vargas. 2021. "Legal Status, Worries About Deportation, and Depression Among Asian Immigrants." *Journal of Immigrant and Minority Health* 24 (4): 827–833.

Yi, Varaxy, Jacqueline Mac, Vanessa S. Na, Rikka J. Venturanza, Samuel D. Museus, Tracy Lachica Buenavista, and Sumun L. Pendakur. 2020. "Toward an Anti-Imperialistic Critical Race Analysis of the Model Minority Myth." *Review of Educational Research* 90 (4): 542–579.

Zhang, Qin. 2015. "Perceived Intergroup Stereotypes, Threats, and Emotions toward Asian Americans." *Howard Journal of Communications* 26 (2): 115–131.

Zhou, Min. 1998. "'Parachute Kids' in Southern California: The Educational Experience of Chinese Children in Transnational Families." *Educational Policy* 12 (6): 682–704.

———. 2004. "Are Asian Americans Becoming 'White'?" *Contexts* 3 (1): 29–37.

Zhou, Min, and Roberto G. Gonzales. 2019. "Divergent Destinies: Children of Immigrants Growing Up in the United States." *Annual Review of Sociology* 45: 383–399.

NOTES

1. In this chapter "Asian American" refers to East, Southeast, and South Asian Americans in the context of the United States. Due to the differential racialization of Native Hawaiians and Pacific Islanders often included in research on Asian American students, these communities were intentionally excluded from this study (Hall 2015; Labrador and Wright 2011; Yi et al. 2020).

    U.S. immigrants and migrants are sometimes studied separately but often analyzed together and/or framed synonymously. Willen (2012) declares that this diverse group "includes unauthorized border-crossers, visa overstayers, failed asylum seekers, and victims of human trafficking, among others, are characterized using a variety of labels. . . . By describing them as unauthorized 'im/migrants,' I aim both to acknowledge this internal diversity and to indicate that distinctions between unauthorized patterns of 'migration' . . . and 'immigration' are often tenuous, shifting, or illusory" (812–813). Considering this, the term "im/migrant" is utilized for this chapter.

    "Mixed-status families" is a term by Fix and Zimmerman (2001), who state that the formation of this type of im/migrant family is generated by U.S. immigration policy, in which parents and children hold varying immigration statuses; this term continues to be used across disciplines to describe im/migrant families who have at least one undocumented member.

2. This chapter uses the term "illegality" to denote the ways "the state criminalizes migrants, drawing analytic focus to legal structures that position undocumented migrants for exploitation" (Reed, Aptekar, and Hsin 2022, 33) and the way "Latino groups are the preeminent target group of both the social and the legal production of illegality" (Menjívar 2021, 91).

3. While the term "'undocumented' is not entirely accurate because many contemporary unauthorized [im/]migrants] possess documents" (Merolla, Ramakrishnan, and Haynes 2013), this chapter uses the term "undocumented" in line with educational and sociology scholarship (Abrego 2019; Enriquez 2015; Suárez-Orozco et al. 2011).

4. A "green card holder" is a permanent resident who has been granted authorization to live and work in the United States on a permanent basis. U.S. Citizenship and Immigration Services grants a person a permanent resident card, commonly called a "green card," as proof of that status (see www.uscis.gov/green-card).

5. Asian im/migrants are people of Asian descent who are foreign-born and have yet to obtain U.S. citizen status.

6. There are about 1.7 million undocumented Asian im/migrants in the United States, which means one out of every six undocumented im/migrants is Asian and one out of every seven Asian im/migrants is undocumented; these demographics include im/migrants from the following countries: India, China, Philippines, South Korea, Vietnam, and Pakistan. Other Asian countries are also included but are not identified due to the small sample (Ramakrishnan and Shah 2017).

7. Immigration-impacted students in this chapter are defined "as those who have been affected by contemporary [U.S.] immigration policies that marginalize undocumented immigrants and individuals with precarious legal statuses . . . [which includes] U.S. citizen students with undocumented family members." See Enriquez et al. (2021).

2

Negotiating Racialized "Illegality"

JESSICA LAW

Traditional ideas of citizenship often elide race, instead focusing on nationality or sovereignty. However, historical examples like Jim Crow segregation and Japanese internment demonstrate that citizenship is unevenly distributed or recognized along racial lines (Ngai 2004). Disproportionate deportations of Black and Latin American people indicate that certain racial groups are not perceived as citizens, regardless of legal status (Golash-Boza 2016). Notions of (non)citizenship and race must be interrogated in relation to each other. A relatively unexamined population is the undocumented Asian population.

The racial narratives about "Asians" and who they are or what they represent have changed over the course of U.S. history, from Yellow Peril to the model minority myth (Saito 1997). It is important to interrogate how contemporary racial narratives impact people's experiences of citizenship today. Given the unique racialization of Asians, the issues undocumented Asians face should be understood on their own terms, not only so that scholars and activists can address them but also to open possibilities for cross-racial solidarity. This chapter discusses findings from a research study I conducted to understand how racial narratives shape how undocumented Asians experience and interpret their immigration status.

In the following sections, I begin with an overview of the theoretical concepts that guide my analysis and a description of the research methods used. The concept of *illegality* is a theoretical anchor for understanding how immigration status confers social exclusions, not just legal ones (De Genova 2002). In the empirical sections, I draw on seventeen in-depth interviews with ethnically diverse undocumented Asian immigrants in Chicago to argue that illegality interacts with other forms of difference, like race, to produce experiences of exclusion that vary across racial groups. The interaction between race and illegality is contingent: the specific racialization of Asians conceals their illegality. I also examine how undocumented Asians leverage institutional categories to resist exclusion and build solidarity.

Literature Review

To examine the social and legal construction of immigration, researchers have foregrounded *illegality*, which De Genova (2002, 427) defines as a particular "social relation to the state" characterized by "forced invisibility, exclusion, subjugation, and repression." Illegality determines not only immigrants' formal rights but also their social membership in society and "their understandings of their place in it" (Menjívar 2006, 1003).

Racialization and illegalization are implicated in each other. Ngai (1999, 92) has argued that U.S. immigration policies have racialized immigrant groups "around notions of whiteness, permanent foreignness, and illegality." In other words, illegality is essential in the construction of "Asian" or "Mexican," as well as others, as groups that are meaningfully distinct and naturally cohesive (Ngai 2004). Studying illegality without accounting for enmeshed axes of difference like race would be to miss the unique consequences of these structures of power (Crenshaw 1991). Scholars have used *racialized illegality* to understand these interlocking systems, specifically for Mexican and Central American immigrants (Enriquez 2019; García 2017; Patler 2014). This analytic is premised on the ideas that certain racial groups become synonymous with illegality and that the actual experience of illegality varies depending on the relevant racial narratives. There is no singular configuration of racialized illegality. Less examined is an "Asian" illegality (see Cho 2017; Hsin and Aptekar 2022).

Although racialization and illegalization may appear totalizing, individuals and groups respond to these processes (Haney-López 1994). In other words, racial identities can be understood as not only strict examples of state domination but also sites where people contest or consent to power (Brown and Jones 2015; Rodríguez-Muñiz 2017). Drawing on their own interpretative work, people can choose to adopt or dispute group identities. I trace how undocumented Asians understand and respond to their own racialized illegality.

Data and Methods

This study draws on seventeen in-depth interviews conducted in 2017 with undocumented Asians, ages eighteen to thirty-four years old, in the Chicago metropolitan area.[1] Participants were initially recruited from local organizations focused on immigration or Asian American issues, and more were recruited through snowball sampling. Most were undocumented or recipients of deferred status under the Deferred Action for Childhood Arrivals (DACA) program at the time of the interview, while some were formerly undocumented. Five were

Filipino, five were Korean, two were Indian, two were Mongolian, two were Pakistani, and one was mixed-race Korean and Japanese. Although participants discussed ethnic differences, all of them aligned themselves with an "Asian American" identity. The participants self-reported as working class or lower middle class.

Because of their age range, my participants may not necessarily be representative of the undocumented population in Chicago. This is evidenced by the large proportion of participants who had been granted deferred status under the DACA program, which was purposefully restricted to "DREAMers," or youth who were seen to be well deserving by having at least a high school education and no criminal background and therefore eligible for the proposed federal DREAM Act legislation. All but two had received a college education or were enrolled in a higher education institution. Nonetheless, their experiences offer important insights as members of a liminal community in the United States today.

Findings

Based on the interviews, I outline how race and illegality can have varying and sometimes conflicting effects on participants' sense of belonging at different moments. I then argue that the social meanings of "Asian" produce chiasmatic invisibilities: undocumented but not Asian or Asian but not undocumented. In response to these invisibilities, I argue, participants mobilize around specific identities to build solidarity.

Becoming "Illegal"

Because most of the participants were unaware of their family's undocumented status until early adulthood and "legality is not a prerequisite for [social] participation" during childhood (Gonzales 2016, 67), their early experiences were primarily shaped by their *racial* status. Participants came to the United States between the ages of two and thirteen years old. Growing up, they were able to access many spaces and forms of American life, like schools.

Participants reflected on their experiences growing up as racial minorities in areas with small Asian populations. Almost all of them had experienced some form of racial "othering" by peers or neighbors. They expressed a keen awareness of their racial minority status, being hypervisible and socially excluded. For example, Isabel, a thirty-four-year-old Korean woman, recounted that her white and Latinx friends would taunt her every day on the playground, chanting racist rhymes.[2] As the only Asian student, she had thought these incidents were "normal" and inevitable for minorities. As these microaggressions become ordinary occurrences, racial difference appears natural. Race textures their everyday lives and perceptions of their place in society.

Despite the microaggressions, participants conveyed that their racial status did not necessarily prevent them from participating in the social world
around them during childhood. Although almost all of the participants admitted that their sense of self was affected by how others saw them, many maintained that they did belong in the United States. In American schools, they
were able to develop enduring, meaningful relationships to their social environment and peers. Jae, a twenty-one-year-old Korean man, expressed that he
was "as American as you can be," having grown up in "American culture and
adopted these norms." These norms include a faith in the American Dream: "To
be American is to have absolute control of your own life and destiny really. Like
honestly, this is the land of opportunity and I've fully understood that and any
person who comes with the right attitude and hard work and drive, you can do
a lot of things here. . . . I wouldn't have that same experience or opportunity in
Korea, right?" Embedded in these social attachments is a cultural expectation
of social mobility or the promise of the American Dream (Gonzales 2016).
American liberalism, which espouses the principles of equal opportunity and
color blindness, encourages the idea that minorities can make equal claims on
the state and society (Bonilla-Silva 2014). Adopting these values can help foster
a sense of normalcy and belonging, even for those who feel marginalized by
their race. In other words, because their racial difference had not formally pre-
vented them from moving up in the world, the American Dream is alluring and
attainable. This access to the American Dream enables a sense of belonging.

It was when participants discovered their undocumented status and its
broad legal exclusions during their teenage years that their feelings of belonging were threatened. Most participants became undocumented as children
when their families overstayed their temporary tourist or work visas. Many
were unaware of their undocumented status until later in life, often discovering it at the end of high school when they wanted to obtain a driver's license or
apply to college. Christina, a twenty-year-old Filipino woman, did not find out
about her status until she wanted to get a job: "I know a lot of people come with
memories of physically crossing the border and that staying with them their
whole life. I did not find out until I was seventeen years old. I was going into my
senior year of high school and I wanted to get a job at the pool in the summer. I
kept bugging my parents and finally they were like, that's not going to be possible because so-and-so, and they told me." Even among those who had known
about their family's precarious immigration status for most of their lives, many
did not grasp its sweeping implications until they tried to accomplish similar
milestones. Before trying to fill out the application for federal student aid, Layla,
a twenty-year-old Pakistani woman, had thought that she was "like everybody
else" regardless of her undocumented status. She "didn't know what [her status]
meant" until she learned that she would not be able to receive federal college
aid. For these participants, it was only upon realizing that they were barred

from undergoing ordinary rites of passage that they began to understand "what it meant" to be undocumented. It was at this point that they transitioned into illegality. As Gonzales (2016, 12) suggests, these "youthful feelings of belonging give way to new understandings of the ways they are excluded from possibilities they believed were theirs." Batu, a twenty-five-year-old Mongolian man, described this phenomenon: "I really thought [that if] you do good in school, that shit will take you places, you know? And I was at the end of the road and there was no more road. It was like, okay, what do I do now?"

The acute disparity between their expectations for their lives and the actual possibilities available to them resulted in feelings of extreme exclusion that disrupted their sense of belonging. Anand, a thirty-four-year-old Indian man, had been aware of his family's immigration status. At certain milestones, he was confronted by the barriers that came with his undocumented status, causing him to reflect on his American identity: "Yeah, it [undocumented status] did affect [how I felt about myself]. Especially when applying to certain scholarships or funding and whatnot, that's when it really laid bare what it actually meant. That's when I realized that maybe I'm not really American. It's institutional or structural that I'm not. My brother and I, we feel American. I consider myself an American, but especially [when you face] those roadblocks is when you really are able to feel like what the difference was, what the distinction meant." The responses of Christina, Layla, and Anand demonstrate a process of illegalization. Their formal relation to the state protruded in opposition to their long-standing presence and social attachments. Before, as solely *racialized* subjects, they were presumed to have nevertheless been able to navigate U.S. institutions and had felt like they belonged, but through *illegalization*, the power of the state appeared to intervene so devastatingly into their lives and created new feelings of exclusion.

Although participants often spoke of their racial and legal statuses simultaneously, indicating the imbrication of racialization and illegality, many narrated their lives as if those were separate and situationally important. While illegality was a powerful determinant of participants' opportunities and emotional attachment to America, its impact on their identities should not be overstated. Racial exclusion and alienation also came to the fore, sometimes even eclipsing legal status. Helen, a twenty-six-year-old Filipino woman, had found out about her status at eight years old when her family was forced to flee from the state due to fear of deportation. The gravity of being undocumented was immediately made apparent to her given the threat of family separation. With this awareness, Helen had not developed the same belief in the American Dream like her peers: "In the community we grew up in, because it was a lot of wealthy white kids, the message of the school that I went to was always, 'If you believe you can do it, then you can achieve it and we're here to help you.' I remember being sixteen and being like, 'This is all a bunch of crap. This doesn't

apply to everybody.'" Without the prospect of social mobility, racial stratification bore more heavily on her sense of belonging. Although she had grown up
knowing that her family's livelihoods were always at risk, she "thought a lot
more about being Asian than [she] did about being undocumented" during her
early adolescence. She explained,

> Because [race] was always something that I knew about and that was
> always the first thing people saw about me. People see you when you
> grow up in a place that's mostly white people. I don't fault them for this
> because they were young, we were young. But most of my friends who
> were growing up would introduce me to their parents as, "This is my Fili-
> pino friend." . . . Maybe I'm just sensitive. But I was always made aware of
> that, whether it was something as overt as being "This is my Filipino
> friend" or going to events with friends and being like, "Wow, I'm the only
> non-white person here." It was a lot more glaringly obvious to me grow-
> ing up than being undocumented.

Even in brief exchanges, Helen was continually made aware of her racial minority status. She expressed a sentiment shared by many participants that race is
immutably marked on the body and therefore undeniable.

The narrative separation between race and illegality was apparent when
Helen recounted her life as having occurred in three stages:

> I think that maybe from ages eight or nine to fifteen, I felt the impact of
> being Asian more. That was always just more obvious in my day-to-day.
> Maybe from ages sixteen to early twenties was when I felt the impact
> more of being undocumented because at that point, I was just used to
> people acknowledging me as their Filipino friend. But when people
> started getting their licenses or people started applying to colleges and
> stuff, that was where I was like, "I can't do these things" and it had noth-
> ing to do with my race, it had to do with my immigration status. . . . It
> wasn't until [my] early twenties, up until even now, that I started really
> thinking about the impact of existing as both.

There is a curious elision and dislocation of race or illegality in these different
periods. Helen is gesturing toward a form of *racialized illegality* that enables the
perception of one without the other, despite their linkages. Instead of a conflation of race and illegality, the latter gets obscured through the racialization of
Asians in the United States.

Visible Race, Invisible Illegality

Migration of elite labor from Asian countries to the United States facilitated by
the Immigration and Nationality Act of 1965 has led to the conflation of being
"Asian" with educational attainment, professional skill, and legality (Junn

2007). Narratives of Asian success and passivity often appear alongside, and in contradistinction to, narratives of "Mexican" illegality that pervade public discourse (Chavez 2013; Hong 2015). Although many participants remarked that the undocumented population is racially diverse, they observed that the dominant image of one is Latinx. A major consequence of this was that, as undocumented Asians, they were not always perceived as "illegal" or undocumented. William, a twenty-six-year-old Korean man, noted that "we [Asians] are much less of a target for deportation" than other communities. Christina offered a hypothetical situation that illustrates a similar point: "Status is something you can't see, but I think even if I'm on the train or something, I have the privilege of knowing if something bad were to happen, like worst case scenario—ICE [U.S. Immigration and Customs Enforcement] just busted through the CTA [train] doors—I would know that I would not be the first person that they would look at." Their racialization as Asians masks the perception of their illegality on multiple registers. They understand themselves as being neither perceived as an institutional priority for policing and deportation nor visually legible as undocumented to those around them. Instead, they are seen as *model minorities*, or "people who are succeeding in America despite their status as minorities" due to cultural exceptionalism (Saito 1997, 71).

At the same time, Asian Americans are seen as *foreign*. Helen described this as "the idea that Asian folks are always this perpetual foreigner." Foreignness is a central feature of the "social construction of an Asian 'race'" (Saito 1997). To be a foreigner is to be socially excluded, where racial difference exceeds that which can be assimilated into the nation. Joey, a twenty-seven-year-old Japanese and Korean man, described how this idea appears in brief interactions: "Even [a] real Asian American with American citizenship, they would go through public transit, being called 'ching chong' or 'go back to China, go back to Korea.' . . . Whatever people have image of American, Asian American is not part of it. . . . I feel like they would never let us feel like we are American too. I don't think they accept Asian features as part of America." Perceived foreignness takes shape in veiled ways as well. Following her remark about being a perpetual foreigner, Helen added, "I've gotten people even now who casually compliment my English," suggesting that people expect her to speak in broken English. In these examples, "Asian features" and "my English" are signifiers of "Asian" foreignness.

"Asian" illegality, unlike that of Latinx immigrants, is produced through obfuscation and exclusion as they are not presumed to be "criminals" or "illegal." That is, while Latinx immigrants are socially excluded due to a perception of criminality, some Asian immigrants are instead socially excluded due to a perception of foreignness that is not largely criminalized. In other words, the previous comments convey that undocumented Asians are assumed to be foreign but are not regarded as "illegal." Irene, a twenty-eight-year-old Filipino woman, summarized public perception: "Asian people, they're immigrants, but they come here the right way." Participants described that even when others questioned their "Americanness," there was still an underlying assumption of legality and not an accusation of criminality.

The duality of this type of "Asian" illegality—foreign yet legal and noncriminal—enables a chiasmatic relationship between race and immigration status, where one appears to preclude the other in certain circumstances. Just as Helen "felt the impact of being Asian" or undocumented more in different stages of her life, race and immigration status can be analytically and experientially separated. Christina illustrated this phenomenon in her experience as a student and activist navigating different organizations: "How I understand me as a person, as a whole person, there's no way to separate the two [race and immigration status], but then, when I'm just going through life and moving through different spaces, there are so many instances where I have to really leave the 'undocumented' or leave the 'Filipino' at the door when I'm going to certain spaces, so they can be severed there." When I asked her why she thought she deferred her "Filipinoness" in spaces intended for undocumented immigrants and whether she thought that others did something similar, she continued, "I don't know. [pause] Because when I'm going into predominantly undocumented spaces, it's a lot of Latinx people and there are a lot of commonalities between Filipinos and Latinos, but usually I find that my Filipinoness can't really come out more. . . . I think they take [their Latinoness] with them. I don't know why. I don't know the reasons why. It's cool to see though. Okay, they don't have to leave it at the door, but why do I feel like I have to leave mine?" Underlying the impasse here is the perceived incompatibility of "Asian" and "undocumented." On one hand, they are not readily seen as undocumented. On the other hand, participants expressed feeling that their identity as an undocumented immigrant was absent or excluded in spaces intended for Asian Americans. This incompatibility, in turn, results in chiasmatic invisibilities: *undocumented but not Asian* or *Asian but not undocumented*. These invisibilities result in exclusion or isolation in the undocumented and Asian communities.

Regarding the first invisibility of *undocumented but not Asian*, some participants noticed that organizations dedicated to undocumented students were often accessible only to Spanish-speaking people, prioritizing Latinx students. At her university, Irene was actively involved in an undocumented student organization. Although there were undocumented Asian students, including herself, or other non-Spanish-speaking members, she felt excluded. On an interpersonal level, this first invisibility manifests as a language barrier. Participants often indicated that the smaller—perceived and actual—proportion of Asians within the undocumented population meant that they were not represented or accommodated.

Another common example of this invisibility among the students was the lack of institutional support for Asians. Because they were not eligible for federal aid due to their status, many sought out external scholarships designated for undocumented students. Layla and Tuyaa, a twenty-one-year-old Mongolian woman, described similar experiences finding scholarships that were available only for Latinx students:

LAYLA: The way where my Muslim and Pakistani identities are not included in the undocumented one are in terms of when I had to talk to people about finding resources and scholarships and all that stuff. It was predominantly, they were all Hispanic scholarships, Latino scholarships, you had to be this descent, this descent. I never fit in there. I was never a part of that.

TUYAA: That's the most difficult or unique part [about being undocumented and Asian]. We don't get represented a lot. A lot of Asian Americans don't have a support system that a lot of Latino undocumented students have. There are so many programs and organizations that, if they're seeking, it's easier. When I was applying for scholarships, I remember it was just so many Latino whatever whatever. There were not necessarily Asian scholarships for undocumented people.

Tuyaa attributed the scarcity of scholarships to the lack of Asian representation in the undocumented community and conversely to the high level of engagement of Latinx communities that advocate for these resources.

The second invisibility of *Asian but not undocumented* occurred in both undocumented and Asian spaces. Irene recounted her experience first joining the undocumented student organization:

When I got involved, I was the only Asian person and would be for a while until my friend got involved, also Filipina. It was interesting because when I started going to meetings, people didn't know I was undocumented. I connected with them maybe June [that year] and then [that] September was when I was like, "Oh, I'm undocumented." Pretty much every meeting, people would go around, "I'm so-and-so and I'm undocumented," and I would just go and say my name, so people wouldn't know. . . . It was interesting because the assumption was that I wasn't undocumented because I was Asian. There were a couple other Asian people there, but they were pretty explicit about being an ally, a supporter, co-struggler.

Unlike the other Asian members who had announced that they were not undocumented, Irene did not disclose her immigration status, thereby creating an ambiguity that had then been tacitly resolved by prevailing expectations about Asians. She was presumed to be like the other Asian members, "an ally, a supporter," rather than a fellow undocumented immigrant. This invisibility also created a demand for representation, where Irene's "Asianness" superseded her identity and experience as an undocumented immigrant: "When I told people I was undocumented, there became this need to speak for Asian people who don't show up to things, like be the voice of the community because they're silent or whatever. I felt this immense pressure to represent and organize all the Asian people in Chicago because there wasn't anyone else that I knew doing it." Because she was Asian, and one of the few undocumented Asians in the organization, she was expected to organize other Asians. Despite her explicit confession of her undocumented status, that part of her identity was ultimately minimized relative to her race.

When asked about the challenges of being both undocumented and Asian, most participants discussed the lack of resources and discourse around undocumented issues in their respective ethnic communities or the broader Asian American community. They said that their experiences being undocumented often went unacknowledged. Participants attributed this invisibility to either ignorance or stigma. For example, according to William, the Korean American community does not accommodate conversations about undocumented status: "Just being Asian American, it comes with cultural barriers. Speaking about your undocumented status, it is still taboo in Korean American community." He added that he used to be a member of an undocumented "Pan-Asian" youth group that served as a response to that invisibility: "For me, I think a lot of the cultural silence or shame that exists in many different Asian American communities was something to bond over with on a friendship level. That was a commonality that naturally brought us together." William was one of the more fortunate participants in this regard; many other participants discussed the loneliness they experienced growing up. Helen spoke about the profound effect this invisibility had on her: "I never thought there was anybody who would understand what I was going through. . . . It makes you feel like you don't count when talking about immigrants, that your experiences don't matter." While some of the participants drew upon notions of an "Asian" culture that demands passivity, this emphasis on culture can further obscure the structural barriers that undocumented Asians face, which may in turn reify Asian stereotypes and inhibit mobilization for such resources (Buenavista 2018).

Although participants gave different reasons for their experiences of isolation, the confluence of them reproduces the racialized illegality of Asian immigrants—the image of them being foreign yet legal and noncriminal. Their illegibility as undocumented allows them certain privileges, such as self-assurance of the relative lack of attention from state authorities. Even for those who are forthright about their immigration status, their racialization sometimes conceals their perceived illegality and thus the challenges they face as undocumented immigrants. The chiasmatic invisibilities present difficulties in both their personal lives and their political efforts, forcing them to find different ways to navigate the sociopolitical terrain.

Becoming In/Visible

Because most participants were young and students at the time of the interview, they were able to access social institutions like schools that then fostered a tactical understanding of the law as maneuverable (Abrego 2011). They felt capable of navigating and resisting their circumstances. Although all participants affirmed the profound consequences of racialization and undocumented status, they also expressed a wide range of responses and strategies. Some elected to take advantage of the invisibilities, while others opted to organize against them. Strategies for organizing took on two forms, centered on either race or immigration status. Understanding the political salience of the categories of "Asian / Asian American" or "immigrant" (Brown and Jones 2015; Calavita 2010; De Genova 2002), activists mobilized these identities to organize collectively.

Although the invisibility of "Asian" illegality has an isolating effect, some saw that obfuscation as advantageous. Some participants felt that the relative invisibility of undocumented Asians vis-à-vis "Mexican" illegality meant that they were less vulnerable. Here, invisibility constitutes a strategy for survival. Other participants similarly described that their approach to managing their illegality was to "lay low." Even those who actively organize for immigrant justice are strategic about disclosing their undocumented status and rely on that invisibility. By embracing their invisibility, these participants can pass as citizens, or at least legal. In doing so, they reproduce a dichotomy of invisible/visible.

The paradigm of in/visibility in immigrant organizing is most evident in the "Coming Out of the Shadows" movement born in Chicago in the early 2010s, which relied on the tactic of disclosing one's undocumented status for collective mobilization in spite of individual fears (Enriquez and Saguy 2016). In the realm of Chicago activism, the primary obstacles participants described were ignorance of undocumented Asian immigrants and their lack of "power," as represented by their relatively small population. The invisibility conferred by "Asian" illegality undergirds these obstacles. Under this logic of invisibility, those who aspire to end state domination must challenge it by becoming visible discursively, physically, and politically. Irene described visibility as "the antidote to stigma." Contestation took two forms for participants: race-focused and status-focused. They often narrated this divide in their experiences, and many were involved in organizations whose focuses were split as such. At the risk of further reifying this divide, I discuss how participants sought to combat and maneuver their invisibility in these two settings as racialized and illegalized subjects.

Participants whose activism was centered on ethnoracial mobilization adopted or tolerated the panethnic classification of "Asian American," despite their misgivings, in order to become visible through racial unity. For many participants, this term was either insufficient or unsuitable for how they identify. Some argued that "'Asian' is too big of a range" or that it is "important that we are able to distinguish these different ethnicities." William expressed plainly, "I wouldn't go out somewhere and tell somebody I'm Asian American." He laughed before continuing, "That's [*pause*] kind of weird. I wouldn't do that." Despite their personal discomforts, many participants agreed on the social and political use of the panethnic category. While Christina believed that the category unfairly "lump[s] people together," she later added that it can also "bring people together."

The "Asian American" category is culturally and politically established through the "tests and checkboxes" that demand their racial identification. This means that "Asian American" is a group that is commonly recognized while specific ethnic groups may not be. With this understanding, groups are able to mobilize "Asian American" for their own political ends. In this way, "Asian American" becomes a political identity that counteracts their invisibility:

ANAND: "Asian American" itself has been defined by the community but as well as by, at least in America, by the U.S. Census Bureau, in other words by the government. . . . Many people are realizing that they may be Brown, but as far as policies are concerned, they are identified as Asian American. I think that considering our numbers, our goal there is to find commonality so that we can ensure that policies are implemented do not negatively impact our community and that includes the entire Asian community, whether it's Vietnamese, or Chinese, or Indian, or Filipino.

IRENE: I think in the way that we've been racialized as Asian Americans and in the sort of narratives around test stats and education achievement, it's super problematic. When I think of "Asian American" as political identity, it's very much around shared histories and shared experiences of oppression. And shared ways we've been exploited and very much explicitly. In laws and in the immigration system. Stereotypes. It can be powerful because these are things that have been ascribed to us as a group of people who are super different, but the ways that we've been grouped together, okay, we can use that to grow our numbers, build our power.

As organizers, Anand and Irene argued that the Asian American identity allows them to bolster their "numbers" and thus their visibility as a powerful population. Although these participants recognize that they are seen as "Asian" institutionally and interpersonally, they do not totally surrender themselves to these categories. Rather, the identities that they take on are determined out of a strategic maneuvering and awareness of others' perceptions.

Alongside its political salience, the visibility of "Asian American" engenders a community that may be more accessible due to its reach. As participants remarked, isolation is a characteristic and product of their invisibility as undocumented Asians. By investing in "Asian American," some participants have been able to create new connections. Joey described a group that was formed through an Asian-focused organization: "Especially for undocumented people, community is important because we feel alone in this fight. . . . I went to meeting for [Asian American organization] that was just for us undocumented and the three of us got together. That was nice. Because I know that was safe because we share the same issues, same kind of desperation." While this undocumented-specific space was important, Joey added that the broader Asian American community remains crucial: "I think it's too limiting if it's just for undocumented community. Undocumented community should be supported by other Asian community who are already naturalized. That would be much more helpful because if we alone are just in the same group, then I think we would be too distrusting to ask for other help, where there could be other help available but we just don't know because we are so afraid." The visibility of the Asian American community performs a shielding function that can preserve the invisibility of its vulnerable members. By leveraging a different visible marker, undocumented Asians can protect against isolation and regulate their public presence while not endangering their safety. In this ongoing tension between self-identifying as Asian American and mobilizing collectively under its banner, there is a simultaneous refusal and embrace of the category.

"Immigrant" as a concept and identity is similarly produced through law, where its taken-for-grantedness has been constructed through the "cognitive power of legal classifications" (Calavita 2010, 35; De Genova 2002). "Immigrant" becomes a way of understanding common experiences or shared histories and uniting across racial lines. During college, Helen found solidarity with others on the basis of their struggles as immigrants:

> When I was going into these spaces that were mostly fellow undocumented folks, there was a lot of young people that were my age, but it was pretty much 95 percent Latinos. It was strange because it was like, I'm in this space where a lot of these folks who are in here share a lot of similarities to me in terms of their background, their—I didn't realize at the time—but their trauma and my trauma, and my anxieties and all of my insecurities and all of my struggles, which was a whole different kind of experience from sitting in these rooms with mostly Asian Americans who had similar upbringings to mine but our struggles, the things that we dealt with growing up were very different.

She contrasted her experience among "fellow undocumented folks" with that in Asian American organizations on her campus, indicating that "Asian American" proved inadequate. Instead, Helen saw "undocumented" or "immigrant" as identities around which she and others could find commonality and combat their invisibility. Although these affiliations often emerge from violent histories of colonization, there is a strength in these connections, as Irene noted, that can offer avenues of activism that "raise visibility."

In response to their invisibility and illegality, these undocumented Asian immigrants strategically maneuvered their illegibility through careful deployment of particular identities. It was at times advantageous for themselves to maintain the shroud that their race provided them, though this move fails to challenge racist narratives about, or build solidarity with, other groups. In other moments, especially in activist contexts, participants would adopt the panethnic category of "Asian American" to become visible. In doing so, they did not acquiesce to institutional classification; instead, they used its social currency for their social activism. Similarly, some participants united with others under the banner of "immigrant" or "undocumented" to bridge racial difference and act collectively. While the use of such identities may appear to further reify and reproduce the very invisibilities—undocumented but not Asian or Asian but not undocumented—that they are situated in, it empowers them to move toward the dissolution of their illegality.

Conclusion

Racist domination remains at the foundation of U.S. society, structuring everyday interactions and institutional access. Beyond just legality, citizenship is a "matter of belonging, including recognition by other members of the community" (Glenn 2002, 52). Given this, citizenship is inseparable from race (Ngai 2004). This study demonstrates how social membership, or citizenship as lived, is mediated by race and legal status for undocumented Asians. By examining the experiences of undocumented Asian Americans today, we may gain a greater understanding of the entanglement of race and citizenship and its consequences for belonging. It is evident that citizenship, in both the legal and the social sense, is inseparable from processes of racialization. In the same way, the injustices that immigrants in the United States have endured and continue to face are linked to racism. Ideologies of color blindness or multiculturalism may tell us that racial inequality can be resolved through an ignorance of race (Bonilla-Silva 2014; Segal and Handler 1995). Opposition to this, however, should not be a commitment to racial essentialism or the flattening of racial difference. Instead, as this study has begun to do, the connection between race and immigration must be interrogated in all of its specificities. By failing to account for the differences in the experiences of undocumented Asians, in relation to both each other and other racial groups, such as Latinx and Black populations, scholars and activists risk reifying the narratives and stereotypes that subject one group to deportation and another to invisibility. This study begins to disarticulate the logics of racialization and citizenship. Through this, hopefully resistances to domination, like the ones explored here, can be imagined and liberatory forms of belonging can be forged.

REFERENCES

Abrego, Leisy J. 2011. "Legal Consciousness of Undocumented Latinos: Fear and Stigma as Barriers to Claims-Making for First- and 1.5-Generation Immigrants." *Law & Society Review* 45 (2): 337–370.

Bonilla-Silva, Eduardo. 2014. *Racism Without Racists: Color-Blind Racism and the Persistence of Racial Inequality in America.* 4th ed. Rowman & Littlefield.

Brown, Hana E., and Jennifer A. Jones. 2015. "Rethinking Panethnicity and the Race-Immigration Divide: An Ethnoracialization Model of Group Formation." *Sociology of Race and Ethnicity* 1 (1): 181–191.

Buenavista, Tracy Lachica. 2018. "Model (Undocumented) Minorities and 'Illegal' Immigrants: Centering Asian Americans and U.S. Carcerality in Undocumented Student Discourse." *Race, Ethnicity and Education* 21 (1): 78–91.

Calavita, Kitty. 2010. *Invitation to Law and Society: An Introduction to the Study of Real Law.* University of Chicago Press.

Chavez, Leo R. 2013. *The Latino Threat: Constructing Immigrants, Citizens, and the Nation.* 2nd ed. Stanford University Press.

Cho, Esther Yoona. 2017. "A Double Bind—'Model Minority' and 'Illegal Alien.'" *Asian American Law Journal* 24: 123–130.

Crenshaw, Kimberlé. 1991. "Mapping the Margins: Intersectionality, Identity Politics, and Violence Against Women of Color." *Stanford Law Review* 43 (6): 1241–1299.

De Genova, Nicholas. 2002. "Migrant 'Illegality' and Deportability in Everyday Life." *Annual Review of Anthropology* 31 (1): 419–447.

Enriquez, Laura E. 2019. "Border Hopping Mexicans, Law-Abiding Asians, and Racialized Illegality: Analyzing Undocumented College Students' Experiences Through a Relational Lens." In *Studying Race Relationally*, edited by Natalia Molina, Daniel Martinez HoSang, and Ramón Gutiérrez. University of California Press.

Enriquez, Laura E., and Abigail C. Saguy. 2016. "Coming out of the Shadows: Harnessing a Cultural Schema to Advance the Undocumented Immigrant Youth Movement." *American Journal of Cultural Sociology* 4 (1): 107–30. https://doi.org/10.1057/ajcs.2015.6.

García, San Juanita. 2017. "Racializing 'Illegality': An Intersectional Approach to Understanding How Mexican-Origin Women Navigate an Anti-Immigrant Climate." *Sociology of Race and Ethnicity* 3 (4): 474–490.

Glenn, Evelyn Nakano. 2002. *Unequal Freedom: How Race and Gender Shaped American Citizenship and Labor.* Harvard University Press.

Golash-Boza, Tanya. 2016. "The Parallels Between Mass Incarceration and Mass Deportation: An Intersectional Analysis of State Repression." *Journal of World-Systems Research* 22 (2): 484–509.

Gonzales, Roberto G. 2016. *Lives in Limbo: Undocumented and Coming of Age in America.* University of California Press.

Haney-López, Ian. 1994. "The Social Construction of Race: Some Observations on Illusion, Fabrication, and Choice." *Harvard Civil Rights–Civil Liberties Law Review* 29 (1): 1–62.

Hong, Grace Kyungwon. 2015. "Neoliberalism." *Critical Ethnic Studies* 1 (1): 56–67.

Hsin, Amy, and Sofya Aptekar. 2022. "The Violence of Asylum: The Case of Undocumented Chinese Migration to the United States." *Social Forces* 100 (3): 1195–1217.

Junn, Jane. 2007. "From Coolie to Model Minority: U.S. Immigration Policy and the Construction of Racial Identity." *Du Bois Review: Social Science Research on Race* 4 (2): 355–373.

Menjívar, Cecilia. 2006. "Liminal Legality: Salvadoran and Guatemalan Immigrants' Lives in the United States." *American Journal of Sociology* 111 (4): 999–1037.

Ngai, Mae M. 1999. "The Architecture of Race in American Immigration Law: A Reexamination of the Immigration Act of 1924." *Journal of American History* 86 (1): 67–92.

———. 2004. *Impossible Subjects: Illegal Aliens and the Making of Modern America*. Princeton University Press.

Patler, Caitlin. 2014. "Racialized 'Illegality': The Convergence of Race and Legal Status Among Black, Latino/a and Asian American Undocumented Young Adults." In *Scholars and Southern Californian Immigrants in Dialogue: New Conversations in Public Sociology*, edited by Victoria Carty, Tekle Mariam Woldemikael, and Rafael Luévano. Lexington Books.

Rodríguez-Muñiz, Michael. 2017. "Cultivating Consent: Nonstate Leaders and the Orchestration of State Legibility." *American Journal of Sociology* 123 (2): 385–425.

Saito, Natsu Taylor. 1997. "Model Minority, Yellow Peril: Functions of 'Foreignness' in the Construction of Asian American Legal Identity." *Asian American Law Journal* 4 (1): 71–96.

Segal, Daniel A., and Richard Handler. 1995. "U.S. Multiculturalism and the Concept of Culture." *Identities* 1 (4): 391–407.

NOTES

1. This research study was approved by the University of Chicago's Institutional Review Board.

2. All names used in this chapter are pseudonyms.

PART TWO

Community-Based Methodological Approaches and Reclaiming Representations of Asian Undocumented Immigrant Experiences

3

Tsismis/Chisme as an Undocumented Community-Responsive Tool

Co-Conspiratorial Research to Action

TRACY LACHICA BUENAVISTA

As a Pinay scholar whose community's presence in the United States is a consequence of the American colonization of the Philippines, I have strived to use decolonizing approaches to research to guide my praxis, or those practices that decenter white-supremacist perspectives and processes of knowledge construction, sharing, and documentation. I have worked alongside undocumented immigrant communities for the past two decades and in doing so have become attuned to the need for reflexivity with regard to how research processes often harm those vulnerable to state violence. In particular, because undocumented immigrant communities are often excluded from the academy, outsider researchers—or those who are not directly impacted by the systems we write about—such as myself, run the danger of conducting work that is more likely than not extractive. However, because I also consider myself simultaneously co-conspiratorial with undocumented peoples, I learned many lessons from organizing and offer a candid reflection about what I believe are the real limitations of a research-driven process of social action with regard to undocumented immigration.

"Co-conspirators" are those who recognize from a privileged standpoint the disenfranchisement of racialized others and the ways they benefit from such disparity but choose to commit to justice practices in which they work alongside—and toward outcomes that center—marginalized communities (Love 2019). Such work requires co-conspirators to be self-reflective and deeply contend with their privilege toward the development of authentic relationships necessary to conduct transformative work. Inspired by abolitionist discourse, as well as the work of other scholars who contend with the nuance of what it means to be in community with undocumented people (Abrego and Negrón-Gonzales 2020), I explain in this chapter how I seek to be co-conspiratorial in my work with undocumented immigrant students and how such an approach can illuminate the research and knowledge construction processes undocumented immigrant communities are already engaged in on a daily basis but are rarely recognized as such. Specifically, I ponder the role of *tsismis* or *chisme* as a community-responsive research tool toward shifting how scholars, practitioners, and students can support undocumented immigrants. The terms *tsismis* in Filipino and *chisme* in Spanish generally refer to gossip, but I argue that they represent a strategic form of information sharing among undocumented immigrant communities and their allies. In the following sections, I share how I came to work with undocumented communities, the lessons I learned from my work with Asian American and undocumented students, the role of research in serving undocumented communities, and how centering tsismis/chisme as a research practice is instructive in how to center undocumented student knowledge toward social action.

How I Come to the Work

It is important to contextualize how I came to work with undocumented immigrant communities as a co-conspiratorial, outsider researcher. I never intended to develop a work agenda attentive to undocumented immigration. My scholarly focus was the college access and retention of U.S. Filipino students and how the relationship among education, immigration, and labor in the Philippines facilitated the formation of the Filipino diaspora. However, to understand this relationship it is necessary to examine how these forces construct undocumented communities in "receiving" countries and subsequently shapes the material realities of Filipino students and families affected by undocumented immigrant status.

The history of American colonial schooling in the Philippines combined with a Philippine economy characterized by a labor brokerage system facilitated (and continues to facilitate) the mass migration of Filipinos to the United States (Guevarra 2009; Rodriguez 2010). Today more than four million Filipinos live in the United States; approximately 370,000 U.S. Filipinos are undocumented (Davis and Batalova 2023). Yet the number of undocumented Filipinos in the United States is likely larger due to underreporting as well as nonlinear migration patterns in which Filipinos migrate from other countries prior to settling in the United States. Often characteristic of the undocumented Filipino experience is the acquisition of undocumented immigrant status through overstaying or visa expiration and/or labor trafficking (Buenavista 2018; Francisco and Rodriguez 2014).

Over the years, my work with U.S. Filipino students led several of them to reveal to me their undocumented immigrant status and the ways it shaped their navigation to and through U.S. higher education. As I was trained in critical ethnography, my work is immersive and requires that I work with U.S.

Filipino students to understand their meaning making as racially minoritized individuals within higher education and, eventually, the undocumented immigrant community. I credit them with sharing their experiential knowledge to provide nuanced ways to understand the intersection among racist nativism, militarism, and carcerality to complicate the discourse on undocumented immigration and education (Buenavista 2012, 2018).

My own positionality as a daughter of Filipino immigrants who were underemployed in the United States led me to pursue an academic career that centered a scholar-activist agenda. My father immigrated to the United States as a U.S. Navy enlistee and benefited from military-facilitated naturalization and family reunification processes that enabled him to petition my mother. They started our family as Filipino settlers in military-occupied Hawai'i. Our collective experiences as U.S. Filipinos moved me to pursue documenting the psychological, socioemotional, and material harm that migration entails, including stress related to labor exploitation, socioeconomic insecurity, family separation, and anti-Asian racism. Yet while my immediate family and I experienced some challenges that were similar to undocumented Filipino families, our American citizenship protected us from the common repercussions associated with resisting marginalization—a privilege I was reminded of from the many lessons I learned from working with students and community organizers.

Lessons from Undocumented Asian American Students

I often think about how research with Asian Americans supports and advances movements, policies, and practices that disrupt systems of power. And the type of research necessary to do this. Storytelling is central to uncovering how U.S. Filipinos intimately embody their marginalization and strategies to resist it (Francisco-Menchavez 2021). My family history and the migration stories of undocumented Filipino students demonstrate how immigrant presence and sociopolitical realities are manifestations of decades of policymaking between the Philippines and the United States. For example, one student I worked with became undocumented during her adolescence as a result of overstaying tourist visas her family used to visit her grandfather, a Filipino World War II veteran. In another instance, an undocumented student had pursued military service as a possible option to legalize his status after being encouraged by his uncle—the patriarch of his family who, like my father, had entered the United States decades prior through enlistment in the U.S. Navy while still in the Philippines. These stories pushed me to interrogate the role of militarism in shaping Asian American educational experiences despite a political context that discouraged my inquiry (Buenavista and Gonzales 2010–2011, 2012).

Around 2007, I continued to work with Filipino students but also organized with immigrant students to establish institutional and community-based resources for undocumented students in Southern California. In my daily interactions with these two separate projects involving two related groups, I realized that Filipino students—those with U.S. citizenship or undocumented immigrant status—as well as undocumented Asian American students increasingly articulated an interest in military enlistment as a strategy to afford college. Filipino students and undocumented Asian American students shared overlapping histories, including American military intervention in their families' countries of origin and/or family history with military service. For undocumented Asian American students, the aspiration toward U.S. military enlistment was also informed by public discourse on military enlistment programs like Military Accessions Vital to the National Interest (MAVNI), a recruitment strategy that disproportionately targeted certain Asian American immigrant subpopulations (Buenavista 2012).

At this time, it was also the height of the nationwide DREAMer movement to pass the federal Development, Relief, and Education for Alien Minors (DREAM) Act. While an earlier iteration of the DREAM Act had been introduced in 2001, in 2007 the DREAM Act garnered bipartisan support due to provisions that would have provided a pathway to residency for some undocumented immigrants through U.S. military service. Due to my family history and my perspective as a scholar located in education and ethnic studies, I hold an antimilitarization standpoint. I am intimately familiar with the ways that servicepeople of color, especially immigrants, serve as fodder in the U.S. military. I openly shared my critique of a militarized immigration reform strategy and particularly with community members I worked with, including a former student and friend, Tam Tran.

Tam Tran and Shifting Undocumented Student Discourse

Tam Tran was an undocumented Vietnamese American scholar, activist, and filmmaker who I mentored while we were at UCLA and beyond, and until her untimely passing in 2010 when she was a graduate student at Brown University. She gained prominence for her 2007 congressional testimony in support of the proposed federal DREAM Act in which she explicitly depicted her family's refugee story and the challenges of being stateless in the United States (Tran 2007). More importantly, she countered stereotypical depictions and laid out the contributions of undocumented immigrants by highlighting her educational perseverance and aspirations, despite the persistent barriers faced by undocumented immigrant communities. Tam's work—alongside hundreds of other undocumented immigrant youth across the United States—galvanized the "undocumented and unafraid" movement, which entailed young people without legal status participating in political advocacy and art making, direct actions, and other civic engagement practices toward comprehensive immigration reform.

Following her 2007 testimony, Tam and I were working on bringing attention to the experiences of undocumented Asian Americans. We cowrote an encyclopedia entry on undocumented Asian American immigrant students (Buenavista and Tran 2010), which was partially based on an academic paper we presented at the annual meeting for the Association of Asian American Studies in 2009 along with prominent undocuservices practitioner-scholar Dr. Angela Chuan-Ru Chen. To our knowledge, this work was among the earliest within the field of Asian American studies and ethnic studies to examine the intersection of race, undocumented immigration, and student experiences. I share my work with Tam not only to document her scholar-activist contributions to the field of ethnic studies education but also to illuminate the lessons we—scholars, practitioners, and community members—can learn from those who have deep experiential knowledge.

However, one point of contention between me and Tam was in regard to public discourse on the federal DREAM Act. I was highly critical of the military provisions of the DREAM Act, while Tam was one of the public faces of the proposed legislation. While I tried to conduct research that would show the potential implications of a militarized immigration strategy, Tam and other undocumented immigrants were at the center of public narratives that depicted its benefits. Between us, we had lengthy discussions on what it meant for her to be an Asian American face of the undocumented immigrant student movement and someone who would benefit from a pathway to legalization through the educational attainment measures laid out by the federal DREAM Act. In what ways did her position reify the Asian American model minority trope and a discourse of legal resident pathways defined through notions of deservedness? And how did my antimilitarization stance represent an idealistic politic defined by my privilege as a second-generation U.S. citizen? In other words, what "right" did I have to stand on my principles knowing that my political position would likely not materialize into legal limbo or, at worst, deportation? While Tam and I remained in loving community with one another, she eventually revealed to me that there was "word on the street" that other community members were wary of my critique and went so far as to discourage students from working with me in fear that my research on the militarization of immigration policy would hurt their movement.

Ultimately, it was not my research by any means that shifted the discourse on "DREAMers." Rather, it was the failure of Congress to pass any meaningful immigration reform and the subsequent move from a respectability politics to an unapologetically undocumented approach to advocacy by immigrant organizers who spoke more openly on the intersection of racist nativism and carcerality. In *We Are Not Dreamers*, Leisy J. Abrego and Genevieve Negrón-Gonzales (2020) curate a collection of scholarship by and for undocumented individuals to depict their incredibly nuanced and intersectional experiences.

Instead of outsider researchers who relied on and held up damage-centered stories of DREAMer students who were all-American with exception to their immigration status, undocumented individuals themselves constructed their own desire-based portrayals that reimagined their legal limbo as a human rights violation caused by decades of racist nativist policies and sentiment, and their joy and thriving as resistance to such state violence (Tuck 2009). Learning from work produced by formerly and currently undocumented scholars, in conjunction with my personal experience with Tam, and my continued work with undocumented communities has rendered me vulnerable to a constant state of reflection. In reflecting on lessons that I learned from undocumented immigrant communities, the one I interrogate in this chapter is the idea of research as socially constructed and the marginalization of knowledge produced by those who are experientially systems-impacted.

Weaponization of "Data-Driven" Decisions

My relationship to Tam and other undocumented student activists and the evolution of the undocumented immigrant movement continue to shape my work. My work is also guided by what Chen (2013; Chen and Rhoads 2016) identified as a transformative resistance praxis that characterizes undocu-ally intentions and projects—reflection and action that seek to challenge inequities experienced by undocumented immigrant students and shift institutional culture. For a decade, I have served as a co-principal investigator and faculty mentor for the Dreamers, Resources, Empowerment, Advocacy, and Mentorship (DREAM) Center at California State University, Northridge (CSUN) in the San Fernando Valley of Los Angeles. The CSUN DREAM Center is among the earliest and largest in the twenty-three-campus CSU system. We have served thousands of students who are undocumented and/or from mixed-status families through academic, student services, legal advocacy, and mental health and wellness programming. The DREAM Center is composed of two professional staff and between eight and ten student staff. While our "undocuservices" are necessarily fluid and subject to ever-changing institutional, state, and federal policies, much of our work is challenged by constant institutional requests for research to justify the allocation of monies to the center. Simultaneously, colleges and universities rarely provide institutional support to collect and analyze research necessary to contextualize our work. To this day, we remain funded by grant money that we must reapply for each year, which requires administrative work that at times contributes to the burnout of an already overworked and underpaid staff.

While there are many good reasons to make "data-driven" decisions in higher education, when it comes to working with undocumented students, the need for research to justify our budget and programming requests is really in response to a neoliberal culture of resource scarcity and risk management of a space that is almost exclusively occupied by those who are Black, Indigenous, and People of Color (BIPOC). When we have encouraged administrators to be bold in their support for undocumented students, they perpetually express a fear of being audited for their use of state or federal funds for undocumented people. Further, similar to other undocuservices projects in higher education, the lack of a large sample size or easily quantifiable metrics to show our outcomes of working with students is weaponized and used to keep our work and our students on the margins. For example, we can show that relative to the other CSU campuses CSUN serves a disproportionate number of students who are classified as eligible for Assembly Bill 540 (AB 540)—a formal status that makes students eligible for in-state fees and, as a result of parallel legislation, certain forms of state financial aid. However, institutions do not maintain data on these students and there is no accurate recordkeeping of the diversity of students who are "out of status" beyond this state designation. AB 540 students also include some who are not necessarily undocumented but benefit from the legislation. In other words, there is no way to accurately measure the totality of students we serve, as students are undocumented in diverse ways and are from mixed-status families.

My experience navigating a data-driven culture in the context of serving undocumented immigrant communities has often facilitated a need to research from the ground up. In other words, instead of attempting to conduct research *on* undocumented students, my primary role as a co-conspirator scholar has been to pay attention to undocumented students' and allies' everyday research practices and to translate their information gathering into narratives deemed compelling by institutional players who hold the resources we need to function. And one such everyday research practice that I've come to be informed by is tsismis or chisme.

The majority of undocumented students I work with are Tagalog- or Spanish-speaking immigrants. *Tsismis* in Filipino and *chisme* in Spanish are often colloquially reduced to gossip, or unverified rumors of everyday phenomena. I am usually the first and only Pinay faculty member they have ever known and among a few that they might have met off campus, before they even enrolled as students. This has been an entry point to work with undocumented students across ethnic and racial lines and to help frame their current experiences in the context of overlapping histories. Rapport building both on and off campus has made me privy to students' concerns in more meaningful ways, as they will often tsismis or chisme with me. And the tsismis/chisme has become an important tool toward deep understanding of undocumented student needs, solutions, and worldmaking.

Tsismis/Chisme as Counterstorytelling

Among BIPOC communities, tsismis/chisme is nuanced word-of-mouth communication. In a study of migrant information-seeking practices at the U.S.-Mexico border, Newell, Gomez, and Guajardo (2016) found that "at the in-between space of life at the border, word of mouth—not technology—is the most important source of information for [undocumented] migrants" (182). In context of the criminalization of immigration, word of mouth does not present any material evidence that might be potentially incriminating for individuals who are and/or might support undocumented people. Yet word of mouth is a practice that does not stop at the border. Among undocumented students and allies, word of mouth in the form of tsismis/chisme also serves as a storytelling mechanism, an oral history tradition in the present.

One of my colleagues, the late Pinay historian Dr. Dawn Bohulano Mabalon, often used to say that history is "really tsismis (gossip) with footnotes" (Mabalon and Tintiangco-Cubales 2022, 367). She knew that foundational to tsismis are stories, witnessed accounts, and testimonies that then became translated multiple times into information learned as the stories were passed on. Her observation helped me to recognize that tsismis/chisme was a community-based research practice, an everyday method of information gathering, interpretation, and sharing. In research terms, it is on-the-ground data collection, analysis, and dissemination, and primarily among those who have already developed some rapport or engaged in some community building such that there is trust. I argue that with such a framing there is much to be learned from engaging in tsismis/chisme, especially with communities who historically experienced harm in context of research. And while I refer to tsismis/chisme because of my work with undocumented immigrants who are Filipino- or Spanish-speaking, this form of story sharing occurs across other cultural communities.

From my work with students, I learned that it is generative to pause and observe how Asian Americans and other BIPOC communities are already participating in processes of inquiry in their efforts to disrupt the systems of oppression that condition their experiences. We also need to contend with the fact that some of these research practices are not deemed valid enough, empirical enough, or systematic enough. Again, while it is often reduced to hearsay, in my work tsismis/chisme has been tantamount to the critical practice of counterstorytelling among the Filipino and Latine undocumented immigrant communities that I work with. For example, in the moment that Tam shared with me that I had essentially been "blocklisted" or "cancelled" because of my anti-militarization research, I understood the experience as an attempt by vulnerable communities to protect their advocacy work and what they considered at the time to be the most viable opportunity to remain in the United States. The

DREAMer movement for all intents and purposes was a counterstory to stereotypical portrayals of undocumented immigrants and a move toward a pathway of humanization.

Education critical race theorists Daniel Solórzano and Tara Yosso (2002) define counterstorytelling as "a method of telling the stories of those people whose experiences are not often told (i.e., those on the margins of society). The counter-story is also a tool for exposing, analyzing, and challenging the majoritarian stories of racial privilege. Counter-stories can shatter complacency, challenge the dominant discourse on race, and further the struggle for racial reform" (32). Counterstories can challenge majoritarian stories of racial privilege and dominant discourses on race and racism, and I would add notions of citizenship and nativism. Undocumented immigrants use tsismis/chisme to illuminate their collective experiences with carcerality and material insecurity as well as how to resist these conditions. If researchers were to really immerse themselves in what young people do on the ground, they would be attentive to tsismis/chisme as legitimate efforts to demonstrate the embodied social, political, and economic challenges that shape their lives. In the following section, I lay out moments in the CSUN DREAM Center that helped me to recognize how engaging in tsismis/chisme can facilitate youth-driven, institutional, and community-based initiatives.

Tsismis/Chisme as Deep Observation

In 2017, undocumented students and allies came into the DREAM Center or shared with me on their many group chats comments including the following:

> Did you see what was happening next door? I saw that they were setting up.

> Someone said ICE [Immigration and Customs Enforcement] will be there. I heard it was CBP [Customs and Border Protection].

> They [student government] said they [administrators] knew; yes, the admin knew and didn't bother to tell us.

> People are going to show up anyway. They're organizing already.

The tsismis/chisme the students shared was regarding the participation of Department of Homeland Security entities at the annual career fair, which was held in a huge auditorium directly adjacent to the DREAM Center, the hub of undocumented student activity.

Hearing and reading these statements in isolation can lead one to believe that what the students shared was all speculation. But taken together, the tsismis/chisme represented deep observation of the institutional culture they navigate on a daily basis. Because of the hypersurveillance that shapes their

everyday lives, undocumented students are among the most perceptive individuals I have ever worked with. They often see, hear, and feel shifts in their
environments. They read energies. And their read was correct.

U.S. Customs and Border Protection (CBP) recruiters were scheduled to be
at the career fair, which was confirmed by students who purposely registered
to verify CBP's participation. The cumulative sentiment of impending danger
and their prompting of institutional allies to follow up on their hunches led us
to engage in emergency intervention plans with campus administrators.
Unfortunately, administrators were more concerned with the environment
that CBP officers would walk into and called on campus police to surveil the
action that students organized in response. Administrators felt threatened
because they were not privy to the tsismis/chisme. Rather than sit with students to learn of their concerns, they overresponded with increased police
presence and attempts to block undocumented students from participating in
the career fair.

The Utility of Tsismis/Chisme

Among undocumented students, tsismis/chisme also serves as a fact-finding
practice and illuminates issues that need immediate attention. For example,
from early in my career to even now, students often find me via word of mouth.
When I meet students, they typically share that they heard from a friend of a
friend who knew of a Filipino professor in Asian American studies who could
help. Often the primary friend was a student in one of my classes or the various
student organizations I advised. Tsismis/chisme facilitated each instance of
outreach or contact and in this way served as the impetus of resource seeking
and fact-finding.

In 2020, tsismis/chisme was also of utility at the height of the pandemic.
Since institutional closures challenged our ability to easily serve students seeking services, online check-ins and text messages became the primary form of
communication. In these brief encounters, students would frequently make
statements such as "Did you hear . . . ?" "Did you know?" "Did so-and-so ever
reach out?" and "So-and-so told me this and I heard from someone else the
same thing." As faculty and staff, many of us served as first responders to the
various crises that undocumented students and families faced when institutions physically shut down. Because we did not have the benefit of students
dropping in, we found ourselves checking in more frequently, a vast majority of
our time being spent on piecemealing tsismis/chisme to comprehend larger
stories we no longer had the advantage of learning about in one overarching
interaction with multiple students in a community space. Rather, tsismis/
chisme became one way to learn what was collectively happening with students
and in absence of student accessibility to undocumented student support

spaces and highlighted what issues warranted our attention and that we needed to prioritize in our work.

· Tsismis/Chisme and Community-Responsive Praxis

During the first year of the COVID-19 pandemic, tsismis/chisme represented a collective counterstory that served as the basis for the establishment of a community-based, non–institutionally affiliated mutual aid project, the Undo-cuFund. One pressing issue was the material insecurity exacerbated by the ineligibility of undocumented immigrants for federal relief programs, particularly those undocumented immigrants who were ineligible for the Deferred Action for Childhood Arrivals (DACA) program, and as a result these individuals also had no pathway to legally work in the United States. Tsismis/chisme depicted the real lack of access to the very resources intended to assist the most vulnerable communities during a very difficult time.

In context of the UndocuFund, tsismis/chisme was a nonlinear data-gathering, analysis, and data-sharing process that became integral to fathom the extent to which undocumented immigrant communities were harmed and excluded at multiple levels of COVID-19 response. Tsismis/chisme revealed the holes in the media discourse surrounding institutional efforts that claimed to serve pandemic survivors. Students' tsismis/chisme about themselves and what they heard about other students and community members became the impetus for action. Along with undocuservices practitioners Daniela Barcenas and Madison Villanueva, we held these stories and together collectively determined that a mutual aid fund would be most effective in meeting the immediate needs of our students.

Upon conceptualizing the idea, we informally consulted with undocumented students to whom we were closest. Students frequently articulated to us the various barriers to financial support programs: ineligibility, lengthy application processes, time constraints, inaccessibility to online applications, limited funding, and little to no outreach to individuals informing them of such programs. While to students these articulations were instances of them sharing their individual stories during check-ins, my co-conspirators and I were story holders and able to recognize the disparities as collective and systemic. Ultimately it was tsismis/chisme—not a formal needs assessment—that facilitated the establishment of a mutual aid fund that redirected community contributions to undocumented and other systems-impacted community members.

Tsismis/chisme also guided us toward the collective decision to ensure that any mutual aid was community-based and non–institutionally affiliated. I used federal stimulus checks provided to certain citizens during the pandemic to jumpstart a fundraising campaign and encouraged others to do the same and collected donations ranging from $5 to more than $1,000 to create a community pot of money. To date, we have provided more than $75,000 in on-the-ground, community-generated microgrants in the absence of effective and efficient institutional mechanisms for aid. Microgrant recipients are solely based on educator and community organizer referrals and have funded basic needs such as food, medicine, and shelter to tuition and DACA renewals. The emergence of the UndocuFund is exemplary of how advocates can conspire alongside undocumented immigrants and translate their stories into direct action that centers their needs and capacities.

Tsismis/Chisme as a Research Tool Toward Transformation

As much as I believe in the practice of research as a necessary part of academic life and its potential to play an important role in political advocacy, I have come to terms with the fact that the research we consume is likely due to its ability to be publishable. And these studies have minimal direct benefit for the people at the center of the work more than the scholars who conduct the research as a mechanism to maintain their material security. This reality is no more apparent than in research on undocumented students, which historically can be characterized as deficit-based or damage-centered. Thus, as a scholar who works with undocumented immigrant organizers, it is important to ask the following:

How can we think of research in more expansive ways?

What do we deem as legitimate forms of inquiry?

What does it mean to take a community-responsive and people-centered approach to research versus an approach that centers institutions and academic enterprise?

How might reconceptualizing research to include the varying ways of generating and sharing knowledge inform direct action and contribute to social movements?

The goal of my chapter has been to promote a conversation regarding how expansively thinking about research—and beyond how scholars, practitioners, and students are socialized in the academy—can open up the possibilities of engaging with disenfranchised communities in more meaningful ways and toward social action. The colonial origins of research often condition us, as researchers, to impose what we deem as legitimate mechanisms of inquiry, and in doing so we miss opportunities to understand how young people draw on their cultural intuition to construct knowledge and enact community-responsive efforts to effectively and efficiently gain access to the resources they need.

Yet I want to clarify that I am not advocating that tsismis/chisme in and of itself is a research method that anyone can just go out and use. So as to avoid information extraction, tsismis/chisme as community-generated knowledge must be treated with deep respect and by individuals who have already established trusting relationships. Such relationships enable co-conspirators to discern when disenfranchised peoples are sharing stories with or without an expectation to address any needs that are revealed, and/or if such stories are even ours to share. However, in general, it is particularly important to recognize the utility of tsismis/chisme as a research practice for direct action, in a space and context where traditional research approaches have been historically harmful to the community. Tsismis/chisme is only one example of how we can center community cultural knowledge to reconceptualize what we consider valid research practice in our efforts toward social change. And more consideration for such research practices will better position the potential of our work as scholars, practitioners, and students to serve as an intellectual arm of social movements.

REFERENCES

Abrego, Leisy J., and Genevieve Negrón-Gonzales, eds. 2020. *We Are Not Dreamers: Undocumented Scholars Theorize Undocumented Life in the United States*. Duke University Press.

Buenavista, Tracy Lachica. 2012. "Citizenship at a Cost: Undocumented Asian Youth Perceptions and the Militarization of Immigration." *Asian American and Pacific Islander Nexus* 10 (1): 101–124. https://doi.org/10.36650/nexus10.1_101-124_Buenavista.

———. 2018. "Model (Undocumented) Minorities and 'Illegal' Immigrants: Centering Asian Americans and US Carcerality in Undocumented Student Discourse." *Race Ethnicity and Education* 21 (1): 78–91. https://doi.org/10.1080/13613324.2016.1248823.

Buenavista, Tracy Lachica, and Jordan B. Gonzales. 2010–2011. "DREAMs Deterred: Filipino Experiences and an Anti-Militarization Critique of the Development, Relief, and Education for Alien Minors Act." *Asian American Policy Review* 21: 29–37.

Buenavista, Tracy Lachica, and Tam Tran. 2010. "Undocumented Immigrant Students." In *Encyclopedia of Asian American Issues Today*, edited by Edith Chen and Grace Yoo. Greenwood.

Chen, Angela Chuan-Ru. 2013. "Undocumented Students, Institutional Allies, and Transformative Resistance: An Institutional Case Study." PhD diss., University of California, Los Angeles.

Chen, Angela Chuan-Ru, and Robert Rhoads. 2016. "Undocumented Student Allies and Transformative Resistance: An Ethnographic Case Study." *Review of Higher Education* 39 (4): 515–542.

Davis, Caitlin, and Jeanne Batalova. 2023. "Filipino Immigrants in the United States." *Migration Information Source*, August 8. https://www.migrationpolicy.org/article/filipino-immigrants-united-states.

Francisco, Valerie, and Robyn Magalit Rodriguez. 2014. "Globalization and Undocumented Migration: Examining the Politics of Emigration." In *Hidden Lives and Human Rights: Understanding the Controversies and Tragedies of Undocumented Immigration*, edited by Lois Ann Lorentzen. Praeger.

Francisco-Menchavez, Valerie. 2021. "Kuwentuhan as a Method: Migrant Filipino Workers and Participatory Action Research." In *Handbook of Social Inclusion: Research and Practices in Health and Social Sciences*, edited by Pranee Liamputtong. Springer.

Guevarra, Anna Romina. 2009. *Marketing Dreams, Manufacturing Heroes: The Transnational Labor Brokering of Filipino Workers*. Rutgers University Press.

Love, Bettina L. 2019. *We Want to Do More Than Survive: Abolitionist Teaching and the Pursuit of Educational Freedom*. Beacon.

Mabalon, Dawn, and Allyson Tintiangco-Cubales. 2022. "Filipina/x/o American Waves and Eras." In *The SAGE Encyclopedia of Filipina/x/o American Studies*, edited by Kevin Lao Yabut Nadal, Allyson Tintiangco-Cubales, and E. J. R. David. SAGE.

Newell, Bryce Clayton, Ricardo Gomez, and Verónica E. Guajardo. 2016. "Information Seeking, Technology Use, and Vulnerability Among Migrants at the United States-Mexico Border." *Information Society* 32 (3): 176–191. https://doi.org/10.1080/01972243.2016.1153013.

Rodriguez, Robyn M. 2010. *Migrants for Export: How the Philippine State Brokers Labor to the World*. University of Minnesota Press.

Solórzano, Daniel G., and Tara Yosso. 2002. "Critical Race Methodology: Counter-Storytelling as an Analytical Framework for Education Research." *Qualitative Inquiry* 8 (1): 23–44. https://doi.org/10.1177/107780040200800103.

Tran, Tam. 2007. "Testimony of Tam Tran." In *Comprehensive Immigration Reform: The Future of Undocumented Immigrant Students*, 14–16. https://www.govinfo.gov/content/pkg/CHRG-110hhrg35453/pdf/CHRG-110hhrg35453.pdf.

Tuck, Eve. 2009. "Suspending Damage: A Letter to Communities." *Harvard Educational Review* 79 (3): 409–427.

4

"Not Your Model Minority"

Undocumented and Multilingual Asian Activists at the Margins of the University

SARA P. LOPEZ AMEZQUITA

If my daughter had wanted to go to the moon, she would have found a way to do it.

–Irene Perez, "My Fearless Daughter"

On May 18, 2007, Tam Ngoc Tran did the inconceivable and "outed" her undocumented immigration status by testifying in front of the U.S. Congressional Immigration Subcommittee. Tran was born in Germany to Vietnamese refugee parents who fled Vietnam after the fall of Saigon. When she was six years old, her family immigrated to the United States and filed a petition for political asylum. Their petition would be denied several years later, and in the United States Tran would become undocumented and stateless (Wong and Ramos 2011). Tran believed in the power of stories, and the power of telling her own story. She believed that if the American people would learn about how complex and exclusive the nation's immigration system was, they would (re)consider immigration reform. In telling her story in Congress, Tran feared the danger that doing so would bring to herself and her undocumented family members, and as Wong and Ramos (2012) explain, her fears were not unfounded: "Given [Tam's] own undocumented status, [testifying] was an act of considerable personal courage. Three days later, ICE [Immigration and Customs Enforcement] agents staged a predawn raid on her family's home in Orange County and took her parents and brother into custody. Tam reached out to members of Congress and immigration attorneys and succeeded in getting her family released and stopping their deportation" (5). Tam Ngoc Tran and Cinthya Felix, whose mother, Irene Perez, is quoted in the epigraph above, were fierce, strategic, and innovative undocumented immigrant activists as well as leaders in the struggle for immigration reform and the (re)introduction of the federal

Development, Relief, and Education for Alien Minors (DREAM) Act, which has failed to pass since 2001 (Alcindor and Stolberg 2017). Tran and Felix were close friends, who had—against all odds—become graduate students at Brown and Columbia, respectively. Before Tran and Felix could realize many of their dreams, they lost their lives in a car accident: "Their tragic passing has galvanized the movement [that] they left behind" (Wong and Ramos 2012, 3).

The immigrant rights movement certainly owes much of its growth to "self-outed" undocumented immigrant young adults, who often labor in the face of extreme national measures that criminalize and profit from racialized bodies (Gonzales 2016; Muñoz 2015; Truax 2015). Undocumented immigrant young adults and their communities have been central voices for contesting, challenging, and shifting many of the debates on citizenship and social justice in the United States today.

In any given week, undocumented immigrant young adults "in the movement" are conducting workshops for immigrant communities in various languages, preparing presentations for university officials and faculty members, visiting high school and college classrooms to create awareness about the immigrant experience in the United States, and/or occupying legislators', governors', and senators' offices across the nation.[1] Related to this work, undocumented immigrant young adults are also engaging in specialized writing practices, which include but are not limited to legal and community translation (Flores 2018; Gonzales 2017). The questions arise: How do undocumented youth come to learn and engage with these forms of writing often deemed to be largely academic? For example, how did Tam Ngoc Tran use writing and advocacy in navigating national legal bureaucracies to have her parents and brother released from immigrant detention? Moreover, what might we make of the ways in which students like Tran and Felix "documented" and wrote their undocumented lived experiences? These are some of the central questions that have driven my research. Specifically, the important nuances of identity, language (in oral and alphabetic-text communication), and undocumented immigrant status have come together to take a central role in my ethnographic research with undocumented immigrant young adults.

Recently, literacy and writing studies scholars have turned their attention to the function of literacy as a meaning-making practice in transnational communities. Scholars in these intersecting fields have focused on how these emergent literacy practices intersect (or not) with school-based literacies (de Block and Buckingham 2007; Guerra 1998; Lorimer Leonard 2017). Given this turn, these scholars have also interrogated the ways in which strongly sedimented schooling practices no longer meet the demands and possibilities of writing and communication in late modernity (S. Alvarez 2017b; García, Ibarra Johnson, and Seltzer 2017; You 2016). This shift has become most salient in higher education, where not only has the demand for writing and writing courses increased but numerous scholars have made important calls to amplify the vision of what constitutes writing, and academic writing specifically (Brandt 2015; Horner and Kopelson 2014). To this end, academic writing has become widely understood as a set of emergent literacy and language practices often reified in and through higher education.

Scholars working with transnational communities have gone to great lengths to show how academic writing practices can (and do) gain attunement through the very practices of doing and introspection, and how a writing orientation can cultivate students' cultural and linguistic pluralism (S. P. Alvarez 2018; S. Alvarez 2017a, 2017b). For undocumented immigrant youth, however, looking at academic writing from this perspective can present limitations, even from the very point of economic and institutional access to higher education. Undocumented young adults in the immigrant rights movement are building and advancing these academic practices in their activism, using their literacies across languages, in ways that would be deemed "academic" in a scholastic setting, but in this case are contextually bound to community activism and governmental policy. As I have argued elsewhere, "The undocumented young adults I have worked with surpass many of the goals and expectations set for courses designed to 'teach' students academically" (Alvarez 2023, 122) and do so through a multilingual orientation. They are engaging in what I describe as activist literacies, academic writing practices that are particular to these young adults' context, embodied lived experiences, and differing positionalities.

To magnify the plurality of voices tied to the undocumented immigrant experience and highlight the crucial role that undocumented young adults in the immigrant rights movement play in cultivating writing and multilingualism, this chapter undertakes a critical analysis of the ways undocumented Asian immigrants, the fastest growing population of undocumented communities in the New York area (Migration Policy Institute 2015; Ramakrishnan and Shah 2017), can also find themselves at the margins of the university. Drawing from data collected as part of a three-year ethnography of the multilingual writing practices of twelve "self-outed" undocumented (or DACAmented) young adults in the U.S. Northeast and South, this discussion focuses on the voices of two undocumented Asian young adults who have intermittently been enrolled at a two- or four-year public institution of higher education in New York City.[2] In doing so, I argue that addressing these young adults' experiences as undocumented immigrants and as part of a racial group that, according to one participant, "does not fit the undocumented narrative," allows for a more nuanced understanding of how undocumented Asian immigrant students have developed academic writing practices through their activism as part of their ongoing pursuit of higher education. Working against the common conflation of undocumented immigrant status with a Latinx Spanish-speaking identity, and often Mexican origin nationality (Ribero 2016; Santa

Ana 2002) which has resulted in the erasure of other racialized immigrant communities, such as Black and Indigenous communities, this chapter contends with the ways assumptions about ethnicity, race, and language operate in the discourse about undocumented immigrant experiences. Simultaneously, this chapter illustrates how highly valued academic writing practices, such as strategic selections of linguistic and cultural forms of language, are being cultivated and sustained through immigration-driven activism and in ways that pay close attention to lived experience and citizenship as an exclusionary measure.

This discussion was prompted by two factors: (1) the ways that the changing demographics of the U.S. immigrant community surfaced in my own ethnographic study, resulting in a participant group that not only spoke to the growing demographic of U.S. Asian communities but also challenged misconceptions about the community and its relationship to undocumented immigrant status; and (2) the need for additional studies in immigration and education that offer a closer look at how immigration, as lived experience, impacts and informs language, cultural practice, and the building of so-called academic writing skillsets.[3] Accordingly, this chapter focuses on two questions that have their origins in the larger qualitative study:

- How do these undocuAsian writers understand the rhetorical value and effects of deploying various languages in their writing on immigrants' rights issues, including what confuses, troubles, or excites them about which language(s) to use, and how to do so in such writing (e.g., translanguaging, transmodality, translocality)?
- More broadly, what might these writers' language practices, and their understandings and views on their practices, contribute to current scholars' understanding of the politics of language practices in writing?

The implications of these questions are of large importance as scholars in education have increasingly turned their attention to the effects of globalization and the growing number of students who identify as multilingual in the classroom continues to steadily rise. At the same time, this is magnified by the fact that discourse on U.S. and global immigration continue to be matters of political and social contention in which undocumented communities face a constant threat of deportation, family separation, and exclusion from institutions of higher education and the country more broadly.

Data Collection

To understand how undocumented immigrant activists practiced and enacted their academic writing practices and multilingualism, I carried out semistructured interviews with participants over the course of three years.[4] The initial set of interviews focused on getting to know the participants' backgrounds as well as their language and writing interests. Follow-up interviews focused on writing samples that participants provided and discussions about language and writing that participants brought up during their initial interviews. Because the study was based on ethnographic fieldwork, it also included observations and action research conducted during immigration-related meetings and national and local rallies, as well as the interviews of two authorized representatives of immigrant advocacy organizations. Given that the main method of text analysis in this ethnography was an adaptation of text ethnography (Lillis and Curry 2010), cyclical conversations via text message and email with the youth about their writing were also added to the data. This chapter focuses on the articulation of one code that emerged out of the research (Saldaña 2016): being undocumented and Asian, and at the margins of the university. This code was traced along a discourse developed from the quote in the title of this chapter, "not your model minority." And while this code is being illustrated here with only two participants, a "smaller sample size," the more than a decade of conversations that have emerged during and after the three-year ethnography result in robust data providing in-depth perspectives on Angie and Mark's lived experiences as members of the Asian undocumented immigrant community, a community that has often been referred to as a "difficult to reach population," or not dispositioned to discuss, disclose, or assume their undocumented immigrant status.

Asian Undocumented Immigrant Young Adults in New York City

As of the 2010 census, the fastest growing population in the United States is Asian Americans, with 43 percent identifying as Asian alone (with no other racial/ethnic demarcation). More specifically, as the NYU Center for the Study of Asian American Health (2018) notes, "New York City (NYC) is the home to nearly 1.2 million documented and undocumented Asian Americans . . . comprising of individuals representing more than 20 countries and 45 languages and dialects." Within this growing racial group there are large differences not only in ethnicity, nationality, and language but also in income and education attainment and, in some cases, two geopolitical migrations within one generation. To examine the struggles that some of these young adults have faced in accessing and achieving their dreams of higher education, I focus on the cases of two participants residing in New York City: a South Korean national who faced the implications of their undocumented status prior to implementation of the Deferred Action for Childhood Arrivals (DACA) program and who now has DACA, and a Filipino immigrant who arrived in the United States shortly before DACA was announced and was therefore deemed ineligible to participate in the program.

Angie

Angie was born in Seoul, South Korea.[5] She migrated to New York City in 1993 at the age of ten. Unlike most recent immigrant young adults who became part of the immigrant rights movement during their adolescent years, Angie became involved in the movement in her late twenties and has become a fierce community organizer in her mid-thirties. Angie related her involvement with the movement to her mother's ways of knowing and immigrant networks in the city (S. Alvarez 2017a, 2017b; Mihut 2014).[6] In 2012, Angie's mother saw a newspaper ad for a free DACA Clinic at the Asian Community of New York (ACNY) and encouraged her daughter to attend.[7] Soon after, Angie would become a community leader for immigration advocacy in that very organization. Today, Angie directs legal clinics, workshops, and empowerment programs with undocumented Asian immigrant youths as well as Asian immigrants more generally. She also participates in multiple local and national immigrant and social justice rallies.

Angie's role is vital to this organization. She provides support to her undocumented and documented immigrant communities and can provide English-language access and translation (both verbally and in writing) to Korean-speaking immigrants in need of assistance. This act of translation, and specifically in the context of "legality," is a much-needed practice in the metropolitan context of a city like New York and the U.S. writing classroom. But Angie has often dreamed and expressed her desire to obtain a four-year college degree in education, specifically in American Sign Language (ASL). As a matter of fact, years before this study Angie took ASL college classes and has since hoped to one day return as a full-time student. At the time that this study was conducted, Angie continued to grow her rich writing and knowledge-making practices but did so outside of the university context.

As scholars in writing and literacy studies have consistently expressed, it is not just that writing "as mass production" has seen a dramatic increase in higher education and the workforce, but that transnational contexts rely upon and increasingly demand transnational approaches to writing (Brandt 2015; Lorimer Leonard 2017). But even such a transnational context does not account for how citizenship, as a form of exclusion, impacts an individual's potential to participate in and benefit from the growing need to cultivate multilingual and academic writing practices. While undocumented immigrant individuals, like Angie, for instance, are learning, engaging, and sustaining multilingualism in transnational contexts, and they are doing so with attention to citizenship, they remain at the margins of the university, and many are deprived of what folks might deem to be traditional college pathways, based on age and time to degree completion.

Simultaneously, because these undocumented immigrant young adults' activist literacies, which meet and exceed the expectations of academic writing in the university, are being cultivated outside the boundaries of higher education and instead in the context of immigrant activism, they are often unacknowledged and/or undervalued as school-bounded literacies. This became most visible when Angie explained how her involvement in the immigrant rights movement and her work at ACNY helped her foster what I identify as her activist literacies—which are at the intersections of translating texts, analyzing and critiquing governmental policy texts, and writing strategically for specific audiences. As Angie recounted,

> Before my involvement with ACNY, and other grassroots organizations, I had no interest [in] study[ing] politics and that's local and federal [politics]. The only education or knowledge I had were introductory courses [in college]. I wasn't up to date on politics, especially [related to the] local level government. I didn't know that local level government has so much impact in our daily lives. I still don't have an interest in politics. I feel like you are forced to learn and keep yourself updated because you need to. And I should. You should. I don't have any desire to get into politics or anything, but I have to know.

Like most participants in this study, Angie is well-versed in U.S. immigration policy. She can name and describe current laws, referendums, and legislative petitions with a level of ease that goes well beyond most U.S. citizens' everyday knowledge of local and national politics. But despite Angie's professional-level credentials and experienced bilingualism (García, Ibarra Johnson, and Seltzer 2017), she has been structurally excluded from spaces of U.S. higher education. Angie completed an associate's degree but was unable to continue her studies because of economic reasons tied to her undocumented immigration status. Undocumented students are ineligible to receive federal financial aid, and in some states, like Georgia, they are formally excluded from attending certain public institutions of higher education and/or receiving eligibility to pay in-state tuition rates (Gonzales and Chavez 2012; Trivette and English 2017). And while in New York State undocumented immigrants may attend four-year public colleges/universities and receive some state funding to do so, the paperwork and time needed to become a full-time student are rarely afforded to undocumented individuals like Angie, who already have many of the adult responsibilities of living (or surviving) in a metropolitan site. Angie's undocumented experience, as a Korean New Yorker, is then distinctively marked by her intersecting identities and how they critically disrupt dominant narratives of Asian and undocumented immigrant experiences in the United States.

Moreover, Angie's involvement with immigrant rights activism, as a Korean-English bilingual transnational of Korean nationality, complicates aspects of multilingualism for settings like New York City. While such spaces claim to be "transnational" or "multilingual," bilingualism has been neither cultivated nor sustained in U.S. schooling. Yet these omissions and her activism have opened up opportunities for Angie to learn to draw and extend her Korean-English multilingual and academic writing practices, as seen in the policy and political work she has developed.

Since becoming involved in immigrant rights advocacy work, Angie has become extremely attuned to the ways in which ethnic communities sustain linguistic and cultural pluralism. Because of the high demand for translation in her work, Angie shared that she feels she has become more introspective about the power and practice of translation, specifically between Korean and English and with different ages of bilingual speakers. In fact, throughout this research Angie offered powerful and insightful theories and practices for translation, some of which are culturally situated and some of which she has adjusted based on her experience working with immigration advocacy drawing on legal documents. As Angie puts it, in her own bilingual practice, "when you are speaking to a halmoni 할모니 [grandmother and elder], you have to be mindful of the difference. It is really important." Angie has shared her own strategies for understanding audience in the process of oral and written communication, and she has done so in a culturally situated and immigrant-attuned form that pays homage to cultural practices of respect and value for the elderly. In other words, she has engaged in what transnational literacy studies scholar Juan Guerra (2016) calls for as necessary academic practice of "rhetorical sensibility." In translating legal discourse, Angie prioritizes relationality and dignity in communicating with speakers in the community.

While this chapter does not focus on the linguistic dexterity and mastery that Angie—or participants in the larger study—employs, Angie's theorization of multilingualism offers insightful perspective into language studies, specifically from the perspective of a member of a racialized ethnic group. Her language practices highlight how rhetorical attunement (Lorimer Leonard 2014) is a desirable practice for college students and graduates. Also, Angie's highly attuned communicative practices and immigration knowledge have led her to take on important leadership roles that move within and beyond the boundaries of social justice and immigration reform. These activist literacies shift and advance academic writing practices and writing knowledge in the context of the professional sphere.

Mark

Like many youth growing up in transnational families, Mark experienced family separation from an early age. Mark was born near Zamboanga City in the Philippines but moved to Manila with his mother at the age of four. Mark's mother sought to give Mark the best education possible, even with their limited resources and income, and she paid for Mark to attend private school in Manila and encouraged him to learn English. At the age of fifteen, he migrated to the United States alone, and though he was not entirely sure what he was getting himself into, Mark knew well enough that he was seeking better opportunities for himself and his hardworking mother. Mark understood that in the United States it was more likely that he and his mother could chart new pathways for themselves, and they could reunite with his cousin—a practicing nurse in the city. Mark's mother followed him to the United States four months later, and since then they have made New York City their home. Mark reads and writes in English and Tagalog, and since his early involvement with the ACNY, he has developed an interest in and attunement to Korean languages. In fact, when I met him he was taking his second Korean class at his four-year public college.

As is the case with many millennial youths, for Mark information often travels and circulates best through digital channels, including social media (Block and Buckingham 2007). In fact, this is how Mark found ACNY. While in high school, Mark quickly realized that his undocumented immigration status would prove a significant challenge to attending college and getting a job, so he looked online for local organizations that could help him learn more about how to cope with his immigration status. And despite the multiple federal and local policies of exclusion, which in many ways make colleges and universities in the United States as some of the most inaccessible places for undocumented youth, when I met Mark he had already managed to pay for and attend two semesters of college, taking one to two courses per semester at a time. In addition, Mark was a committed member of his university's undocumented immigrant student community. He attended all their meetings and strategically challenged the perspective that undocumented immigration is a struggle exclusive to Latinx communities. Mark shared resources and information about events empowering immigrant communities, and he made it a point to look at immigration from a community perspective that understood that immigration intersected with many other issues and aspects of a person's life. In fact, Mark often argued that the group's meetings should work to be introspective of how immigration and undocumented immigrant status affected a person's lived experiences. To some extent, this presented a level of tension during the group's meetings at the university, as the youth leading this group seemed, according to him, less familiar with current immigration policies and debates. For Mark, these meetings were focused largely on integrating students in the college life, but college life had everything to do with local, state, and national policies that embraced them as undocumented students while ignoring the significant structural barriers they faced.

Mark explained that before getting involved with immigration advocacy groups, and before confronting his undocumented immigration status—a year into his life in New York—he and his mom were somewhat out of touch with politics and their impact on people's everyday lives:

Back then [when he was somewhat unaware of the implications of being undocumented] politics was never a thing for me. I guess that is like a saying we have: you don't know what you lost until you lose it. Figuring out I don't have all of these papers, discovering . . . that these papers are part of a system that is often manipulated by politics. [For instance, you should know about] people who implemented the state ID of New York. . . . [You should know about] people possibly taking rights away from you, especially now. Now, it is super terrifying. . . . Oh with Obama, [my mother] was not as worried. Now, I've never seen her watch more American TV.

As was evident during the interview, Mark recounted viewing his activist work as an opportunity to learn about his immigration status and as a form of schooling outside of school—as community literacy. Mark also shared that he felt that through advocacy work he was able to be more in tune with his world and has since gained a better sense of how local and national laws directly impact his communities. Additionally, in the context of a white-supremacist 2016 presidential election and presidency (2017–2021) that built on the hate and fear of immigrants, Mark and his mother felt the urgency to be informed and work to defend their rights as human beings.

Rising up for human rights has become an important practice for Mark, which concerns all aspects of his life. And like Angie, Mark too has gained important academic practices through his activist engagement and emergent activist literacies. Often as the only Asian person in his college undocumented immigrant student organization meetings, which were predominantly directed and attended by Mexican, Latinx, and West Indian members in New York City, Mark generally referred to this as placing the group "in check." He explained that he often sought to guide group members in thinking more critically about being undocumented as a status that was not solely a Mexican, Latinx, or Caribbean issue. He did this by constantly asserting Tagalog and Korean in any activity the group conducted and trying to recruit new members to the group. He discussed the need to translate materials in these languages and added terms from these language groups as part of the immigration-oriented work they were doing. However, as Mark recognized, he was placed in a difficult position because as he and other Asian undocumented immigrant young adults in this study posed, "Asian people have a harder time speaking openly about their undocumentation, even with other Asians." And as Mark and most communities of color in metropolitan sites have learned to recognize, "Latinos aren't so united either," meaning differences in migration patterns, educational attainment, locality, and racialization also posed differing dispositions in cultivating solidarity.

Activist literacies move within and across academic practices. These literacies, which involve advocacy and close analysis of lived experience, challenge academic practices not only on the premise that they are solely developed in and through higher education but also in the sense that they are grounded in a person's lived experience, in this case that of being an undocumented immigrant. Mark's active participation in both ACNY and his university's undocumented immigrant students' group, shows the many ways in which his activist literacies opened opportunities for him to voice his concerns and experience as a Filipino undocumented immigrant wanting to obtain a college degree. In voicing his concerns and amplifying the voices of fellow Asian immigrants also affected by undocumentation, Mark demonstrates his strategic moves toward visibility in oral and written communication. Furthermore, Mark's attention to how, for example, the very problem of visibility is at the intersection of other issues in the immigration movement is an example of how he has crafted informed opinions based on research and patterns of community participation.

Here, I want to clarify that Mark's observations about the patterns of participation in particular groups are quite in line with research and can be expanded through historical examinations. For instance, the understanding that not all Latinx communities see immigration or immigration advocacy in the same way but that Latinx communities have also been historically impacted by colorism, anti-Blackness, and, in the U.S. context, anti-Mexicanness is central to recognizing how these issues play out in the contemporary politics of immigration and citizenship.[8] For example, as Preston and Alvarez (2016) have highlighted, the 2016 election seems to have caused a rift in the usual Latinx Republican majority in Florida, in which Latinx groups including Cubans, Colombians, and Venezuelans have generally voted in conservative ways. These shifts even to the internal makeup and voting behavior of the U.S. Latinx immigrant community may be indicative of some of what Mark referred to when stating that "Latinos aren't so united either" with regard to the topics of immigrant activism and comprehensive immigration reform. Thus, including Mark's voice as an Asian, specifically a Filipino undocumented young adult growing up in a working-class single-parent home in New York City, is also about becoming more mindful of the nuances of ethnicity, nationality, and class in discussing immigration and cultural and linguistic plurality. Looking more closely at these nuances also helps in better understanding how undocumented Asian young adults like Mark struggle to attain and face tremendous hardship in reaching higher education. As an Asian and undocumented individual, Mark's storysharing (as opposed to storytelling) of his experiences and fears as an undocumented person—alongside his mother—demonstrates strategic rhetorical moves as he navigates through and with his activism and advocacy.

The fear of "having no rights" that Mark and his mother have experienced since their arrival to the United States is not unfounded and to a great extent became a reality in the past six years when Mark's mother was diagnosed with breast cancer. Mark has helped his mother with translating medical documents, attending doctor's appointments, and providing pre- and postop home care. Mark has become a consistent advocate for his mother. His activist literacies have then proven to be dynamic in that he has learned to strategize community activist practices in the advocacy he passionately engages in for his mother and her health. As Mark shared with me, he has realized that more interpretation services are needed in medical sites in New York City. Greater understanding about trauma and how trauma is dealt with in immigrant and undocumented immigrant families is also needed. This struggle has made Mark more intro- spective of how despite being an advocate for his mom and immigrant commu- nities in the United States, there are no policies that protect them in this area, and accordingly Mark has turned to writing more than ever before. He is writ- ing for himself, as a knowledge-making practice, and to better understand the whirlwind that he has experienced since his mother received her breast cancer diagnosis, and he is also writing out of demand for all the paperwork related to his mother's medical situation.

Mark is also using his writing skills in applying for work positions. He is send- ing out messages and emails in the hopes of landing a work opportunity that can help him and his mother become more financially stable. Mark's multilingual practices and activist literacies have had real ramifications for his and his mother's lived experiences. They have allowed him to navigate his positionality as an undocumented immigrant and challenged him to understand how writing can be a reflective practice. But writing and literacy also have their limitations. Mark had to abandon his hopes of completing a professional degree in computer science and has since reformulated what he could pursue "more practically." When I first met Mark, he demonstrated his awareness of how it would take a longer path to com- plete his four-year degree. Mark talked about how taking one to two classes a semester "was not enough to finish on time," as in the four-year timeline for a four- year degree, but continuing higher education was a vision he sustained for him- self. More recently, however, Mark has turned to getting an aesthetician license and finding immediate employment in this profession. Mark's undocumented immigrant status, his family circumstances, and, more importantly, the lack of formal support available from his four-year public institution forced him out. Returning to college will continue to be a labor that will depend entirely on him.

Discussion: Multilingual Professionals Without a Bachelor's Degree

It is important to also contextualize a discussion of Angie's and Mark's experiences—and the disparities they face being Asian and undocumented—by acknowledging their dreams of completing four-year college degrees and the impact their dreams have had on their own personal and activist journeys. To do so, it is useful to frame their experiences as defying the so-called model minority myth and its emphasis on immigrant exceptionalism and social mobility. In doing so, I demonstrate how immigrant young adults' voices can and should be discussed within the parameters of their lived experiences as well as the many forms of marginalization they face as undocumented individuals hailing from a plurality of ethnic, linguistic, and racial communities. On the one hand, undocumented immigrant young adults can display outstanding writing and professional practices as students, immigrants, DREAMers, and family members. On the other hand, they regularly face ideological and physical exclusion from the place they have learned to call home—simultaneous inclusion and exclusion or a provisional form of inclusion predicated upon their ability to adapt to the status quo of the U.S. nation-state. I also focus this discussion in relation to what Lorimer Leonard (2017) has presented as the "deep contradictions" about multilingualism as "both personal and professional asset and condemned as ethnic, racial, or cultural deficit" (125). For example, as the Spanish language has become hypervisible and demonized in the context of immigration, other languages have rarely entered the discussion. Yet these languages are certainly present in spaces like ACNY, where both Angie and Mark worked and volunteered for several years. Along these lines, Nguyen and Kebede (2017) have shown that the U.S. immigrant population has grown dramatically and is shifting the racial and ethnic makeup of the country. These changes have become most salient in schools that must now work to serve increasingly diverse and multilingual student populations in their classrooms. For example, they echo a finding that has now become widely known to many people in the United States: that "Spanish is the most common language spoken at home in the United States after English" and that multilingualism is not limited to the confines of the Spanish/English dichotomy (Nguyen and Kebede 2017).[9] In fact, after Spanish, "Chinese, Tagalog, Vietnamese, French, Korean, Arabic, German and Russian" are the languages most spoken today aside from English, and the incidence of these languages of course varies from region to region.

This shift in immigrant population demographics is not meant to be overtly determinant, as Bhojwani (2017) has cautioned, and indeed "demographics is not destiny," but based on the experiences of undocumented immigrant young adults who are part of the 1.5 generation, demographics matter for multilingual and cultural sustainability. Population demographics have a great deal to do with how schools and policymakers respond to immigrant youth, sometimes for the better and sometimes for the worse. But these youth matter and these demographic shifts compel us as scholars to ask the very questions that frame the larger study. Such questions include the following: What might the language and writing practices of 1.5-generation multilingual undocumented immigrant young adults as well as their understandings and views of their practices contribute to current understandings of the politics of such practices? These demographic shifts also compel us as researchers who work closely with directly impacted community members to ask questions related to the schooling experiences and trajectories of students like Angie and Mark: How can we better envision (and design) equitable educational spaces to support all students? Related, how can we better support undocumented immigrant young adults so that they too can achieve their dreams of higher education?

Implications

My examination in this chapter of Angie's and Mark's experiences at the margins of the university has several implications for fellow scholars invested in social justice and immigration reform. First, Angie's and Mark's experiences of being "pushed out" or denied access to higher education prior to and following DACA demonstrate the need for a fuller understanding the experiences of undocumented immigrant young adults, for whom "undocumented" is not a master status but an experience that is interwoven with their U.S. racial/ethnic identities and lived experiences. Second, these two narratives prompt those of us who do research at the intersections of language, education, and immigration to pay closer attention to race, ethnicity, and class as part of the experiences of immigrants, specifically undocumented immigrant young adults. This approach also asks us to broaden discussions that have largely focused on the U.S.-Mexico border as a foundational component of U.S. immigration discourse and to make visible how the coming together of these multiple narratives helps nuance our understanding of undocumented immigrant young adults' lives. Doing so will yield three important outcomes. First, it will provide increased visibility for immigrant groups whose historical and social lives have been invisibilized within overarching narratives of immigration to the United States. Second, it can support critical introspection regarding the effects of racial/ethnic identity and geographic context on the institutional barriers that members of the community face (e.g., the heightened rates of deportation that undocumented Black immigrants experience as compared to their peers from other racial/ethnic backgrounds; Morgan-Trostle, Zheng, and Lipscombe 2016). Third, such an approach may provide valuable insight into the prospect of cross-racial/ethnic solidarity and coalition building as in the case of activists Tam Ngoc Tran and Cinthya Felix.

In closing, Angie's and Mark's experiences as undocumented young adults and multilingual writers, who have developed activist literacies through their advocacy work and at the margins of the university, point to the continued importance and need to look beyond academic and professional writing practices in higher education toward the sphere of activists' daily lives. Academic literacies are for a limited, often disembodied audience, but activist literacies have real audiences, real effects. Activist literacies effect change.

REFERENCES

Alcindor, Yamiche, and Sheryl Gay Stolberg. 2017. "After 16 Futile Years, Congress Will Try Again to Legalize 'Dreamers.'" *New York Times*, September 5.

Alvarez, Sara P. 2018. "Multilingual Writers in College Contexts." *Journal of Adolescent & Adult Literacy* 62 (3): 342–345.

———. 2023. "Multilingualism Beyond Walls: Undocumented Young Adults Subverting Writing Education." In *Writing on the Wall: Writing Education and Resistance to Isolationism*, edited by David S. Martins, Brooke R. Schreiber, and Xiaoye You. Utah State University Press.

Alvarez, Steven. 2017a. *Brokering Tareas: Mexican Immigrant Families Translanguaging Homework Literacies*. State University of New York Press.

———. 2017b. *Community Literacies en Confianza: Learning from Bilingual After- School Programs*. National Council of Teachers of English.

Bhojwani, Sayu. 2017. "Alternative Facts and Extreme Vetting: Immigrants and American Democracy." Keynote presented at the 2017 Mellon Faculty Diversity Program, New York, November.

Brandt, Drandt. 2015. *The Rise of Writing: Redefining Mass Literacy*. Cambridge University Press.

de Block, Lisbeth, and David Buckingham. 2007. *Global Children, Global Media: Migration, Media, and Childhood*. Palgrave Macmillan.

Diaz, Eduardo. 2014. "The Nuevo South: A Changing Landscape." *HuffPost*, September 13.

Flores, Tracey T. 2018. "Breaking Silence and Amplifying Voices: Youths Writing and Performing Their Worlds." *Journal of Adolescent & Adult Literacy* 61 (6): 653–661. https://doi.org/10.1002/jaal.733.

García, Ofelia, Susana Ibarra Johnson, and Kate Seltzer. 2017. *The Translanguaging Classroom: Leveraging Student Bilingualism for Learning*. Caslon.

Gonzales, Laura. 2017. "But Is That Relevant Here? A Pedagogical Model for Embedding Translation in Technical Communication Courses Within the US." *Connexions* 5 (1): 75–108.

Gonzales, Roberto G. 2016. *Lives in Limbo: Undocumented and Coming of Age in America*. University of California Press.

Gonzales, Roberto G., and Leo R. Chavez. 2012. "'Awakening to a Nightmare': Abjectivity and Illegality in the Lives of Undocumented 1.5-Generation Latino Immigrants in the United States." *Current Anthropology* 53 (3): 255–281.

Guerra, Juan. 1998. *Close to Home: Oral and Literate Practices in a Transnational Mexicano Community*. Teachers College Press.

———. 2016. "Cultivating a Rhetorical Sensibility in the Translingual Writing Classroom." *College English* 78 (3): 228–233.

Horner, Bruce, and Karen Kopelson, eds. 2014. *Reworking English in Rhetoric and Composition: Global Interrogations, Local Interventions*. Southern Illinois University Press.

Lee, Erika. 2015. *The Making of Asian America: A History*. Simon & Schuster.

Lillis, Theresa, and Mary Jane Curry. 2010. *Academic Writing in a Global Context: The Politics and Practices of Publishing in English*. Routledge.

Lorimer Leonard, Rebecca. 2014. "Multilingual Writing as Rhetorical Attunement." *College English* 76 (3): 227–247.

———. 2017. *Writing on the Move: Migrant Women and the Value of Literacy.* Pittsburgh University Press.

Mignolo, Walter D. 2005. *The Idea of Latin America.* Wiley-Blackwell.

Migration Policy Institute. 2015. "U.S. Unauthorized Populations from Asia, Central America and Africa Have Grown the Fastest Since 2000." http://www.migrationpolicy.org/news/us-unauthorized-populations-asia-central-america-and-africa-have-grown-fastest-2000-new-mpi.

Mihut, Ligia A. 2014. "Literacy Brokers and the Emotional Work of Mediation." *Literacy in Composition Studies* 2 (1): 57–79.

Morgan-Trostle, Juliana, Kexin Zheng, and Carl Lipscombe. 2016. "The State of Black Immigrants: Part II: Black Immigrants in the Mass Criminalization System." NYU Immigrant Rights Clinic.

Muñoz, Susana M. 2015. *Identity, Social Activism, and the Pursuit of Higher Education: The Journey Stories of Undocumented and Unafraid Community Activists.* Peter Lang.

Nguyen, Chi, and Maraki Kebede. 2017. "Immigrant Students in the Trump Era: What We Know and Do Not Know." *Educational Policy* 31 (6): 716–742.

NYU Center for the Study of Asian American Health. 2018. "Asian Americans in the U.S." https://med.nyu.edu/asian-health/about-us/asian-americans-us.

Perez, Irene. 2012. "My Fearless Daughter." Translated by Rocio Trujillo. In *Undocumented and Unafraid: Tam Tran, Cinthya Felix, and the Immigrant Youth Movement,* edited by Kent Wong, Janna Shadduck-Hernández, Fabiola, Inzunza, Julie Monroe, Victor Narro, and Abel Valenzuela Jr. UCLA Center for Labor Research and Education.

Preston, Julia, and Lizette Alvarez. 2016. "Florida's Changing Latino Population Veers from G.O.P." *New York Times,* October 3.

Ramakrishnan, Karthick, and Sono Shah. 2017. "DATA BITS a Blog for AAPI DATA." http://aapidata.com/blog/asian-undoc-11n7/.

Ribero, Ana Milena. 2016. "Citizenship." In *Decolonizing Rhetoric and Composition Studies: New Latinx Keywords for Theory and Pedagogy,* edited by Iris D. Ruiz and Raúl Sánchez. Palgrave.

Saldaña, Johnny. 2016. *The Coding Manual for Qualitative Researchers.* SAGE.

Santa Ana, Otto. 2002. *Brown Tide Rising: Metaphors of Latinos in Contemporary American Public Discourse.* University of Texas Press.

Trivette, Michael J., and David English. 2017. "Finding Freedom: Facilitating Postsecondary Pathways for Undocumented Students." *Educational Policy* 32 (6): 858–894.

Truax, Eileen. 2015. *DREAMERS: An Immigrant Generation's Fight for Their American Dream.* Beacon.

U.S. Citizenship and Immigration Services. 2018. "Consideration of Deferred Action for Childhood Arrivals (DACA)." https://www.uscis.gov/DACA.

Wong, Kent, and Matias Ramos. 2011. "Undocumented and Unafraid: Tam Tran and Cinthya Felix: Two Activists and Colleagues Remember Cinthya Felix and Tam Tran, Renowned Leaders in the Immigrant-rights Movement." *Boom California,* March 15. https://boomcalifornia.com/2011/03/15/undocumented-and-unafraid-tam-tran-and-cinthya-felix/.

———. 2012. "Introduction: Tam Tran and Cinthya Felix Undocumented and Unafraid." In *Undocumented and Unafraid: Tam Tran, Cinthya Felix, and the Immigrant Youth Movement,* edited by Kent Wong, Janna Shadduck-Hernández, Fabiola, Inzunza, Julie Monroe, Victor Narro, and Abel Valenzuela Jr. UCLA Center for Labor Research and Education.

You, Xiaoye. 2016. *Cosmopolitan English and Transliteracy.* Southern Illinois University Press.

NOTES

1. The term "in the movement" emerged from my research as a self-reference that undocumented immigrant young adults have used in their activist discourse to refer to their immigration related advocacy work.

2. "DACAmented" refers to the youth who have been granted status under the Deferred Action for Childhood Arrivals (DACA) program. For more information about the program, see the USCIS website: www.uscis.gov/DACA.

3. The material presented in this chapter draws from a larger qualitative study that asks how language-minoritized and transnational immigrants navigate, practice, and sustain bilingual and bicultural literacies *with* and *through* their immigrant advocacy and writing.

4. This research study was approved by the University of Louisville's Institutional Review Board.

5. Per IRB approved guidelines, participants were provided the opportunity to exercise their right to select what name appears in this chapter—and the research at large. Angie selected to maintain her authorship here and thus that is the name that is used.

6. Painfully aware that her daughter had been excluded from the family's green card petition because she had "aged out," Angie's mother looked out for her daughter in the best way she could. She relied on her long-term literacy practice of reading the local Korean newspaper to look out for any immigration-related news that could help Angie in coping with her undocumented status.

7. All organization names are pseudonyms.

8. See Mignolo (2005) on how "coloniality" functions in the modern world.

9. Perhaps, what is not widely understood about this fact is the diversity that is captured within this Spanish statistic, which speaks to Mexican variations of Spanish and Spanglish.

5

Sacred Silhouettes

The Legacy of Brown Girl Joy Productions

AMRITPAL KAUR

AMANDEEP KAUR

JASPREET KAUR

Note to Readers

Dear Reader,

As you journey through the pages of this chapter, we invite you to hold close fragments of your own past, the pieces of your own story that define who you are. Every thread of memory, every moment of loss, joy, and every whisper of longing contributes to this rich, intricate existence of ours. Let the echoes of your childhood laughter, the tender touch of loved ones, and the places you have called home fill your heart with a sense of belonging and love.

As you read this chapter, may you discover the beauty in your own narrative, may you feel the presence of those you have lost, their love and guidance forever woven into the fabric of your being. May you find strength in the stories of those who came before you, and may their journeys inspire you to navigate your own with courage and grace.

And as you walk through the corridors of your own history, may you be reminded of the resilience within you, the unbreakable spirit that has carried you through life's twists and turns. In sharing our story, we hope to connect with you on this journey of remembrance, and together, may we find solace and strength in the tapestry of our shared human experience.

With heartfelt gratitude,
Amrit, Jaspreet, Aman

Departures at Dawn

The sun had not yet kissed the fields of Manakpur. Our Pind lay quietly under a blanket of stars. The crisp, early morning air clung to our

FIGURE 5.1 Narinder Kaur (left) and Tarsem Singh (right) standing on top of a hill, overlooking the San Fernando Valley. Still from "Sacred Silhouettes," Brown Girl Joy Productions' unreleased film.

mud-brick veranda and courtyard walls, whispering through narrow lanes like a tender farewell. Inside our home, I stirred in my sleep, my dreams filled with the laughter and warmth of my Nani's embrace, the playful chases with my older cousins Sarbjit, Gurjit, Ranjit, and Sukha, the late-night slurred lullabies sung by my uncles lingering in the background.

At 3 A.M., my mother gently woke me, the soft glow of a diya casting long, soft shadows across the room, illuminating our packed suitcases. I rubbed my eyes, still in my dreamy haze, confused by the urgency. My little sister lay cradled in my Massi's arms, still peacefully dreaming.

This wasn't like the other early morning departures.

My aunts and uncles, cousins and friends, all crowded us. On any other day, it would have felt normal to have us all at home together. They embraced us one by one; their expressions a mixture of forced smiles and lingering sadness. My mother's youthful face and bright eyes were a canvas of mixed resolve and hidden sorrow.

Kundi Massi held me tightly as we reached the small car waiting outside the home gates. I clung to her, tears streaming down my face as she anchored me in her embrace. "I don't want to go . . . I want to stay with

Pal Maama and Bhabi," I cried, my little voice breaking as my confusion turned into desperate realization.

Nani's hands, worn with years of love and labor, gently cradled my tear-streaked red cheeks. Her touch was soft but trembling, a reflection of the sorrow she tried to mask for her dearest daughter and grandchildren.

"Putt, you must go now. Your mother is waiting," Nani murmured, her voice thick with emotion. "You are crossing seven seas, but you will all return to me, to us."

Brimming with an unspoken depth of love and quiet sorrow, Nani's gaze lingered on mine, her eyes holding more than I could ever comprehend. In that fleeting moment, she seemed to memorize every detail of me. Her hands, soft and warm, brushed against my cold face, and with that touch, all her blessings, her strength, her unspoken prayers came to me.

Kundi Massi held me even closer with a firm grip, trying to lend me her own strength.

My Nani's arms found my mother—her child—one final time. The hug was more than a mere gesture; it was the surrender of a lifetime's love, a silent ache that throbbed in every heartbeat. This wasn't like her wedding day in 1996, when Nani had sent her daughter off with joy and hope. This time, Nani was sending her into an unknown beyond, to a place no one could reach, where no hands could ever pull her back.

The weight of that moment, of that goodbye, clung to the air, the silence heavier than any words could ever be. In that space, all they had was each other, and the silent understanding that the love between them would transcend every boundary, every distance, every lifetime until the end of time.

"It's okay, putt," Kundi Massi whispered in my ear, her voice a soothing balm. "We'll be together again. Remember, your Nani's love and our blessings are always with you, wherever you go."

As my mother approached us, my chest felt like it was pressing in on me. I wanted to ask so much, but the lump in my throat kept me silent. My Nani's words and the comforting presence of my Massi wrapped around me like a protective blessing.

I looked up at my mother, seeing the reflection of the far away Manakpur lights in her eyes. They glistened with unshed tears as we piled into the car.

My mother and Nani's home, with its familiar courtyard where I had played and roamed with wobbly footing, seemed to beckon me back. The smell of the earth, the sounds of the Pind waking up with the first light, and the warmth of my family's love would soon become distant memories.

As the car rumbled down the road, I pressed my face to the window, trying to memorize every detail of Manakpur shrinking into a fading silhouette against the dawn sky.

I wondered if the Pind knew we were leaving, if it felt the weight of our absence already, just like my Nani was feeling the cold air settle into the warm hugs she gave us.

Every mile took us further from Manakpur, yet every mile echoed with the promises my mother and Kundi Massi whispered softly to us of new beginnings in the faraway City of Angels and the promise of being reunited with our father once more.

My heart ached with grief too big for words and too big for me to understand at nearly four years old, a sense of loss that settled deep within me for decades to come. I did not know then that I would never again walk those dusty paths or feel the familiar warm hands of my Nani patting my tiny head with eternal blessings.

As I ruminated on these words for the last year, I kept coming back to the true essence of that morning. It was more than just a move; it was a farewell to a part of my soul, a chapter closed too soon. I realize I will never return to Punjab, not as the little girl who left nor as the adult who carries the weight of those unspoken farewells, the goodbyes without the goodbyes.

Punjab traveled with us, tucked away in the stories and memories that will forever be a part of who we are.

Home, I've come to know, is not just a place but the love, honor, and memories we carry with us wherever we go.

—Amritpal Kaur

Embracing the Tapestry of Identity

Welcome to a chapter where the tapestry of Sikh heritage and the multigenerational immigrant journey in America are intricately woven by Brown Girl Joy Productions, founded by three sisters. We embark on a storytelling odyssey that explores the landscapes of memory, aspiration, and resilience. From the serene fields of Punjab beneath starlit skies to the vibrant Gurdwaras of Southern California, our stories transcend borders and challenge the status quo. Within these narratives, we unravel the complexities of identity, navigating the sociopolitical landscapes that often silence our voices. Through our heartfelt storytelling, we illuminate the richness of our culture and reclaim, reimagine, and amplify narratives with the authenticity and depth that only we can offer.

"Sacred Silhouettes: The Legacy of Brown Girl Joy Productions" embodies our mission to celebrate the profound beauty, magic, and resilience within the diasporic Sikh community. It symbolizes our commitment to shedding light on the often-overlooked stories and experiences that have shaped us. We hope that through these narratives we not only educate and inspire but also foster empathy and understanding across cultures.

As family members who are filmmakers and storytellers, we recognize the importance of representation in shaping perceptions and challenging systemic biases. Through our artistry, we seek to reclaim our identities from the shadows of misrepresentation and erasure, offering a platform for voices that have been silenced for far too long. When we say we are going beyond representation and reclaiming identities, we are talking about *reshaping and reimagining* what it means to exist, live, and thrive within the sociopolitical landscape of today. It's not about assimilation or "fitting in," it's about creating something new—where our voices are not just represented but empowered to shape the world around us.

By spotlighting and embracing our stories, we hope to inspire collective conversations that transcend borders, time, and prejudice. Together, let us embark on a path of discovery and transformation, forging a more inclusive and compassionate world where every voice is heard and every story matters.

Echoes of Resilience: A Brief Journey Through Sikh History and Struggle

Our family's immigration journey is situated within a larger history of the Sikh diaspora. We offer a broad historical overview of the circumstances in which Sikhs immigrated from South Asia to the Global North. While it may be painful to read, this is history that is often decontextualized, erased, or minimized and thus important to honor by remembering and documenting.

Punjabis were the first group of individuals of Indian descent to immigrate to the United States and much of North America, with most identifying as Sikhs. The Sikh Foundation states that "between 1903 and 1908, about 6,000 Punjabis entered North America (Canada) and nearly 3,000 crossed into the United States," separated into two different groups. One group consisted of illiterate laborers and agricultural workers, and the other consisted of upper-caste educated "professionals and students" (Kang n.d.).

Punjabi laborers were responsible for the majority of manual labor at railroad construction sites from 1907 to 1909. Some Punjabi laborers immigrated from Canada to Washington State to escape anti-Asian hate, but unfortunately they also encountered prejudice in America. As an example, in 1907 in Bellingham Mill, Washington, white workers raided and looted the living space of Punjabi laborers (Cahn 2008). The goal was to drive the South Asian population out of town to prevent "illegal South Asians [from] taking jobs from Americans." Over four hundred Punjabis were arrested and jailed for attempting to flee the violent raids, and many jumped from windows to escape being whipped and dragged onto the streets naked. The raids achieved their goals; within days after the raids the population of South Asians completely dwindled in Bellingham.

Punjabis as a whole were referred to as the religious and ethnic group "Hindu," despite most of them following the Sikh religion (Hochschild and Powell 2008). This not only created errors in the U.S. census but began a century-long misclassification of Punjabi Sikhs. Much of the anthropological work being done in the limited Sikh and Punjabi archives and nonprofit organizations in Canada and the United States today has focused on gathering sufficient information to correct past historical language and terminology referring to members of the community. Moreover, Canada's de facto ban on immigration from Asia in 1908 resulted in the large-scale immigration of Punjabis to Washington State and later to other states (Government of Canada 2025). By 1910, there were over six thousand Punjabis residing in California, and most identified as practicing Sikhs.

At this time anyone of Indian descent was not allowed to own property or a business, a result of racist and xenophobic legislation in the United States. They were however allowed to own "one building [that was] a place of worship," which led to the building of the first Gurdwara in 1912 in the Northern California city of Stockton (Lucas n.d.). These Sikhs created the Khalsa Diwan in 1909 to unite Sikhs within Stockton and figure out a way to actively practice Sikhi in a foreign, Western country that did not want them there in the first place. The Gurdwara in Stockton became a sanctuary for East Indian people of all different religions to worship and socialize together. The Stockton Gurdwara became one of the epicenters of bustling Punjabi culture and led to the creation of smaller and "illegal" community spaces for Punjabis.

Due to most of the early Indian immigrants being both Punjabi *and* Sikh, many of the community-based organizations were religious and held Sikh gatherings and prayers; they were attended by Indians of all religions. Because Gurdwaras were the only legal meeting place for Indians, naturally there was a formation of political activists working toward decolonizing India from British rule and fighting against anti-Indian and anti-Punjabi naturalization laws in America. One of the significant achievements of this Gurdwara was the founding of the Ghadar Party (revolt/rebellion party), which led the charge on anti-colonialism and anti-British sentiments. This party became the center of community building in 1913 as it not only brought Indians of all religions together around collective anti-British sentiment but also united Indians back in India to begin the rebellion against British rule. Sikh migrant workers were therefore at the forefront of the Indian nationalist movement and vital in popularizing the Ghadar Party among Indian populations all over the world.

While the Ghadar Party's efforts to free India were unsuccessful, India gained its independence on August 15, 1947, codified in the Indian Independence Act. The reality behind this joyous occasion lay in the graves of over one million Sikhs, Muslims, and Hindus who were forced out of their homes due to this "independence" resulting in the partition of India into a Hindu-majority India and Muslim-majority Pakistan.

Over fourteen million Sikhs, Muslims, and Hindus found themselves seeking refuge to avoid interreligious violence and military organized riots taking place in Punjab (Perkins n.d.). Reports state that at least one million people passed away, but due to the partition the bodies of many families were forever lost and thus not counted (Brocklehurst 2017). The Rawalpindi massacre, the Mirpur massacre, and the Kamoke train massacre are only a few of the many massacres that occurred in Punjab. Punjab, the indigenous home of Sikhs, found itself as the burial ground for the burned and mutilated bodies of close to a million Sikh men, women, and children.

Following the division of India, the remaining Sikhs within Punjab found themselves underrepresented in government positions despite being the majority in the region. The dominance of Hindu-majority government officials in decision-making roles left many Sikhs feeling disconnected and excluded from political processes during the process of national rebuilding. This lack of representation contributed to feelings of alienation among Punjabi Sikhs while hindering their ability to influence policies that directly impacted their communities and general welfare.

These actions sowed seeds of unrest and culminated in more turbulent events in the 1980s, setting the stage for heightened conflict between Sikh communities and the Indian state for decades to come. The call for Khalistan, an independent Sikh state, gained traction in the early 1980s as Sikhs felt politically and economically sidelined. Many Sikhs, including Sikh militant Jarnail Singh Bhindranwale, believed that the Indian government did not acknowledge the uniqueness of Sikh identity and struggles as a minority religious group within India following the 1947 partition.

Tensions escalated in June 1984 with the launch of Operation Blue Star, where the Indian government, led by Prime Minister Indira Gandhi, ordered a military operation to remove Bhindranwale and other Sikh militants barricaded in the Golden Temple in Amritsar, the holiest Sikh shrine. It is reported that over ten thousand pilgrims visited the Golden Temple to celebrate Gurpurab, the martyrdom of Guru Arjan Dev ji, and were not given prior warning of the ensuing assault, contrary to Indian military claims. The operation caused significant damage to the Golden Temple and resulted in the deaths of many civilians, including children, and militants. Following Operation Blue Star, tensions between the Sikh community in India and the Indian government heightened.

The situation took a tragic turn on October 31, 1984, when Prime Minister Indira Gandhi was assassinated by her two Sikh bodyguards, Satwant Singh and Beant Singh. While Sri Harmandir Sahib and Amritsar felt the direct impact of Operation Blue Star, it was the assassination of Indira Gandhi that shook the entirety of the Sikh community in Punjab and Delhi. The ensuing riots lasted for five days, with smaller outbursts of violence persisting for weeks afterward.

Under the leadership of elected officials like Jagdish Tytler, Hari Krishan Lal Bhagat, and several officials from the Indian National Congress, about three thousand Sikhs were massacred in this genocide, with unofficial records and personal accounts from many Punjabi Sikh families putting that number over twenty thousand in all districts of Punjab. During this period, the Indian government was accused of inhumane, organized crimes against Punjabi Sikhs in the name of exterminating terrorism in India. A famous Bollywood actor incited violence during this time by stating "khoon ka badla khoon" (blood for blood) on national television and encouraging the masses to arm themselves against the "traitors" of India (Rana 2011). There were strategic manhunts in which many Punjabi Sikh men were kidnapped, tortured, murdered, and imprisoned without just cause or evidence of terrorism. Policemen rounded up men with turbans and beards in vans and either set those vans on fire or organized massive shootouts. Many Sikh men left their homes the morning of October 31 and never returned to their families. Punjabi Sikh women were not safe either. Hundreds of women were abused, sexually assaulted, and kidnapped; some were never found alive. Families were burned alive, Sikh-owned businesses were ambushed, and young Sikh boys with patkas were brutally slaughtered. The Indian government continued to utilize these tactics well through the 1990s and early 2000s on Sikh civilians.

This conflict significantly strained Sikh-Indian relations, leaving a lasting impact on Sikh communities worldwide. While the demand for Khalistan has diminished in popularity since the 1990s, the scars of the 1980s still influence the sociopolitical landscape in Punjab and India, with many Sikhs still seeking justice for the events of the 1980s. The Indian government has yet to answer or hold itself accountable for these atrocities. The military to this day denies the claims made by survivors of Operation Blue Star, who stated they were given no warning to vacate the Golden Temple before the indiscriminate shootings took place.

As a result of these events and instability from the political and economic climates in India, many Punjabi men, who wore the traditional Sikh dastars and long beards, fled to Western countries in record numbers during the 1980s and 1990s. Families uprooted their lives in their homeland, sold their ancestral farmland, and sought refuge abroad. Hoping to rebuild their homes, thousands of Sikhs fled to the United States in search of economic and political stability.

The Impact of Post-9/11 Discrimination

In the aftermath of 9/11, Sikhs in America became targets of discrimination, with over three hundred documented violent incidents within the first month alone, as reported by the Sikh Coalition (n.d.). The first person killed in retaliation for the attacks was a turbaned Sikh man, Balbir Singh Sodhi. His murderer exclaimed that he wanted "to kill some towelheads" (O'Kelley 2021). The post–9/11 era led to the creation of the Immigration and Naturalization Service (INS) Special Registration, implemented by Immigration and Customs Enforcement (ICE) (ACLU 2025). This registration, part of the War on Terrorism, unfairly targeted immigrants from predominantly Muslim countries, including Sikhs, leading to the unjust deportation of over thirteen thousand individuals under the guise of national security threats.

In the midst of these harrowing experiences, the injustices our community members endured rarely found a place in mainstream discussions about justice and social issues in the United States, even within Black, Indigenous, and People of Color (BIPOC) circles. Despite the efforts of organizations like the ACLU and the Sikh Coalition, media coverage and broader public discourse often justified the need for national security rather than confronting the human rights violations that were a direct result of the War on Terrorism. This lack of recognition perpetuated a cycle of marginalization and invisibility for Sikhs, making it even more challenging to secure acknowledgment and seek justice in the aftermath of those traumatic post–9/11 policies.

Striving for Justice: Sikh Resilience in India and America

The parallels between India and the United States underscore the global struggle for Sikh communities, where political persecution and xenophobia continue to undermine our rights and safety.

The current climate in India presents a challenging landscape for Sikhs, marked by systemic discrimination and political marginalization under Hindu nationalist leadership. Sikhs in India face ongoing challenges related to religious freedom, cultural identity, and political representation. Instances of desecration of Sikh Gurdwaras, false accusations of terrorism, and targeted attacks highlight the precarious position of Sikhs within India's sociopolitical framework. The lack of accountability for past atrocities, such as the 1984 anti-Sikh riots, continues to strain Sikh-Indian relations and hinder efforts for reconciliation and justice.

Meanwhile, in the United States, the misunderstanding and stereotypes of Sikh immigrants as dangerous "terrorists" continue to manifest in violence against the Sikh community today. We are living in a post–9/11 world where a rise in mass shootings at Gurdwaras, school bullying, hate crimes, and workplace discrimination remain realities for Sikhs. In 2012, as community members at a Gurdwara in Oak Creek, Wisconsin, prepared *langar*, a white supremacist murdered seven Sikhs (Harmeet Kaur 2022). In 2021, a mass shooter at a FedEx in Indianapolis killed eight employees, four of whom were Sikhs (B. Kaur 2022). In the aftermath of both of these shootings, Sikhs gathered in Gurdwaras to mourn, rebuild, and heal through our faith and community as a guiding light. We write about these moments of violence to show that creating visibility for Sikhs and immigrants is not a matter of privilege or luxury but rather a necessity to create safe spaces and communities.

Gurdwaras: The Heart of Our Faith and Resilience

In our Gurdwaras, we seek solace, but even these sacred spaces are tainted by the ever-present threat of violence. In our community, children grow up hearing stories of martyrdom not just from past centuries, but from their own lifetimes. They learn to live with the dual burden of preserving their faith while guarding against the prejudices that come with it. This duality shapes our community's psyche, fostering a blend of pride and perpetual vigilance. Each incident of violence is not just an attack on individuals but an assault on the fabric of our communal identity. We remember the faces of the victims, not just as statistics but as brothers, sisters, sons, daughters, fathers, and mothers whose lives were cut short by hatred and ignorance. The ripple effects of these tragedies extend far beyond the immediate families, shaking the entire Sikh diaspora and leaving us grappling with grief and fear.

Our faith and the Gurdwara remain a source of hope and strength for us. These sacred spaces allow us to come together, to heal, and to reaffirm our commitment to the values of equality, service, and compassion. The Gurdwara is a symbol of our community, a place where we find peace even amid the chaos, and where our shared identity gives us the strength to keep moving forward despite the challenges we face.

Our Family's Story: The Strength That Carried Us

Our family arrived in the United States in 2000, stepping into a country that promised opportunity but often greeted us with hostility. Just a year later, the September 11, 2001, attacks cast an immediate shadow over our lives, as suspicion and violence against Sikhs surged. The symbols of our faith—our turbans and our unshorn hair—became targets for hate. In those precarious years, our parents, Narinder Kaur and Tarsem Singh, carried the immense weight of both survival and dignity, shaping our understanding of resilience, love, and sacrifice in ways we would come to fully grasp only much later.

Narinder Kaur: A Mother's Strength in an Unfamiliar World

When our mother, Narinder Kaur, arrived in the United States, she carried more than just the hopes of a better life—she carried the burden of raising a family in a world she had yet to understand. She did not know the language. She did not know where to buy school supplies. She did not know whom to turn to when fear and isolation crept in. But despite it all, she became our first teacher. In the dim light of our one-bedroom apartment, while the world outside seemed unpredictable and unwelcoming, she was the one who taught us our ABCs. She shaped our early world with lessons not only in language but in resilience.

Every day, she lived in fear—fear of what could happen to our father when he stepped outside, fear of how she would protect us in a country that saw us as outsiders. And yet, she met each day with unwavering determination. She built a home within four small walls, ensuring that even in a world that did not yet embrace us, we would always know love, safety, and the strength of our roots. Her quiet sacrifices, her sleepless nights, her silent prayers were the foundation upon which we stood, learning not just how to navigate a new world, but how to do so with pride in who we were.

Tarsem Singh: Defiance in the Face of Fear

While our mother held the home together, our father, Tarsem Singh, worked relentlessly to keep it standing. He labored seven days a week as an underpaid cashier at a 7-Eleven, a job that demanded everything from his time, his health, to his sense of safety. He did it without complaint, believing that his sacrifices would pave the way for something greater.

In the years following 9/11, the risks he faced as a turbaned Sikh man in America became even more pronounced. He knew that every moment spent outside the home carried the possibility of violence. He knew that to simply exist as himself was to invite danger. And yet he never wavered. He refused to hide who he was. He refused to strip away the symbols of his faith to make others more comfortable. He would often respond to his supervisors and friends requests to cut his hair and beard with "je goli vajdi ah fe vaj jave parr sir ton pagg ni launi" (If I get shot, then I get shot, but I refuse to take off my turban).

These were not just words; they are a testament to the unshakable spirit of our father, to the legacy of Sikh resistance, and to the pride of a people who have endured centuries of oppression and still stand tall. In an era when many Sikh men and boys were forced to choose between their safety and their identity, our father's defiance was an act of rebellion. His turban was not just fabric—it was dignity, it was sovereignty, it was a declaration that his existence would not be dictated by fear.

Even now, the weight of those years lingers. The trauma of being targeted for who we are is not easily forgotten and continues. In our mother's perseverance and our father's courage, we learned something invaluable: that our existence is an act of resistance, that our faith is our strength, and that no matter the challenges, we carry within us the power to rise, to heal, and to move forward even through the difficult heart space it takes to do so.

Sikh Representation: Navigating Sociopolitical Spaces and Identities

In the United States, Sikh characters are often misrepresented or entirely absent from mainstream media. One glaring example is the television show *Outsourced* (2010–2011), in which a Sikh character, Gupta, is depicted as a socially awkward, bumbling office worker, seemingly content to be the object of ridicule. By casting Sikhs in such a light, the show not only trivializes Sikh culture but also perpetuates our invisibility. It fails to provide an authentic portrayal of our lives, our struggles, and the complexities of our identity as Sikhs in America.

These portrayals are not just misguided—they are dangerous. They feed into a broader narrative that diminishes our existence, making us seem like caricatures rather than complex individuals with rich histories, beliefs, and lives. This kind of representation, or lack thereof, perpetuates ignorance and fuels bias, which inevitably translates into real-world violence and discrimination. It is no coincidence that after 9/11 hate crimes against Sikhs soared, as many Americans, unfamiliar with our faith, misidentified us simply because of our outward appearance. These portrayals make a mockery of our faith, which we have fought to preserve for centuries, including the right to maintain our *kesh* (uncut hair) and *dastars* (turbans) as integral parts of our identity.

Narrative Threads: Weaving Our Storytelling Legacy

In contrast to the stereotypes on screen, the first stories we heard were from our mother in our native rhythmic language of Punjabi. She would tell us about the *khets* (farmlands) and *galliyan* of the village in which she grew up. Our parents were from a time when photography was not widely accessible in pinds and smaller shahars, so our family history was passed down as oral stories. We learned that our mother's words contained entire worlds. Her oral stories were a bridge to a different time and place that we could not travel to physically, but we were given the tools to imagine. From a young age we were fascinated by our mother's ability to tell stories that made us feel rooted, even though, in reality, we were in limbo as undocumented immigrants in a post–9/11 world. We came to understand storytelling as an art form about creating feelings and imagination.

Our first attempt to participate in this tradition of storytelling was in high school. As part of the Community Rights Campaign and Bus Riders Union, we spent time on buses getting petition signatures to change the punitive truancy ticket policy within the Los Angeles Unified School District. We saw firsthand how our classmates, particularly Black and Brown students, were unfairly punished for being late to class and criminalized through the school to prison pipeline. We learned how to craft a compelling and quick story to convince strangers to sign the petition. Our words as storytellers were able to move a person from being a complete stranger with different political views to empathize and then take action. Similar to our parents, we were encouraging the listeners of our stories to envision a radically different world than the one we currently live in.

But our excitement quickly became exhaustion. We realized that every single signature required us to keep advocating and proving that the humanity of Black and Brown students matters. It was also not always safe to approach strangers on a bus as undocumented Sikh teenagers. Grassroots organizing work is necessary and effective but often demands excessive vulnerability and unpaid labor especially from impacted community members.

We discovered filmmaking as an avenue that protected our safety and sanity and gave us more agency over our narratives. With film, we did not have to keep repeating the same information in exchange for one signature. Instead, we could reach people beyond our five-mile radius and the larger Los Angeles County. There were more tools to protect our identity and the identities of our fellow community members who were sharing their personal lived experiences. Most importantly, through film our words and stories have longevity to create a lasting impact.

As undocumented Sikh immigrants, we are under constant threat of historical erasure or misrepresentation. The only thing we truly own is over our voices. For us, storytelling is not a luxury or an act of creative self-expression. It is a means of survival, a way to protect the people we love, and a declaration that people like us exist. Too often, low-income Black and Brown communities are researched and portrayed through a deficit lens, framed as inherently broken or lacking. This framing is not just inaccurate; it is dehumanizing. In contrast, community-rooted storytelling reveals the ingenuity, resilience, and creative strategies that arise from living within constraint. The difference between stories told by outsiders and those told from within is not just about perspective. It is about truth. Outsider narratives often flatten, pathologize, or exoticize. Stories from within carry nuance, memory, and lived accountability. We do not see ourselves as "giving a voice to the voiceless." That framing wrongly implies that other underresourced people have no voice of their own, a paternalistic narrative that often allows those in power to speak for us rather than to listen to us and make space for us.

We aim to honor our parents and others by reflecting them as we truly see them: as people whose small, everyday acts have quietly shifted the discourse of family lineages and generations to come. Though our parents may never be called "artists" in the formal sense, they were in many ways the first artists and change makers we ever knew. Their creativity took shape in survival, from tailoring secondhand clothes and painting our small apartment a new color every other year, to telling oral stories that stitched the past to the present. These acts were not decorative or optional. They were ways of coping, resisting, and keeping us connected to something larger than our immediate circumstances.

Their storytelling helped us remember where we came from and imagine what could be. It did more than preserve history. It created forward motion. It gave us the momentum to endure, and eventually, the foundation to tell stories of our own.

From Langar to Liberation

Our ability to endure and the ethos of us as individuals, siblings, and storytellers is rooted in the time we spend at the Gurdwara. During our childhood, our parents cooked *langar*, a communal meal served to anyone regardless of caste, religion, socioeconomic status, sexuality, or gender. Traditionally, everyone eats langar sitting on the ground to symbolize equality among all people. As kids when we climbed onto stools to knead dough to make roti, we were learning that it is possible to embody a philosophy of equality in everyday life. It is not an abstract concept to treat people as equals and to dignify them with respect. For Sikhs, langar is about the fundamental belief that equality means every human being deserves to have access to basic necessities like food and water. Most importantly, langar is a joyous time, from the cooking to the serving and eating. Different types of labor, volunteering to cook, donating ingredients, and serving the food, are valued equally.

Sikhism offers an egalitarian alternative to the way the caste system created a hierarchy in South Asian society. Often lower-caste people would sit on the floor, out of sight from higher-caste people who were allowed to sit on chairs to eat. The idea of *seva*, selfless service, like langar is to actively practice, seeing other beings as part of one interconnected whole. Sikhi transcends borders and social constructs of differences between people. We saw that our parents were not just going to the Gurdwara to pray for the safety and prosperity of our family. The Gurdwara was also a place where they could connect with the community and hear, even if it was in passing or phrased as jokes, that we were not the only family that was struggling.

Sikhism's egalitarian aspirations have deeply shaped our political consciousness and the way we think critically about power, identity, and social constructs. But we also know that Sikhi, as it is practiced today, is not without its contradictions. Across Punjab and the diaspora, casteism continues to harm Dalit Sikhs through social exclusion, violence, and erasure, often in spaces like the Gurdwara itself. We have witnessed how anti-Blackness, homophobia, and patriarchy persist in our communities, even when they are quietly ignored or spiritually rationalized. These contradictions fuel our work. In both our storytelling and our community labor, we turn to the core values of Sikhi, seva, sarbat da bhala, and justice, through an intersectional lens. We do not romanticize the Gurdwara. Instead, we hold it accountable to its own highest ideals. We believe that if the Gurdwara can be a place of nourishment and sanctuary, it can also be a site for transformation. To us, the global spread of Gurdwaras is not just a religious footprint. It is a blueprint. Wherever Sikhs gather, there is the potential to build infrastructure for social repair, collective care, and radical change. Our commitment to filmmaking and storytelling is shaped by this very possibility that the places that shaped us can also evolve, and that justice must begin at home.

Reclaiming Our Narratives and Empowering Voices

Central to our work is the authentic representation of our communities. As such, we are committed to confronting the shallow, often one-dimensional portrayals of our identities that often reduce us to stereotypes. Our goal is to represent the complex layers of our experiences, acknowledging the barriers we face while remaining rooted in our cultural heritage.

As Amrit, Jaspreet, and Amandeep, our commitment to storytelling is deeply personal. The stories we tell through "Sacred Silhouettes"—both as an unreleased documentary and in this chapter—are about more than history; they reflect the ongoing struggles and triumphs of Sikh communities in America. We understand the power of our voices to reshape narratives that have long been misrepresented or ignored. Our work draws strength from our lived experiences, the resilience of our ancestors, and our determination to create new legacies that challenge dominant storytelling frameworks.

This commitment also extends beyond casting Punjabi characters. We actively seek to provide opportunities for individuals without a background in film to tell their own stories behind the camera. Through our films and social impact projects, we hope to instill pride in our heritage, educate others about our community's journeys, and advocate for change that reaches far beyond the screen.

Our Filmmaking Practice: Holding Love, Loss, and Lineage

One of our most recent films, *Zindagi Dobara* (Life Again), was created with this same ethos. The story, written by Amritpal Kaur, follows Mahi, a Punjabi Sikh teen who loses her parents in a tragic accident and is sent to live with an estranged aunt, Dilreet, whom she has never met. The two begin to navigate their grief, uncovering family secrets and confronting generational trauma.

This film is a tribute to our Nani, who passed away in 2018, inspired by the distance we felt from her after leaving India in 2000. We never had the chance to reconnect before she passed, and the stories we carry with us remain unspoken, leaving a void in both our hearts and the legacy of our family.

Through *Zindagi Dobara*, we explore the complexities of generational and cultural differences—particularly how our Punjabi Sikh identities intersect with the experiences of LGBTQ+ individuals. The film delves into the process of unlearning taboos and the transformative power of healing and self-discovery. It shows how Mahi and Dilreet, two people from different generations, find common ground, leading to emotional and spiritual rebirth.

We aim to challenge expectations and create space for queer South Asians to imagine futures free from the constraints of tradition. For many LGBTQ+ individuals, the path to healing or overcoming trauma can feel impossible. *Zindagi Dobara* offers a glimpse of what that healing could look like, even in the midst of great pain.

Through this story, we have witnessed firsthand how storytelling can bridge gaps—between generations, between personal struggles and collective identity, and between the versions of ourselves we once struggled to see and the selves we're becoming. Just as "Sacred Silhouettes" honors the resilience of Sikhs in America, *Zindagi Dobara* works to spark an important conversation: How do we heal when history and tradition have erased parts of who we are? We believe stories like these have the power to soften hearts and open new doors to love and acceptance.

Beyond Filmmaking: Building Bridges and Uplifting Communities

At Brown Girl Joy Productions, filmmaking and storytelling are acts of *seva*—rooted in a commitment to creating narratives that go beyond entertainment. Our work is about uplifting and transforming communities, especially those that have long been marginalized.

Growing up in a mixed-status immigrant family, we have always navigated the complexities of dual identities—of balancing the cultural values of Punjab,

India, with the realities of our lives in America. Our experiences as undocumented immigrants shape much of our work, offering a space to confront stereotypes while expressing our personal and collective stories. Our stories become a necessary reflection of our lives against a backdrop of systemic injustices.

Our mission extends beyond the screen. We recognize the challenges faced by our community—like barriers to health care, education, and creative resources—and we are driven to empower those who share our circumstances. In 2020, in response to the challenges presented by the first Trump administration, we organized virtual film events in collaboration with community stakeholders. Over two months, we engaged over 550 South Asian community members in the San Fernando Valley and the broader Los Angeles County, guiding them through the U.S. census process. By fostering trust and providing multilingual resources, we helped people navigate their fears, underscoring how participation could secure resources for underserved communities. This moment reminded us that our work has never been limited to the mediums of film and art. It is about building trust, carrying memory, and mobilizing communities toward collective liberation. It is in that spirit that we turn to remembrance and resilience.

In Remembrance, In Resilience

Our story is not just our own—it is a continuation of the sacrifices, dreams, and resilience of those who came before us. From the hushed goodbyes in Manakpur to the turbulent migration journeys of Sikh families across time, from the scars of partition to the echoes of post–9/11 discrimination, our history and present day are a testament to both struggle and survival. Yet, in every departure, in every challenge, we have carried forward something far greater: the unshakable spirit of our people.

Through Brown Girl Joy Productions, we have sought to reclaim our narratives, to honor the silences imposed upon our histories, and to amplify the voices that demand to be heard. Our storytelling is more than a creative pursuit—it is an act of defiance, an assertion of identity, and a means of forging belonging in a world that has often refused to make space for us.

The stories of our parents, of our community, and of our faith are woven into every frame of our films, and every word of this chapter. We carry their strength in the memories of our mother teaching us resilience through the simplest acts of care and in our father's unwavering pride, despite the dangers of being visibly Sikh in white America. These are not just personal recollections but universal truths that bind us to a larger struggle for justice, dignity, and representation.

As we move forward, we do so with the knowledge that our past does not define our limitations; it shapes our power. The resilience of our ancestors, the perseverance of our community, and the legacy of Sikhi continue to guide us toward a future where our voices are not only heard but also honored.

Our history is one of movement and memory, and through storytelling, we have built something permanent: a home within each other, a place where our past, present, and future come together, forever intertwined.

In the words of Guru Nanak Dev Ji, *"Recognize the whole human race as one."* May we continue to walk this path with courage, carrying the love, lessons, and stories that have shaped us, ensuring that no voice is forgotten and no story fades into obscurity.

Acknowledgments

Thanks to Nirvikar Singh, distinguished professor of economics, University of California, Santa Cruz. We dedicate this chapter to those who left everything behind, to those who are left behind and not forgotten, and to the countless Punjabis across the globe who long for a motherland, a Punjab, they may never return to. In perpetual gratitude to our creators, Tarsem Singh and Narinder Kaur, who weaved dreams for us to build in this lifetime.

REFERENCES

ACLU. 2025. "National Security Entry-Exit Registration System." https://www.aclu.org/issues/immigrants-rights/immigrants-rights-and-detention/national-security-entry-exit-registration.

Bindra, Onkar Singh. "Baba Jawala Singh and Baba Wasakha Singh, Founding Fathers." In *Sikh-American Establishments and Their Journeys, 1912–2012.* Pacific Coast Khalsa Diwan Society.

Brocklehurst, Steven. 2017. "Partition of India: 'They Would Have Slaughtered Us.'" *BBC News*, August 11. https://www.bbc.com/news/uk-scotland-40874496.

Cahn, David. 2008. "The 1907 Bellingham Riots in Historical Context—Seattle Civil Rights and Labor History Project." Seattle Civil Rights & Labor History Project. https://depts.washington.edu/civilr/bham_history.htm.

Dalrymple, William. 2015. "The Mutual Genocide of Indian Partition." *New Yorker*, June 22. http://www.newyorker.com/magazine/2015/06/29/the-great-divide-books-dalrymple.

Gibson, Margaret A. 1988. *Accommodation without Assimilation: Sikh Immigrants in an American High School.* Cornell University Press.

Government of Canada. 2025. "Significant Events in the History of Asian Communities in Canada." May 1. https://www.canada.ca/en/canadian-heritage/campaigns/asian-heritage-month/important-events.html.

Hirvi, Laura. 2013. "Identities Negotiated through Dress(Ing)." In *Identities in Practice: A Trans-Atlantic Ethnography of Sikh Immigrants in Finland and in California.* Finnish Literature Society.

Hochschild, Jennifer L., and Brenna M. Powell. 2008. "Racial Reorganization and the United States Census 1850–1930: Mulattoes, Half-Breeds, Mixed Parentage, Hindoos, and the Mexican Race." *Studies in American Political Development* 22 (1): 59–96.

Kang, Jasbir Singh. n.d. "Punjabi Migration to United States." Sikh Foundation. https://www.sikhfoundation.org/PunjabiMigration_JSKang.html.

Kataria, Shyamal. 2016. "'We Suffered the Most': Sikh Refugee Perspective on Partition." *South Asianist Journal* 4 (2): 62–77.

Kaur, Brahmjot. 2022. "A Year After FedEx Shooting, Sikh Americans Honor Victims." *NBC News*, April 15. https://www.nbcnews.com/news/asian-america/year-fedex-shooting-sikh-americans-honor-victims-rcna24559.

Kaur, Harleen. 2022. *Crossroads of Belonging, Safety, and Sovereignty: Sikh Punjabi Negotiations of Statecraft and Racecraft from Colonial Punjab to Imperial United States.* University of California, Los Angeles.

Kaur, Harmeet. 2022. "The Oak Creek Massacre Signaled the Rise of White Supremacist Violence. But the Warnings Went Unheeded." *CNN*, August 5. https://www.cnn.com/2022/08/05/us/oak-creek-shooting-anniversary-white-supremacy-rise-cec/index.html.

Lucas, Greg. n.d. "Stockton Is Home to Nation's First Gurdwara." California State Library. https://celebratecalifornia.library.ca.gov/stockton-is-home-to-nations-first-gurdwara/.

Mann, Gurinder Singh, Paul David Numrich, and Raymond B Williams. 2001. *Buddhists, Hindus and Sikhs in America.* Oxford University Press.

O'Kelley, Kaley. 2021. "Sikh Family Speaks About Forgiveness, Community in Honor of Mesa Man Murdered After 9/11." *ABC 15 Arizona*, September 9. https://www.abc15.com/news/region-southeast-valley/mesa/sikh-family-speaks-about-forgiveness-community-in-honor-of-mesa-man-murdered-after-9-11.

Ong, Paul M., Edna Bonacich, and Lucie Cheng. 1994. *The New Asian Immigration in Los Angeles and Global Restructuring.* Temple University Press.

Perkins, C. Ryan. n.d. "1947 Partition of India & Pakistan." Stanford University Libraries. https://exhibits.stanford.edu/1947-partition/about/1947-partition-of-india-pakistan.

Punjabi and Sikh Diaspora Digital Archive. n.d. "Stockton Gurdwara." https://punjabidiaspora.ucdavis.edu/contributions/religion/stockton-temple/.

Rajan, Sebastian Irudaya, et al. 2016. *Migration, Mobility and Multiple Affiliations: Punjabis in a Transnational World.* Cambridge University Press.

Rana, Yudhvir. 2011. "1984 Riots: 'Why Nobody Noticed Amitabh Bachchan Spewing Venom in India." *Times of India*, October 21. https://timesofindia.indiatimes.com/india/1984-riots-Why-nobody-noticed-Amitabh-Bachchan-spewing-venom-in-India/articleshow/10429011.cms.

Sikarwar, Dharam. 2019. "Mirpur Massacre 1947: When 18 Thousand Hindus Got Killed by Pak Soldiers, Due to Negligence of PM Nehru: The Youth." *1947 Archive.* https://www.theyouth.in/2019/11/26/mirpur-massacre-1947-when-18-thousand-hindus-got-killed-by-pak-soldiers-due-to-negligence-of-pm-nehru/#google_vignette.

Sikh Coalition. n.d. "Fact Sheet on Post–9/11 Discrimination and Violence Against Sikh Americans." https://www.sikhcoalition.org/images/documents/fact%20sheet%20on%20hate%20against%20sikhs%20in%20america%20post%209-11%20.pdf.

Singh, Gurharpal. 2024. "Partition Violence, Mountbatten and the Sikhs: A Reassessment." *Sikh Formations.* https://doi.org/10.1080/17448727.2024.2318874.

Singh, Nirvikar. 2016. "Cosmopolitanism, Tradition and Identity: Framing the Sikh Experience in California." *Sikh Research Journal* 2 (1). https://doi.org/10.62307/srj.v2i1.118.

Srivastava, Ram P. 1986. Review of *From India to America. Journal of Comparative Family Studies* 17 (1): 139–142. http://www.jstor.org/stable/41601589.

"Stockton Sikh Temple: Sikhnet." n.d. *SikhNet Play—Sharing the Love of Gurbani.*

PART THREE

Family, Faith, and Navigating Higher Education in the United States

6

Given and Chosen Family

The Central Pillar for Undocumented Asian College Students' Value for Civic Engagement

CYNTHIA MARIBEL ALCANTAR

RACHEL FREEMAN-WONG

VICTORIA KIM

'INOKE HAFOKA

TRISHA MAZUMDER

SET HERNANDEZ

Undocumented college students are some of the most civically engaged members of society. Their civic involvement as activists has resulted in major movements that have created more equitable policies and programs for undocumented immigrants (Dao 2017; DeAngelo, Schuster, and Stebleton 2016; Forenza, Rogers, and Lardier 2017; Saldivar 2017; Wu 2018). Part of their civic participation stems from their own experiences with racism, xenophobia, and other oppressions that create barriers to full incorporation into the United States. Some undocumented immigrant youth become civically engaged to be proactive and cope with the frustration about the restrictions they face (Gonzales 2016; Muñoz 2008; Perez et al. 2009, 2010; Suárez-Orozco, Hernández, and Casanova 2015). For others, their interest in civic engagement stems from a sense of responsibility to family and their own communities (Katsiaficas et al. 2016). Family—both given (the families children grow up with) and chosen (the families children and adults choose to join)—plays an integral role in the civic development of undocumented college students (Alcantar et al. 2023; Andolina et al. 2003; McIntosh, Hart, and Youniss 2007; Murray and Mulvaney 2012; Pancer 2015; Pavlova et al. 2016).

Although family is a key pillar in the civic participation of undocumented students, undocumented families are continuously vilified in the national discourse around immigration reform. For example, politicians and public figures spoke poorly of immigrant parents as they denounced the proposed Deferred Action for Parents of Americans and Lawful Permanent Residents (DAPA) program, an executive order announced by President Obama in 2014, that would have provided relief from deportation for undocumented parents of U.S.-born and lawful permanent resident children. In a *CNN* article in 2015, Judge Hanen, a federal judge in Texas, was quoted as saying that the state of Texas "stands to suffer direct damages from the implementation of DAPA" (Mullen and Diamond 2015). DAPA was proposed as an expansion of Deferred Action for Childhood Arrivals (DACA), an executive order instated in 2012 that provides temporary protection against deportation and work permits for eligible undocumented adults. DAPA would have reduced the number of families who have been separated because of deportation, as deportation negatively impacts families' everyday lives (Dreby 2012; Valdivia 2021). Unfortunately, no parents were ever able to apply for the program (Solórzano 2022) because DAPA was halted by the U.S. Supreme Court in 2016. The fight to reunite immigrant families and pass federal immigration reform for families continues.

This chapter discusses the significant role that family plays in the development of civic values among undocumented Asian immigrants. We focus this chapter on undocumented Asian students given that they are the second largest undocumented group, yet there is a dearth of literature on this population (Buenavista 2012; Escudero 2012, 2020; Gogue et al. 2021). Much of the literature on the civic engagement of undocumented college students has focused on Latinx undocumented communities (Forenza, Rogers, and Lardier 2017; Gonzales 2008; Hinton 2015; Katsiaficas et al. 2018; Perez et al. 2010; Rogers et al. 2008; Seif 2011; Suárez-Orozco, Hernández, and Casanova 2015; Terriquez 2017). Yet of the estimated 11,047,000 undocumented immigrants in the United States, about 15 percent were born in countries across Asia (Migration Policy Institute 2019).

Scholars have found that "family support is key to civic development" for Asian / Asian American students (Bi, Lam, and Chung 2021, 138) both documented and undocumented (Wui and White 2023). Additionally, "understanding familial ties to immigration and displacement can help AAPI [Asian American and Pacific Islander] students understand the ways in which their families have demonstrated leadership in their pursuit of a better life for their family and community" (Gogue et al. 2021, 105). Building on this growing body of literature, this chapter presents portraits of three undocumented Asian college students with a particular focus on their conceptualization of family and its role in developing their civic values.[1] We were interested in exploring two research questions:

1. How do undocumented Asian students describe both given and chosen family?
2. How have these students' families influenced their civic values and participation?

Each of the three portraits in this chapter highlights how given and chosen families influence the civic values of undocumented Asian students. This occurs particularly through the intergenerational and intragenerational transmission of civic values and a broader conceptualization of family in the lives of undocumented Asian students.

The authors of this chapter have worked directly with undocumented students and their families, and undocumented Asian and Pacific Islander communities specifically, in various capacities as researchers, practitioners, and activists with immigration advocacy organizations, higher education institutions, and K–12 schools. All authors come from immigrant backgrounds (Latina, Pacific Islander, Asian, and Eastern European / Jewish) and communities with family and friends who are undocumented, which have fueled their passion for engaging with this topic. Some of the participants' experiences were similar to what the authors have witnessed through their own communities and work, allowing the authors to bring a collectively unique perspective. In addition, Mazumder's educational and professional training in photography allowed for a more extensive and detailed analysis of the participants' family maps, including providing a critical lens to analyze participants' choices in colors or position of individuals drawn.

Methods

The data for this study stemmed from a larger participatory action research (PAR) project that was part of a national community-based participatory action research (CBPAR) study that focused on the lived experiences of undocumented students in higher education (Teranishi, Suárez-Orozco, and Suárez-Orozco 2015).[2] The PAR project findings presented in this chapter drew data from the national CBPAR project to engage undocumented and allied undergraduate and graduate students in a research project to understand the experiences of undocumented undergraduate students and to inform the policies and practices to better support this population in higher education.

This chapter focuses on the experiences of three undocumented Asian students from a pool of eighteen undocumented students who participated in the PAR project. The small sample size is reflective of the undocumented population's regard for being a hard-to-reach population in research, especially undocumented Asians (Alcantar et al. 2023; Azmitia 2024; Ro et al. 2021). In fact, the project's PAR and CBPAR approaches were intentionally employed to reach this hard-to-reach population and engage, collaborate, learn from, and address the needs of diverse and often less known undocumented student populations (Alcantar et al. 2023; Katsiaficas et al. 2016; Katsiaficas et al. 2018; Teranishi, Suárez-Orozco, and Suárez-Orozco 2015). Although the literature on undocumented college students has grown exponentially in the past decade, it remains limited compared to studies on non-undocumented students; and of the limited literature on undocumented students, even less documents the experiences of undocumented Asian students. Focusing this chapter on the experiences of three undocumented Asian students contributes to the growing, albeit limited, literature on this population and raises awareness to inform policies and practices to better support this group.

We addressed our research questions by constructing portraits (Lawrence-Lightfoot and Hoffmann Davis 1997) of three undocumented Asian students (two born in the Philippines and one who is Chinese and was born in Taiwan) based on in-depth semistructured interviews and family identity maps (Katsiaficas et al. 2016; Sirin, Katsiaficas, and Volpe 2010) collected by the PAR project. Centering the portraits of three participants allowed us to provide a rich and in-depth perspective of the lived experiences of undocumented Asian community members. During the interviews, the researchers asked participants to draw what they consider to be their family. The family maps were then reviewed by the researchers during the interviews. This approach allowed participants to visually and artistically express themselves and researchers to present complex themes through narratives and portraits of research participants. The portraits, corresponding data collected, and PAR approach allowed us to gather thick descriptions of how undocumented Asian students defined their family and how their family has influenced their civic values and participation.

The Role of Family in the Civic Development
of Undocumented Asian Students

This chapter presents three portraits of undocumented Asian college students related to family and civic engagement. The findings draw attention to the central role of given and chosen family in supporting undocumented Asian students' civic development and engagement. In the first portrait (Figure 6.1), Stacy, a twenty-two-year-old Chinese student born in Taiwan, demonstrated the intergenerational transmission of civic engagement, where one generation passes on civic values to the next. In the second portrait (Figure 6.2), Joshua, a twenty-five-year-old Filipino student, demonstrated the intragenerational transmission of civic engagement, where values of civic engagement are passed on within one generation. Last, Annie, a twenty-one-year-old Filipina student, represented the expansion of the notion of family to incorporate friends and demonstrated their impact on her civic development in her portrait (Figure 6.3).[3]

Stacy: Intergenerational Civic Development

Stacy is a Chinese student born in Taiwan and raised in Northern California by her undocumented immigrant single mother, who played an integral role in Stacy's civic development as a student activist. She identifies as Chinese, and as an undocumented woman. Stacy looks to her mom, who shares these identities, for guidance and role modeling, which is reflected in her family portrait (Figure 6.1). Stacy drew herself and her mom, standing side by side on the same line, with her mother in a strong stance with her hand on her hip, looking at

FIGURE 6.1 Stacy's portrait, Intergenerational Civic Development.

Stacy. In contrast, Stacy is drawn with both hands in the air, making a gesture of questioning or reluctance and, in a sense, waiting for her mother's direction. The portrait seems to demonstrate Stacy's mom taking a leading and guiding role with Stacy being the recipient of her mother's guidance.

Stacy faced challenges within her family, particularly regarding her choice to major in political science in college. She stated, "Oh, we have to go into the science and math, or you have to be quiet about what you want to do with your study. I definitely had to battle that a lot, with my friends' circle and my relatives, of what I really want to study." Even though Stacy was expected by others to pursue a major in one of the STEM fields, she resisted expectations put on her and advocated for her own interests by majoring in political science instead. Stacy's experience being an undocumented immigrant and her awareness of the challenges and needs of the undocumented community through her involvement with immigrant advocacy organizations helped cultivate a passion for social activism. Stacy's mother, in contrast to her extended family, provided emotional and spiritual support and took a stance supporting Stacy's decision to major in political science. When Stacy was asked about the expectations her mother had of her to be successful, she stated, "She's [Stacy's mom] like, 'No, you have to find a meaning of what you do, and then you'll be happy about it.' . . . My family is very Buddhist. So, we've always been detached from material wealth, in a way. . . . Finding meaning is a very Buddhist perspective, and in another thing, you have to be able to, you know, find meaning and help the people around you. You have to work on yourself before working on other people. . . . My mother pretty much shaped my expectation for myself."

Stacy's desire to pursue a degree in political science to help others like herself and the importance of her mother's support and influence in this decision were demonstrated in her drawing. To the left of the figures of herself and her mother, she drew two heads representing the entire undocumented Asian community in the United States. Stacy considered all undocumented Asians as part of her family, given their shared undocumented and racial status. The family values Stacy learned through her mother, such as "help the people around you," assisted her in developing a deeper understanding of community. As undocumented Asians share similar burdens (e.g., challenges related to racialized immigrant and undocumented backgrounds), Stacy believed undocumented immigrant status and racial identity were interconnected communal experiences.

Stacy's mother also supported her activism. For example, Stacy shared, "She is very supportive of me coming out to public about my status. Actually, she's the person that pushed me to do it. Which is very weird. She never stopped me from applying to political science. She is a huge advocate for a lot of things that I am passionate about." This advocacy helped Stacy gain the courage to publicly share her undocumented status and participate in advocacy efforts to help other undocumented students. From Stacy's perspective, most parents of undocumented children are not likely to support their children in publicizing their legal status due to fear of deportation or the stigma around being an undocumented immigrant. Through her activist work, Stacy has continued to be involved with supporting undocumented students and has had many opportunities to engage, share, and hear stories from other undocumented Asians. The connections Stacy has made in the undocumented Asian community, due to her openness as an undocumented person, have allowed her to extend her family beyond her mother and relatives to also include the undocumented Asian population in the United States.

Stacy has frequently disclosed her undocumented status with others as a way to raise awareness and share resources. Given her spiritual stance on success, Stacy has deliberately engaged in efforts to provide support for undocumented students by participating in undocumented immigrant advocacy organizations. Stacy became involved in activism in her second year in community college in 2012 when DACA was established:

> Because of DACA, I kind of [came] to realize that, well okay, what about the other people that were excluded on this? And so that was when my wish to become more active. . . . I mean, if people [are] giving [me] power, I should use that power. So that was how I came about, and at that time, I was an intern in a different organization that focuses on workers' rights. So, a lot of my work kind of intersect one another, . . . it was a truly empowering

moment that maybe I can actually combine all of this, and then whatever power I have from having DACA maybe make some changes.

Through one advocacy organization that focused on providing support for undocumented Asian Americans, Stacy helped develop "a whole series of workshops for the California Dream Act. . . . We were able to utilize that resource and replicate that resource at different [college] campuses."

Stacy's portrait demonstrated the intergenerational transmission of civic capacities and highlighted her mother as foundational to her civic development through her encouragement to pursue her degree in political science, to publicly share her undocumented status, and to develop a civic value of helping others. This portrait extended past literature on the influence of parents in the civic development of individuals by examining the role of undocumented parents.

Joshua: Intragenerational Civic Development

The sun was shining, birds were in the sky, and a large tree was situated between a house and Joshua's immediate family. This was what came into Joshua's mind when he was asked to draw who he considered to be his family (Figure 6.2). Joshua immigrated with his family from the Philippines at the age of fifteen, and family is central to his life. His experience navigating life in the United States became even more challenging when his father had to return to

FIGURE 6.2 Joshua's portrait, Intragenerational Civic Development.

the Philippines, leaving him, his mother, and his two brothers in the United States. As the oldest of three boys, Joshua understood his role was to provide for his family.

After he completed high school, the idea of attending college as an undocumented person became overwhelming to the point that Joshua felt it was unattainable: "Whatever happens, happens. . . . There was no plan for me. I just wanted to work. I could help my family, and higher education was not something I really plan[ned] for or really wanted to finish." With the absence of financial support to pay tuition and as the eldest in the family, Joshua worked to help provide for his family. However, after a year, his parents wanted to find a way to get Joshua back into school: "My parents pushed me to finish my education because they always told us that that's the only thing they can give us, a proper education. That's also the one reason we came to America, so we can get a good education."

Joshua began attending a community college while continuing to work. His younger brother Soren earned a degree from a national top-tier four-year institution, Pacific Coast University (pseudonym). Soren was a key factor in Joshua regaining interest in school. "He [Soren] really wanted me to finish college, and he really pushed me . . . he showed me what to do [regarding the college application process]. . . . I asked him to proofread my personal statement. And then he asked everyone to proofread it." Soren was actively involved in student organizations focused on immigrant advocacy. Observing Soren's involvement with one of the largest undocumented immigrant youth conferences in the nation, Joshua shared how he felt: "Wow, this is something where there's a community for me." Joshua discovered there were many resources available to him by being a part of this organization.

After Joshua earned his associate's degree, Soren shared that the California Dream Act could give Joshua the opportunity to transfer to Pacific Coast University, like his brother, and pursue a bachelor's degree. Soren's influence and support helped Joshua connect with people who sought out ways to be a voice for marginalized communities, and he was able to find community at Pacific Coast University. "Being involved with [the undocumented student organization on campus] has really given me a good support, good network. I can find resources; it's a big help for me. I can get people to talk to who are your friends, who are your family, and when you're having a difficult time in your life, they can actually give you advice, they give you emotional support that sometimes you will need as a student." The research on the influence of family in the civic development of individuals has often focused on parents (Kelly 2006; White and Mistry 2016), as in the case of Stacy, or even older siblings who influence younger siblings (Chan 2011). However, Soren portrayed a nontraditional influence as the younger brother impacting his older brother's civic development and participation. Joshua's narrative demonstrated the intragenerational development of civic values in a family.

Annie: Family of Friends as a Bridge to Activism

Annie grew up in a large Filipino community in Southern California and began her college education at Pacific Coast University (pseudonym) immediately after high school. While in college, Annie formed close friendships with her peers, especially fellow undocumented students in the student-led organization on campus. She described her friends as being like family. When asked whom she considered family, she stated, "Family is a loved one that you create. The love that you create with other people, it doesn't necessarily have to be blood. . . . It's really the people that you choose to be happy with and like the people that you don't give up on because I know my family and I—my immediate family and I don't—we don't always get along, but we keep trying, and I think that's what counts." Annie strongly valued her connections with her friends and credited them for encouraging her civic development by connecting her with resources.

Annie described how as a college student her friendships grew stronger and more closely connected. Many of these friends helped Annie navigate opportunities, including answering her questions about financial aid and suggesting helpful housing options. For example, she said, "I don't like going [to the financial aid office] anymore . . . I just ask friends if I have any other questions." This support led Annie to develop a sense of civic responsibility, in other words, a responsibility to give back to campus organizations that support and advocate for undocumented students while at the same time sharing these resources with other undocumented youth.

In addition to her friends, community members at her university provided Annie with a strong sense of home. For example, Rosie, a staff member at a church near the university, provided a second home for many undocumented students. Annie said of Rosie, "[She] genuinely cares about her students . . . and no matter what, you know she had your back." Annie's friends and community were civically engaged in helping Annie find resources and a sense of belonging.

This strong sense of community led Annie to feel more comfortable sharing her own immigration status publicly. Her family of friends was especially important when her given family was not as supportive of her decision to become an outspoken activist about immigrant rights because they were scared for their family's safety. Annie said her family's "expectation is just [be] quiet, and just kind of breeze through college, and don't really tell anybody about your status." But as her time at Pacific Coast University continued, Annie developed deeper connections with her friends, and this sense of belonging allowed her to feel more comfortable being an activist. She eventually shared her story in a published book and often spoke on behalf of the undocumented student group. She developed an understanding with her parents, saying, "I understand why they're scared, and they have a right to be scared, but I think they're starting to

FIGURE 6.3 Annie's portrait, Family of Friends as a Bridge to Activism.

see my side." While her family played an instrumental role in connecting her with resources and encouraging her success in education, her family of friends provided critical support in her aspirations to be an activist.

The central focus of friends and family in Annie's life was encapsulated in the family portrait she drew during her interview (Figure 6.3). The figures on the outside of the circle are her friends. "These are my friends, and they're . . . I guess they're like everywhere. I have friends here in LA, and I have friends on the East Coast who I'm really close to, so . . . they don't always have to be with me physically or geographically." The multiple colors that represent her friends symbolize the diversity of her friend group in terms of race/ethnicity and geographical location.

Inside the circle are her father, her mother, and her two younger sisters. She described the circle around them as protection from the outside world and inside the circle being their ethnic community: "They kind of stick to our own ethnic community too, um, so I feel like they don't know as much as I do, outside. So, I feel like I'm trying to shelter them in a way." Moreover, her family is the only family within her extended family who has undocumented members (her father has a visa and her mother is undocumented), so she was also representing the isolation that her family feels. Interestingly, she said she did not draw herself in the picture because she sees herself as an "outsider" with her family because she goes to Pacific Coast University and her family doesn't "know as much as [she does]" about immigration news and politics. Omitting herself may also have represented her selflessness in valuing the well-being of her family and friends over herself. Annie's portrait demonstrated the influence of friends as "family" in her civic development and how they provided the navigational and emotional support that led Annie to develop a sense of civic responsibility to help others through activism.

Discussion

This research demonstrated how family—both given and chosen—is a central pillar of activism against an oppressive society for undocumented immigrant students. More specifically, Stacy's portrait demonstrated the intergenerational transmission of civic values, particularly from her mother, of helping others and supporting her decisions to engage in activism. Stacy's mother's support of her disclosing her status publicly is noteworthy, considering that research studies have found that undocumented parents are often keen to keep their immigration status a secret so they are not deported (Cuevas 2021; Yoshikawa 2011). In a study with undocumented Chinese parents, Yoshikawa (2011) found that parents were hesitant to engage in public programs for fear of deportation.

Joshua's portrait demonstrated the intragenerational transmission of civic engagement between siblings and highlighted what McDevitt and Chaffee (2002) call the "trickle-up influence" of political socialization. However, in Joshua's case, this trickle-up influence was initiated by the younger brother in the civic development of his older brother, as opposed to the focus on children influencing their parents as conceptualized by McDevitt and Chaffee.

Finally, Annie's portrait demonstrated the influence of her chosen family, composed of friends who role-modeled civic behaviors by helping her, and in turn she developed her own civic values and practices. Many researchers describe the important role of peers in supporting undocumented students' decisions to engage in activism (Freeman, Iniestra Varelas, and Castillo 2021). Unlike Stacy's mom's support of her coming out publicly, Annie's experience with her family echoed other research findings that Mexican and Chinese undocumented immigrant parents may discourage their children from sharing their immigration status publicly (Cuevas 2021); however, further research is needed to better understand the cultural factors among Asian parents and their approach to the topic of immigration status with their children.

The portraits of the undocumented Asian students in this study clearly reveal the strong yet complicated role of family and the interconnection of race, culture, and context in their civic development and engagement. They discussed how their civic development was influenced by the interconnected and

parallel process occurring at the individual and systems levels, with the participants being shaped by their experiences with family, schools, and the larger
sociopolitical context. For instance, while Stacy's civic development was initially influenced by her mother, it was later impacted by her experiences attending community college during the implementation of DACA. These contexts
combined to cultivate Stacy's civic engagement and her decision to transfer to a
four-year institution with an active civic campus culture.

The findings of this study also add to the literature on the civic development
of Asian / Asian American students and the role of given and chosen family,
immigration status, and sociopolitical and historical contexts. These portraits
have demonstrated the ways in which given and chosen families play a role in
the civic development and engagement of Asian / Asian American students by
highlighting the influence of spirituality, emotional support and encouragement, role modeling, and a deepening sense of community and belonging.

Implications for Research, Policy, and Practice

This chapter has important implications for research, policy, and practice related
to undocumented Asian youth. More research is needed to examine the role of
family in the civic lives of undocumented immigrants and to better understand
their diverse needs and experiences. The Asian racial category encapsulates a
vast group of different ethnicities, languages, cultures, religions, and immigration trajectories and thus represents varied experiences in the United States,
which may influence different forms of family and civic engagement.

Future research should examine the experiences of undocumented Asians
that represent other ethnicities. Additionally, such research could explore
undocumented Asians' other intersecting identities of class, gender, and sexual
orientation. For instance, some undocumented Asian college students' families
may be supportive of their civic engagement while rejecting their queer identity. This juxtaposition thereby impacts their overall wellness and ability to
thrive and achieve their aspirations.

This study also offers deeper insights about undocumented Asian students
for institutional agents (e.g., student affairs professionals, faculty, and administrators) to better understand and support members of this population. Given
that family plays a critical role in the civic development of undocumented
Asian students, institutional agents could provide opportunities for students to
connect their homes to schools, which suggests more student-centered and culturally sensitive practices on campus. Thus, this research calls for more studies
to examine how institutional agents' understandings of undocumented Asian
students are manifested inside and outside the classroom.

This chapter also calls for reconceptualizing traditional Western notions
of family in policymaking. When drafting family-based immigration policy,

policymakers often draw on Western conceptions of the family unit, defined as biological parents and their children, like the case of DAPA. However, this definition of family is not always relevant for people of color who may live with extended family. Moreover, federal policies tend to benefit the undocumented youth population, such as DACA, and exclude older immigrants even though they are much more vulnerable to deportation. When drafting legislation, policymakers should adopt a more nuanced understanding of family and consider undocumented individuals as members of communities and family units.

Finally, this study highlights a need to reconceptualize traditional notions of civic values and civic engagement. Civic engagement is often focused on voting (Coley and Sum 2012). However, this study underscores how undocumented immigrants are civically engaged in our democracy. Policymakers, philanthropic foundations, scholars, and educators should consider adopting more nuanced conceptions of civic values and civic engagement.

REFERENCES

Alcantar, Cynthia M., Rachel E. Freeman-Wong, Victoria Kim, 'Inoke Hafoka, Trisha Mazumder, and Set Hernandez Rongkilyo. 2023. "The Role of Family in the Civic Lives of Undocumented Asian College Students." *Journal of College Student Development* 64 (3): 309–325. https://doi.org/10.1353/csd.2023.a9001171.

Andolina, Molly W., Krista Jenkins, Cliff Zukin, and Scott Keeter. 2003. "Habits from Home, Lessons from School: Influences on Youth Civic Engagement." *Political Science & Politics* 36 (2): 275–280. https://doi.org/10.1017/S104909650300221X.

Azmitia, M. 2024. "Research with Hard-to-Reach Emerging Adult Populations." In *Flourishing as a Scholar: Research Methods for the Study of Emerging Adulthood*, edited by Angela Sorgente, Shannon Claxton, Joseph Schwab, and Rimantas Vosylis. Oxford University Press. https://doi.org/10.1093/oso/9780197677797.001.0001.

Bi, Shan Shan, Chun Bun Lam, and Kevin Kien Hua Chung. 2021. "Sibling Relationships and Civic Engagement: A Longitudinal Study of Chinese Young Adults." *International Journal of Psychology* 56 (1): 138–142. https://doi.org/10.1002/ijop.12685.

Brydon-Miller, Mary. 2001. "Education, Research, and Action: Theory and Methods of Participatory Action Research." In *From Subjects to Subjectivities: A Handbook of Interpretive and Participatory Methods*, edited by Deborah L. Tolman and Mary Brydon-Miller. New York University Press.

Buenavista, Tracy Lachica. 2012. "Citizenship at a Cost: Undocumented Asian Youth Perceptions and the Militarization of Immigration." *AAPI Nexus: Policy, Practice and Community* 10 (1): 101–124. https://doi.org/10.36650/nexus10.1_101-124_Buenavista.

Chan, Wing Yi. 2011. "An Exploration of Asian American College Students' Civic Engagement." *Asian American Journal of Psychology* 2 (3): 197–204.

Coley, Richard J., and Andrew Sum. 2012. *Fault Lines in Our Democracy: Civic Knowledge, Voting Behavior, and Civic Engagement in the United States*. Educational Testing Service. https://files.eric.ed.gov/fulltext/ED532316.pdf.

Cooc, North, and Grace MyHyun Kim. 2021. "The Roles of Racial Discrimination and English in Civic Outcomes for Asian Americans and Pacific Islanders." *Cultural Diversity and Ethnic Minority Psychology* 27 (3): 483–494. https://doi.org/10.1037/cdp0000443.

Cuevas, Stephany. 2021. "Ever-Present 'Illegality': How Political Climate Impacts Undocumented Latinx Parents' Engagement in Students' Postsecondary Access and Success."
Journal of College Access 6 (2): article 5. https://scholarworks.wmich.edu/jca/vol6/iss2/5.

Dao, Loan Thi. 2017. "Out and Asian: How Undocu/DACAmented Asian Americans and
Pacific Islander Youth Navigate Dual Liminality in the Immigrant Rights Movement."
Societies 7 (3): 17. https://doi.org/10.3390/soc7030017.

DeAngelo, Linda, Maximilian T. Schuster, and Michael J. Stebleton. 2016. "California
DREAMers: Activism, Identity, and Empowerment Among Undocumented College
Students." *Journal of Diversity in Higher Education* 9 (3): 216–230. https://doi.org/10.1037
/dhe0000023.

Dreby, Joanna. 2012. "The Burden of Deportation on Children in Mexican Immigrant Families." *Journal of Marriage and Family* 74 (4): 829–845. https://doi.org/10.1111/j.1741-3737
.2012.00989.x.

Escudero, Kevin. 2012. "Organizing While Undocumented: The Law as a 'Double Edged
Sword' in the Movement to Pass the DREAM Act." *Critical Legal Studies Journal* 6 (2):
31–52. https://www.uidaho.edu/-/media/UIdaho-Responsive/Files/law/critical-legal-stu
dies/issues/volume-6/6-2-escudero-kevin.

———. 2020. *Organizing While Undocumented: Immigrant Youth's Political Activism Under the
Law.* New York University Press. http://www.jstor.org/stable/j.ctv1jkoj8j.

Forenza, Brad, Briana Rogers, and David T. Lardier. 2017. "What Facilitates and Supports
Political Activism by, and for, Undocumented Students?" *Urban Review* 49: 648–667.
https://doi.org/10.1007/s11256-017-0413-1.

Freeman, Rachel, Daniela Iniestra Varelas, and Daniel Castillo. 2021. "Building Critical
Bridges: The Role of University Presidents in Collaborating with Undocumented Student Activists." *Journal of College Access* 6 (2): article 12. https://scholarworks.wmich
.edu/jca/vol6/iss2/12.

Given, Lisa M., ed. 2008. *The SAGE Encyclopedia of Qualitative Research Methods.* SAGE.

Gogue, Demeturie T.-L., Rikka J. Venturanza, Aida Cuenza-Uvas, and Mike H. Nguyen.
2021. "The Role of Asian American and Native American Pacific Islander-Serving
Institutions in Reframing Leadership Education." *New Directions for Student Leadership* 2021 (171): 101–111. https://doi.org/10.1002/yd.20460.

Gonzales, Roberto G. 2008. "Left Out but Not Shut Down: Political Activism and the
Undocumented Student Movement." *Northwestern Journal of Law and Social Policy*
3 (2): 1–22. https://scholarlycommons.law.northwestern.edu/njlsp/vol3/iss2/4.

———. 2016. *Lives in Limbo: Undocumented and Coming of Age in America.* University of California Press.

Hinton, Kip A. 2015. "Undocumented Citizens: The Civic Engagement of Activist Immigrants." *Education, Citizenship, and Social Justice* 10 (2): 152–167. https://doi.org/10.1177
/1746197915583933.

Katsiaficas, Dalal, Cynthia M. Alcantar, Edwin Hernandez, Erick Samayoa, Maria Nava Guti-
errez, Oscar Rodriguez Texis, and Zyshia Williams. 2016. "Important Theoretical and
Methodological Turning Points for Understanding Contribution with Undocumented
Undergraduates." *Qualitative Psychology* 3 (1): 7–25. https://doi.org/10.1037/qup0000043.

Katsiaficas, Dalal, Valerie A. Futch, Michelle Fine, and Selcuk R. Sirin. 2011. "Everyday
Hyphens: Methodological Pluralism for Understanding Multiple Selves." *Qualitative
Research in Psychology* 8 (2): 1–19. https://doi.org/10.1080/14780887.2011.572743.

Katsiaficas, Dalal, Edwin Hernandez, Cynthia M. Alcantar, Erick Samayoa, Maria Nava
Gutierrez, and Zyshia Williams. 2018. "'We'll Get Through This Together': Collective
Contribution of Family and Community in the Lives of Latino Undocumented Under-

graduates." *Teachers College Record* 120 (120306): 1–48. https://doi.org/10.1177/0161468
11812001201.

Kelly, Diann C. 2006. "Parents' Influence on Youths' Civic Behaviors: The Civic Context of
the Caregiving Environment." *Families in Society* 87 (3): 447–455.

Lawrence-Lightfoot, Sara, and Jessica Hoffmann Davis. 1997. *The Art and Science of Portraiture*. Jossey-Bass.

McDevitt, Michael, and Steven Chaffee. 2002. "From Top-Down to Trickle-Up Influence:
Revisiting Assumptions About the Family in Political Socialization." *Political Communication* 19 (3): 281–301. https://doi.org/10.1080/01957470290055501.

McIntosh, Hugh, Daniel Hart, and James Youniss. 2007. "The Influence of Family Political
Discussion on Youth Civic Development: Which Parent Qualities Matter?" *Political
Science and Politics* 40 (3): 495–499. https://doi.org/10.1017/S1049096507070758.

Migration Policy Institute. 2019. "Unauthorized Immigrant Population Profiles." https://
www.migrationpolicy.org/programs/us-immigration-policy-program-data-hub
/unauthorized-immigrant-population-profiles.

Mullen, Jethro, and Jeremy Diamond. 2015. "Obama Vows to Abide by Immigration Court
Order." *CNN*, February 17. https://www.cnn.com/2015/02/17/politics/texas-obama
-immigration-injunction/index.html.

Muñoz, Susana M. 2008. "Understanding Issues of College Persistence for Undocumented
Mexican Immigrant Women from the New Latino Diaspora: A Case Study." PhD diss.,
Iowa State University. https://doi.org/10.31274/rtd-180813-17024.

Murray, Gregg R., and Matthew K. Mulvaney. 2012. "Parenting Styles, Socialization, and the
Transmission of Political Ideology and Partisanship." *Politics and Policy* 40 (6): 1106–1130.
https://doi.org/10.1111/j.1747-1346.2012.00395.x.

Pancer, S. Mark. 2015. *The Psychology of Citizenship and Civic Engagement*. Oxford University
Press.

Pavlova, Maria K., Rainer K. Silbereisen, Mette Ranta, and Katariina Salmela-Aro. 2016.
"Warm and Supportive Parenting Can Discourage Offspring's Civic Engagement in
the Transition to Adulthood." *Journal of Youth and Adolescence* 45 (11): 2197–2217.
https://doi.org/10.1007/s10964-016-0511-5.

Perez, William, Roberta Espinoza, Karina Ramos, Heidi M. Coronado, and Richard Cortes.
2009. "Academic Resilience Among Undocumented Latino Students." *Hispanic Journal of Behavioral Sciences* 31 (2): 149–181. https://doi.org/10.1177/0739986309333020.

———. 2010. "Civic Engagement Patterns of Undocumented Mexican Students." *Journal of
Hispanic Higher Education* 9 (3): 245–265. https://doi.org/10.1177/1538192710371007.

Ro, Annie, Michelle Kao Nakphong, Hye Young Choi, Alex Nguyen, and May Sudhinaraset.
2021. "The Association Between Social Ties and Depression Among Asian and Pacific
Islander Undocumented Young Adults." *BMC Public Health* 21 (994): 1–10. https://doi
.org/10.1186/s12889-021-11087-y.

Rogers, John, Maria Saunders, Veronica Terriquez, and Veronica Valez. 2008. "Civic Lessons: Public Schools and the Civic Development of Undocumented Students and Parents." *Northwestern Journal of Law & Social Policy* 3 (2): 201–218. http://scholarlycommons
.law.northwestern.edu/njlsp/vol3/iss2/3.

Saldivar, Steve. 2017. "At Boyle Heights Arts Show 'We Never Needed Papers to Thrive,'
Immigrants Are the Focus and the Stars." *Los Angeles Times*, March 5. http://www
.latimes.com/local/california/la-me-ln-immigration-20170005-story.html.

Seif, Hinda. 2011. "'Unapologetic and Unafraid': Immigrant Youth Come Out from the
Shadows." *New Directions for Child & Adolescent Development* 2011 (134): 59–75. https://
doi.org/10.1002/cd.311.

Sirin, Selcuk R., Dalal Katsiaficas, and Vanessa V. Volpe. 2010. "Identity Mapping: Methodological Implications for Studying Hyphenated Selves." *International Society for the
Study of Behavioral Development Bulletin* 2: 22–26. https://nyuscholars.nyu.edu/en
/publications/identity-mapping-methodological-implications-for-studying-hyphena.

Solórzano, Lizette G. 2022. "'We Are Not the People They Think We Are': First-Generation
Undocumented Immigrant Belonging and Legal Consciousness in the Wake of
Deferred Action for Parents of Americans." *Ethnicities* 22 (1): 24–41. https://doi.org/10
.1177/14687968211041805.

Suárez-Orozco, Carola, María G. Hernández, and Saskias Casanova. 2015. "'It's Sort of My
Calling': The Civic Engagement and Social Responsibility of Latino Immigrant-Origin
Young Adults." *Research in Human Development* 12 (1–2): 84–99. https://doi.org/10.1080
/15427609.2015.1010350.

Teranishi, Robert T., Carola Suárez-Orozco, and Marcelo Suárez-Orozco. 2015. "In the
Shadows of the Ivory Tower: Undocumented Undergraduate in the Uncertain Era of
Immigration Reform." Institute for Immigration, Globalization, & Education, UCLA.
https://escholarship.org/uc/item/2hq679z4.

Terriquez, Veronica. 2017. "Legal Status, Civic Organizations, and Political Participation
Among Latino Young Adults." *Sociological Quarterly* 58 (2): 315–336. https://doi.org/10
.1080/00380253.2017.1296756.

Tolman, Deborah L., and Mary E. Brydon-Miller. 2001. *From Subjects to Subjectivities:
A Handbook of Interpretive and Participatory Methods.* New York University Press.

Valdivia, Carolina. 2021. "'I Became a Mom Overnight': How Parental Detentions and
Deportations Impact Young Adults' Role." *Harvard Educational Review* 91 (1): 62–82.
https://doi.org/10.17763/1943-5045-91.1.62.

White, Elizabeth S., and Rashmita S. Mistry. 2016. "Parent Civic Beliefs, Civic Participation,
Socialization Practices, and Child Civic Engagement." *Applied Developmental Science*
20 (1): 44–60.

Wray-Lake, Laura, and Julia Tang. (2017). "Are They Political? Examining Asian American
College Students' Civic Engagement." *Asian American Journal of Psychology* 8 (1): 31–42.
https://doi.org/10.1037/aap0000061.

Wu, Harrick. 2018. "'Undocu-queer' Artist Julio Salgado on Creative Resistance." *KQED*,
July 5. https://www.kqed.org/arts/13836333/undocu-queer-artist-julio-salgado-on-crea
tive-resistance.

Wui, Ma Glenda Lopez, and Cameron S. White. 2023. *Civic Engagement of Asian American
Student Leaders.* Lexington Books.

Yoshikawa, Hirokazu. 2011. *Immigrants Raising Citizens: Undocumented Parents and Their
Children.* Russell Sage Foundation. https://www.jstor.org/stable/10.7758/9781610447072.

NOTES

1. Portraits, as a product of portraiture, is a social science research methodology that
   blends social science and art to capture the complexities of the human experience
   (Lawrence-Lightfoot and Hoffmann Davis 1997). More details about the method can
   be found in Alcantar et al. (2023).

2. An extended version of this chapter, with additional details on the conceptual framework and methods, can be found in Alcantar et al. (2023).

3. The broader research project, from which the vignettes in this chapter are drawn,
   received Institutional Review Board approval from the University of California, Los
   Angeles (UCLA), and all names used are pseudonyms.

7

"Rooted Around Church"

The Role of the Korean Protestant Church in the Lives of Undocumented Korean Young Adults

ESTHER YOONA CHO

Lydia was nine years old when her mother decided to leave South Korea to embark on a new life in the United States with her two young daughters. Because Lydia's father had been the sole breadwinner, the divorce on top of the transatlantic move made the first few years especially challenging. However, living in a Korean enclave in Southern California with familiar sights and smells, Lydia steadily found her way. Being devout Christians, they made the Korean church ten minutes from their apartment a central part of their newfound lives. Lydia taught Sunday school, sang on the music team, and tutored some of the younger kids, a sure way to make some money when you don't have papers. With the help of DACA and the California DREAM Act, Lydia was able to finish college and now works with foster youth. While she lives an active life, she has struggled with feeling isolated. Being Korean allowed Lydia to fly under the radar and avoid being detected as an undocumented immigrant. Despite being embedded in her church community, no one knew about her status for many years. In fact, well into her adulthood, Lydia thought her family was an outlier in the population of undocumented immigrants, the only undocumented Koreans that existed. It was not until much later when one of her Korean friends "came out" to her about his immigration status that Lydia realized that she was not alone.

Where do Korean undocumented immigrants find a sense of belonging and community as individuals not only living in the shadows (Suárez-Orozco et al. 2011) but the margins of these shadows?[1] Given our current understanding of the mental health needs of undocumented immigrants of Asian origin (Sudhinaraset et al. 2017) and research that reveals the impact of unique interpersonal challenges such as status disclosure on their overall well-being (Cho 2021; Patler 2014, 2018), further examination of the primary social spaces they inhabit is needed. In this chapter, I bring a magnifying glass to a site that has historically played an integral role in the social life of Korean immigrants in the United States—the Protestant Christian church. Like Lydia, more than 75 percent of the thirty-three undocumented Korean respondents I interviewed shared that they were Christian. Even though I did not recruit through church networks nor ask about religion in the interviews, the church emerged organically as occupying an important social function in their lives, motivating me to explore this phenomenon further.

In this work I therefore highlight how the Korean immigrant Protestant church shapes the lived experiences of Korean undocumented young adults. Ethnic nonprofit organizations in general have been found to assume a significant role in facilitating the incorporation and integration of undocumented immigrant communities. These entities have offered spaces of respite and healing for individuals (Gonzales et al. 2013; Gonzales, Terriquez, and Ruszczyk 2014), provided information and resources for education and employment (Cho 2017), and taken the lead in orchestrating major advocacy and activism efforts across the country (Nicholls 2013). Similarly, the Catholic church in the United States, with its growing Latino presence, has been found to be a powerful mobilizing force for the undocumented Latino community, reaching out to its members in an era of heightened uncertainty and trepidation. However, much of our understanding is derived from Latino-based organizations, and less is known about Asian organizations that play a critical role in the day-to-day lives of their coethnic participants. Especially given that undocumented Asian immigrants largely remain hidden and isolated, it is important to understand how their own ethnic organizations and communities shape and address experiences of illegality.

The Study

This chapter is based on semistructured in-depth interviews with thirty-three undocumented Korean respondents in their twenties and thirties as well as interviews with two staff members of Korean community-based organizations (not faith-based). These interviews were completed as part of a larger comparative research study that I conducted from 2015 to 2017 on the lived experiences of Korean and Mexican undocumented young adults in broader Los Angeles and the San Francisco Bay Area in California.[2] Respondents were recruited through purposive snowball sampling, and interviews typically lasted about one to two hours. The vast majority of the Korean respondents, more than three-quarters of them, identified as Christian, and most of them were actively involved in local Korean churches that were composed primarily of 1.5-generation and second-generation Korean peers.[3] Collectively, they attended church regularly, participated in Bible study groups, led music for Sunday services, and socialized with fellow church members outside of structured spaces.

The undocumented Korean young adults I interviewed did not discuss the spiritual benefits of religious life but instead pointed to the indirect effects of church as an organizational entity.[4] Thus, in examining the Korean immigrant church I do consider its role as a significant ethnic social organization (Ramakrishnan and Bloemraad 2008) rather than a religious institution, and the complex ways in which this coethnic community shapes the lives of community members living in legal precarity in the United States. Studying coethnic ties within the undocumented Korean community through the Korean church is appropriate, as the church has been called an extension of the Korean immigrant family due to the important function it plays in and for the Korean American population (Min 1992). This broader institutional context surrounding the undocumented population begs us to look deeper into how the church shapes the lived experiences of undocumented Korean immigrants.

I begin this piece by situating the experiences of undocumented Koreans in the broader context of the Korean immigrant church in the United States. I then dive into my findings that reveal the multifaceted, paradoxical role of the church as an ethnic organization in the lives of undocumented Korean young adults. While one might assume a level of safety within the Korean church due to shared ethnic identity and religious values, I find that the relationship with the church, the primary space where undocumented Korean young adults seem to form connections within the coethnic community, is a complex one. The church simultaneously can be both a space of safety and provision and one where the stigma of illegality is reinforced.

Religion in Korean Immigrant Communities

Several studies have shown that religious organizations provide a sense of home and belonging for immigrant communities. Ethnic religious organizations in particular have served significant nonreligious social functions for immigrant populations in the United States throughout its history, allowing immigrants to cultivate some form of collective identity in a society in which they are minorities (Chen 2008; Hirschman 2004; Levitt 2003; Portes and Rumbaut 2006).

Religious life is also an integral part of the Korean American narrative. Religious organizations have been found to play a consequential role in the civic life of first- and second-generation Korean American communities (and Asian American communities more broadly). Moreover, the United States is home to the largest South Korean immigrant population in the world, with roughly one million Korean immigrants currently residing in the country (Zong and Batalova 2017). A significant proportion of this population, nearly eight out of ten Koreans, are Protestant Christians affiliated with the Korean church and more than 80 percent are very devout, attending church at least once a week for a worship service, Bible study, or another program (Kim, Warner, and Kwon 2001; Min 1992; Min and Kim 2002). In fact, nearly 50 percent come to the United States already affiliated with Christianity and the rest convert upon settlement due to the tight-knit, institutionalized social network that the Korean immigrant church provides (Min 1991). In particular evangelical Protestantism, a branch of Christianity that focuses on bringing others into the faith through the sharing of testimonies, is popular among Korean Americans (Kim, Warner, and Kwon 2001; Min 1992; Min and Kim 2002) due to the history of Western missionaries who brought evangelical religious traditions to South Korea beginning the late nineteenth century. Today there are about 4,500 Korean churches in the United States, where hundreds and thousands of Korean immigrants and their children worship every week (Jang 2018).

"Saving Face" in the Korean Immigrant Church

Extant literature suggests that the Korean immigrant church could be a conflicting space where undocumented Koreans are either embraced into the folds of the community or ostracized due to the stigmatization of their immigration status. Indeed, the Korean church in the United States has been shown to play important social functions for its members, including providing community for church members, offering social services for the Korean community at large, and maintaining Korean traditions (Min 1992). At the same time, however, it can be a place in which individuals cannot escape societal ideas of "success." Korean American congregations have been found to often use religious discourse to uphold cultural values of achievement and prestige (Chai 2001; Chong 1998). In her study comparing Korean American young adults attending predominantly second-generation Korean churches with those attending multiethnic churches, Ecklund (2005) found that the "model minority" trope is reproduced by religious interpretations in Korean churches but not in multiethnic churches. The myth of the "model minority" is further maintained in the Korean church by leaders who have internalized this narrative. For example, Ecklund provides an example of pastors of Korean churches telling their congregants that "acting like a victim" and "acknowledging discrimination or poverty" takes their focus away from God and on themselves. At the same time, leaders and congregants alike would speak of their ambition for education and wealth as "inherent." This discourse of discrimination and poverty as well as achievement and prosperity leads Korean individuals to implicitly distance themselves from ethnoracial groups that they perceive as less successful. One would thus expect for this rhetoric in the Korean American church to affect the sense of identity and belonging of its congregation members who are hearing these words from religious authorities. This may be particularly true for individuals who face more material hurdles on their path toward "success," such as those living as undocumented.

Because being undocumented is often framed as something to be ashamed of, the practice of "saving face" within East Asian societies can also shape how Korean undocumented immigrants navigate and negotiate the challenges of living without legal status (e.g., Chung 2016; Lee 1999). Particularly in a highly concentrated coethnic context such as immigrant churches, it could be even more critical to ensure that one does not "lose face" at the risk of jeopardizing one's reputation across the community. We may expect individuals who are undocumented to struggle with finding support within this space that is otherwise a lifeline for their community. On the other hand, given that it is a religious institution that holds doctrines of compassion and care for the marginalized and disadvantaged, we may expect that some individuals would feel more comfortable being their authentic selves, finding acceptance and belonging in the midst of their stigmatized legal circumstances.

As I discuss in further detail in the sections that follow, my findings show that undocumented Korean young people have a complex, tension-ridden relationship with coethnic community members, with whom they primarily interact through an ethnic organization that is central in the lives of Korean Americans—the Korean ethnic church. Korean churches assume a multifaceted, paradoxical role of simultaneously providing a space of relational, interpersonal safety, while continuing to reify the stigma and shame of undocumented status on both interactional and broader structural levels. Specifically, some individuals find that status disclosure is a risk even within a religious organization with tenets of love and acceptance, which can further exacerbate feelings of isolation and loneliness.

At the same time, the support system that stems from immigrant churches in the United States (e.g., Ebaugh and Chafetz 2000; Ecklund 2006; Hirschman 2004; Min 1992) serves as a significant anchor for some undocumented young adults, offering them a sense of belonging and dignity that is otherwise elusive. Compared to other social spaces, the Korean church can be a haven where they can more readily be their authentic selves and be open about their legal situation, and where they can find a greater sense of meaning and hope in their lives as they entrust themselves to a divine power in the midst of legal liminality (Menjívar 2006).

Church as Haven

The Korean ethnic church served a comprehensive social function for study respondents, who received support and guidance in socioemotional and material ways through the relationships they formed in their church community. The church was also a critical hub of relationships where important information, at times essential to their survival, was circulated. Their church was at the core of their lives, offering a strong sense of community through a network of similarly situated individuals of Korean immigrant background. Their lives revolved around the church, from the friends they made to how they spent their time on the weekends. It was where many of them felt most "at home" and felt a general sense of safety. Julie, who was twenty-four years old at the time of interview, seemed to be a very gregarious and disarming individual who had a diverse group of friends spanning various ethnoracial backgrounds and walks of life. However, ultimately the foundation of her social identity stemmed from the Korean church that she had been attending since she was a young girl: "[Church] has kinda been like the center of my community and my family for life. . . . Korean people are very rooted around church, [it's] kinda like the anchor of our society and everyone else kinda shifts around it. . . . I've been going to the same church since I was ten so I built a lot of strong relationships, everyone knows my family." Julie recognized that church was not only a critical aspect of her and her family's social life, but that it is a cornerstone of her broader Korean community in the Los Angeles area.

In addition to being an organizational context where their social lives were anchored, for some respondents the church also served as a sacred space where they could be vulnerable and open about their tenuous legal situation. Often, undocumented immigrants are incredibly vigilant and private in social situations, taking immense care to ensure that their immigration status does not fall into the hands of untrustworthy individuals. Many young undocumented immigrants strategically navigate their friendships, disclosing their status selectively based on perceived markers of minority background and understanding of the immigrant experience (Cho 2021; Patler 2018). Undocumented Korean young adults in particular have been found to take greater caution relative to their Mexican counterparts; not all of their close friends are considered confidants whom they trust with their illegality (Cho 2021). In the Protestant evangelical tradition at large, however, congregants are encouraged to invite their community members into their personal lives. Being in a shared religious community entails supporting one another through their trials and tribulations, in addition to their joys and celebrations.

When twenty-five-year-old Joanne from the San Francisco Bay Area heard a young man at her church openly share his story of being undocumented and "always feeling alien" with the whole congregation, "it really shocked [her]." She grew up hearing from her parents that even extended family members were not to be trusted. "Just be careful," they would always warn her. Joanne was so accustomed to staying silent, both within her family and at her church growing up, but she had a transformative experience after joining a new church in college:

> The fact that he [Mark] was able to really open up about this, it was unheard of—it wasn't in my frame of reference. Like that would never happen in my world. And it was before a huge group of people, both regulars and nonregulars to church and so I was like, wow, you're willing to share this story with everybody. He was sharing about how he had this feeling of isolation, of secrecy, of never being able to trust anybody, but then he made his decision some time sophomore year [of college], something like that. And [he shared about] the security he gained through belief in Christ and the community that he was welcomed into and the fact that everywhere he turned, he received acceptance not condemnation, and so I think that really resonated with me.

Because of the cultural framework of "saving face" (Chung 2016) that Joanne and her Korean community operated under, when one of her church's congregants so publicly revealed his immigration status, it was an incredibly life-changing moment for her. For the first time she had heard someone else dare to utter the feelings that she had endured in solitude for years. Despite having been in the same congregation for years, Mark and Joanne had not been aware at all of their shared vulnerabilities around their immigration situation. Furthermore, Mark's public testimony was the beginning of a shift in Joanne's own thinking of her immigration status, destigmatizing both the nature of being undocumented as well as the act of disclosing her status. In the evangelical church space, sharing one's testimony is valued and lauded as a way to publicly acknowledge divine sovereignty and will in places of burden, helplessness, and struggle. Through the embrace that Mark had experienced in the church community, when the expectation was rejection, he found more freedom and acceptance around his immigration status in a society that refused to welcome him as their own. Joanne was inspired. She could not open up about her own story immediately, but just a couple weeks after the evening of Mark's testimony she was compelled to take this step:

> Some of the girls [at my church] invited me to their place for like a brunch, and it was there where two girls in the same situation as me were talking about that, and then I was like, oh wait, I'm actually like that too. And I think that was the first time I ever opened up about it. And we had this huge moment of like, oh my gosh, we knew each other

for like a whole semester and we didn't even know about this about each other, and so, yeah, it was like a huge bonding moment.

Mark's testimony had catalyzed openness and transparency for Joanne and her friends. Despite having been a part of the same Christian community for a semester, they had kept their immigration statuses private. However, at the risk of "losing face," they divulged this significant aspect of their lives and in turn found even deeper understanding and belonging. Joanne shared that since this pivotal moment she has been able to "even share it to people not in the church." The socioemotional support she had discovered in her church had given her the agency and courage to share her experience with less shame and fear of judgment.

In contrast to Joanne, twenty-two-year-old Daniel from Koreatown, Los Angeles, told me that he had always been pretty open about his status with friends and church members, even writing a public blog about his experiences at times. Unlike many other respondents, Daniel was well acquainted with the presence of the undocumented Korean population and had several undocumented Korean friends. "We are the undocumented ones," he told me, when describing his friends. Other undocumented families at his church were not as transparent as he was, however. They would privately write about the struggles surrounding their undocumented status on prayer request cards, which would be read only by a select few members of the prayer committee. Daniel, however, would find out about the children in these families from his pastors, leading him to vigilantly support these students navigating the precarity of their status: "At my church I worked with a lot of kids that have the same problems, so I kind of just like mentored them. . . . Usually pastors will let me know. Because you know like their parents would write it in like prayer requests, and [the pastors] know that I've been through it and stuff so they're like 'oh can you kind of [help]?' you know." Because of the magnified culture of "saving face" in the Korean community coupled with the constant reminders from their parents to hide this socially stigmatized part of their lives, many respondents had often been left with no choice but to struggle in silent solitude. Such was the paradox of the spiritual and religious context of the church. While the faith framework placed great value on sharing openly and accepting one another unconditionally as one spiritual family, in some ways their Korean culture of preserving one's reputation and family honor operated more powerfully due to fear of shame and judgment. Even so, individuals like Joanne, her friend Mark, and Daniel found that ultimately sharing their status within their churches did not mean "losing face." Not only did they find a welcoming community who continued to embrace and support them, they were able to find belonging with others who had treaded the same journey and truly understood their stories.

Church as Resource

In addition to the church being a haven for the undocumented Korean young adults I interviewed, I found that the church served as a significant material resource through the member base it provided them (e.g., Kwon 1997; Menjívar 2000). Many scholars have shown that Asian Americans and immigrants generally gain access to economic and social capital through religious organizations, which facilitate upward mobility (Hirschman 2004; Portes and Rumbaut 2006; Warner and Wittner 1998). It was no different for the undocumented young people whom I talked to and their families—that is, if they were willing to share their stigmatized immigration status with their fellow church members. For those who felt safe enough to open about their legal situation, they proceeded to share selectively when they had a specific need and objective. Taking the risk of revealing their status to key actors in their church community was a critical step to garnering information and resources that could mitigate barriers associated with being undocumented, as Patler found in her work with undocumented students in the education system (2018). For example, respondents and their family members gained important information on Deferred Action for Childhood Arrivals (DACA) and in-state tuition, employment, and even access to health care through their church.

ESTHER: So they found out about DACA through their friends or . . . ?

JOSEPH: Yeah. So like in our church we had other families who were undocumented who came . . . who are more advanced in their life here in the States. So they gave us tips and . . . they had their children go to college with DACA, so yeah.

Twenty-one-year-old Joseph from the San Francisco Bay Area found out about DACA from his parents, who were first made aware of the program through other church members with undocumented children. For those individuals who were open about their immigration status with their church community, they were able to support one another by sharing valuable knowledge such as the opportunities available through DACA. For Joseph and his family, as well as other respondents, the primary motivation for these discussions was to access higher education and earn a college degree. Operating within a "success frame" (Lee and Zhou 2015) within which educational and professional achievement are prioritized, Korean parents, despite their difficult circumstances, went to great lengths to mitigate the barrier that immigration status posed for their children's academic prospects.

Undocumented children did the same for their parents, especially when it came to their parents' health. Daniel had graduated top of his class in high school, getting accepted into prestigious colleges and universities across the country. However, because his family could not afford the tuition nor take out loans, he went to a community college and then transferred to a state university nearby. His second semester there, his mom fell severely ill, causing Daniel to take a year off from school, working seventy-hour weeks to help make ends meet. When I asked how his mom was treated for her illness, he responded that "she didn't really get treatment [and] just stayed home." The undocumented population has lower rates of access to health insurance and medical care not only due to public health insurance ineligibility but also due to the fear and apprehension that visiting the doctor could put them at risk of deportation (Hacker et al. 2015; Pitkin Derose; Escarce, and Lurie 2007; Prentice, Pebley, and Sastry 2005). When I gently probed further, Daniel shared that his mom went to a Korean medical center for some form of treatment. While about half of low-income undocumented immigrants qualify for Medi-Cal, and while federally qualified health centers, hospital emergency departments, and community clinics provide free or reduced-price health care coverage for undocumented immigrants (McConville et al. 2015), his mom likely did not want to risk putting her family in such a precarious position.

DANIEL: She went to a clinic through someone from church that knew her position, so like full confidence . . . it was like all confidential. Everything was paid in cash but that's also the reason that I work, because you know if you pay in cash, you gotta pay up front. So like I was working a lot.

ESTHER: How did she know that person?

DANIEL: Church.

ESTHER: Oh okay.

DANIEL: My mom serves in church too. We've all served in church ever since we were born.

Because of the community she had formed in their church, Daniel's mom was able to receive some semblance of medical treatment that otherwise would not have been easily accessible due to their legal situation. Through their connection with this church member, they received the opportunity to pay "under the table" with cash and circumvent the lack of insurance.

Similar to barriers in the health care system, in the absence of legal access to the labor market, informal methods of employment are critical (e.g., Cho 2017). For the vast majority of Korean respondents, the availability of jobs through coethnic networks was a presumed reality that provided basic material benefits despite their legal situation. Twenty-one-year-old Christine, who was attending local community colleges and steadily working toward a bachelor's degree, attributed the facility of finding work to the cultural sentiment of 정 (jeong). Christine seemed to imply that jeong, which roughly translates to a deep emotional bond stemming from shared experience and social responsibility, operates strongly within the Korean American community because of their shared struggles as immigrants and minorities in the United States.

Through the hub of the Korean church, where individuals of all classes and socioeconomic situations intermingle, respondents were able to more readily draw on the capital of their coethnics. Several of those who managed to over-come institutional hurdles in the education system and excel academically tutored the children of more affluent families in the church or their networks. One respondent, twenty-four-year-old Yoonkyung, shared that her mother worked as a full-time receptionist at the dental office that was owned by one of the congregation members, despite not having any training in the area. For a couple of summers Yoonkyung herself worked there as well, supporting the office with her fluent English-language skills for their few English-speaking clients. The church network therefore allowed many respondents to access employment through Korean ethnic labor market niches despite the lack of documentation (Cho 2017). Willing to pay under the table and, in the process, lend a hand to a fellow church member, congregants in the church with greater capital were a vital lifeline for undocumented respondents who asked for help.

The Hostility of Church

Existing scholarship has demonstrated that Korean churches have been the most significant ethnic organization for Korean immigrant communities in the United States, serving an important nonreligious civic function in their lives. This historical role was prominent in the lives of the undocumented Korean young adults I interviewed, but their relationship to the community they found in church was not solely as positive as we might expect based on the literature. A segment of respondents also experienced hostility and shame in this environment where they expected and yearned for acceptance and comfort. Despite the church being a religious institution where unconditional love and acceptance are espoused in key teachings, church members' perception of undocumented immigration status seemed to mirror dominant stigma-laden narratives that cast undocumented immigrants as immoral and undeserving. Some respondents were therefore careful not to disclose their undocumented status "even at church," as thirty-four-year-old Karen shared with me: "You know, I was really embarrassed about the situation and so I never brought it up with my peers. Even at church, I just knew, or I assumed that nobody would really understand the situation or what I was going though, and I don't know why but I felt really, really embarrassed and ashamed of the fact that we weren't legal residents." While respondents had hoped that they would be able to bring their whole selves to the church space and some respondents had positive experiences sharing their immigration status, others upheld protective strategies in this purportedly safe environment in order to shield themselves and their family members from shame. They seemed to have internalized negative tropes about undocumented immigrants themselves and, in addition, assumed that there would be a lack of empathy from fellow congregation members. Many respondents shared that they felt that they were alone in the struggle, thinking that they were the "only Korean undocumented immigrants." Adding to this perceived lack of understanding due to limited awareness of the plight of illegality in the Korean community, some were also very skeptical of the kind of support they would receive from the church: "Like at the end of the day, even other Korean families even at church were like, 'That's kind of your problem and like not mine. And hope things work out for you, but there's nothing that I can or will do to kind of help that way.' So that kind of cold interactions among the community" (Paul, thirty years old). When Paul and his family had solicited help from their fellow church members in times of trouble, they received rejection instead of the support that one would expect from a religious organization. Despite the communal virtues of the Christian faith, an individualistic mentality seemed to exist among the church members Paul encountered. Hurt by the boundaries that were constructed by his own coethnic people, he compared the lack of support and understanding he had experienced within the Korean community to the Latino community. "I see Latinos watching out for each other more," Paul shared.

The church was also a place where respondents felt prompted to disclose their immigration status with their peers, and it was often to explain why they could not go on evangelical mission trips abroad. Generally, respondents were very private about their legal situation because of a perceived lack of shared experience and empathy, limiting disclosure to a select few confidants. However, at times they were prompted, almost forced, to "come out" as undocumented in the church context to explain away another potential source of shame, such as their lack of participation in global mission trips. Engaging in international mission work is perceived as a representation of faith in the Korean evangelical church, and therefore a rite of passage that is expected by the religious community (Ecklund 2006). Hence, twenty-year-old Eric described disclosing his immigration status for the first time with his church friends because they were confused about his lack of participation: "Yeah I mean oh, for my church friends, when we talk about missions and stuff, I can't go to missions because I can't leave the country so it'd always come up during those times and people would always be like hey, are you going on missions this year? And I'd be like no and they'd be like why? And I'd just be like oh because I'm not a citizen." Note that Eric describes himself as "not [being] a citizen," instead of saying "I'm undocumented" or "I don't have papers." He leaves his status vague so as to not get further questioning from his peers.

Institutionally, Korean immigrant churches seem to be wary of any formal or public demonstrations of immigrant rights advocacy. They generally "want to stay out of this political immigration stuff," a staff member at a major Korean community-based organization (CBO) in Los Angeles shared with me. In fact, one organization in the Bay Area had conducted information sessions on the Affordable Care Act for a local Korean church, which garnered a positive response from its members. However, when they reached out to the church to ask if they could also hold sessions about DACA, the church was not interested and refused. Even though the church was willing to tackle issues within their community regarding health care access, they were reticent when it came to education around immigration issues. While these are solely the experiences of two organizational leaders, they have significant implications for outreach practices among Korean CBOs to adequately support the undocumented Korean community and work toward destigmatizing illegality.

These findings complement the research of scholars such as Janelle Wong (2018) and Angie Chung (2005) on evangelical Protestant churches and civic engagement and advocacy. Contrary to studies that have demonstrated the strong role of religious organizations on civic and political participation, this phenomenon has been found to be more complicated for conservative, majority-immigrant religious contexts. Asian and Latino evangelical Protestant churches in the United States do not as readily engage in the civic sphere like their Catholic counterparts, except for issues they deem more directly related to healthy Christian living (Heredia 2011; Mora 2013; Wong, Rim, and Perez 2008).[5] Korean churches in particular, which tend to have conservative leanings, are also shown to be politically disengaged as organizations (Chang 1999), though individual leaders are often politically active outside of the church sphere (Chung 2005). This organizational approach can have broader implications for the stigmatization of illegality within their respective ethnic communities as well as the limited political and civic mobilization around immigrant rights in the Korean community at large.

While Korean churches may choose to focus strictly on spiritual and religious matters as organizations, there have been glimpses of efforts to mobilize the immigrant community through religious coalitions. For example, a national Korean American Sanctuary Church network began in New York in the spring of 2017 with a small gathering of pastors of Korean churches in the United States. It has since grown into an ecumenical effort of more than a hundred churches across the East Coast and its Facebook page has nearly a thousand followers.[6] A 2018 article written about this movement states its goals as the following: "to help immigrant brothers and sisters, Korean and non-Korean alike, avoid deportation; to bring attention to the issue of immigration; and to promote the sanctuary movement and rights of the immigrants" (Manangan 2018). However, the author of the piece makes sure to begin with an argument rooted in religious values: "The Bible is our ultimate immigration values handbook." While Korean churches do not play a prominent role in immigrant advocacy, there is evidence that a gradual movement by church leaders may at least begin to be a symbolic sign of coethnic support for undocumented Korean immigrants.

Conclusion

In examining the functional role of the Korean immigrant church on the well-being of undocumented Korean young adults in California, I have highlighted the complex, often contradictory role of this ethnic organization on their undocumented members. My findings reveal that the Korean church, the primary space where undocumented Korean young adults interact with their coethnic community members, functions as a source of socioemotional and material support, while concurrently being a place where feelings of shame and isolation are reinforced. The church therefore is a space of tension and ambiguity for those on the margins of Korean American society, such as immigrants who are undocumented. For these individuals, their experiences with the church and the social actors that compose it are characterized by amplified risk and amplified reward due to the stigmatized and precarious nature of their legal situation. This study of the Korean ethnic church, which has historically been found to be instrumental in facilitating the integration of Korean immigrants, is particularly illuminating when considering the diversity of the Korean population in the United States by legal residency status.

Particularly given that undocumented Asian immigrants continue to remain largely isolated and on the periphery both in their lived experiences and in broader discourse, more research that sheds light on the presence and impact of their own coethnic organizations on their experiences with illegality is critical. Being connected to immigrant advocacy organizations helps cultivate a sense of belonging and empowerment among undocumented young people (Vaquera et al. 2017), but undocumented Asians are also less likely to find support through these community organizations (Gonzales et al. 2014). For undocumented Asian immigrants, therefore, theirs is an "invisible illegality" that operates as a double-edged sword (Cho 2019). Possessing at least some capacity to "look away" from their immigration situation, as twenty-one-year-old respondent Sangwoo described, allows them to hide from being recognized as "deportable" and stigmatized as "illegal" by enforcement officers, friends, and others. However, it also keeps them hidden from resources that could be beneficial for their psychological and mental-emotional health as well as their educational and professional trajectories. Without institutional supports, undocumented immigrants of Asian origin will continue to be elided not only of material resources but of trusted confidants, community, and a deep sense of belonging. Particularly for these individuals who are on the ethnoracial periphery of the undocumented population, finding social support and a sense of collective identity is instrumental for their holistic well-being.

REFERENCES

Chai, Karen. 2001. "'Beyond Strictness' to Distinctiveness: Generational Transition in Korean Protestant Churches." In *Korean Americans and Their Religions: Pilgrims and Missionaries from a Different Shore*, edited by Ho-Youn Kwon et al. Pennsylvania State University Press.

Chang, Edward T. 1999. "The Post-Los Angeles Riot Korean American Community: Challenges and Prospects." *Korean and Korean American Studies Bulletin* 10 (1–2): 6–26.

Chen, Carolyn. 2008. *Getting Saved in America: Taiwanese Immigration and Religious Experience*. Princeton University Press

Cho, Esther Yoona. 2017. "Revisiting Ethnic Niches: A Comparative Analysis of the Labor Market Experiences of Asian and Latino Undocumented Young Adults." *RSF: The Russell Sage Foundation Journal of the Social Sciences* 3 (4): 97–115.

———. 2019. "Invisible Illegality: The Double Bind of Being Asian and Undocumented." PhD diss., University of California, Berkeley.

———. 2021. "Selective Disclosure as a Self-Protective Process: Navigating Friendships as Asian and Latino Undocumented Young Adults." *Social Forces* 100 (2): 540–563.

Chong, Kelly. 1998. "'What It Means to Be Christian: The Role of Religion in the Construction of Ethnic Identity and Boundary Among Second-Generation Koreans." *Sociology of Religion* 59 (3): 259–286.

Chung, Angie Y. 2005. "'Politics Without the Politics': The Evolving Political Cultures of Ethnic Non-profits in Koreatown, Los Angeles." *Journal of Ethnic and Migration Studies* 31 (5): 911–929.

———. 2016. *Saving Face: The Emotional Costs of the Asian Immigrant Family Myth*. Rutgers University Press.

Committee on Migration of the United States Conference of Catholic Bishops (USCCB). 2003. *Strangers No Longer: Together on the Journey of Hope. A Pastoral Letter Concerning Migration from the Catholic Bishops of Mexico and the United States*. January 22. https://www.usccb.org/issues-and-action/human-life-and-dignity/immigration/strangers-no-longer-together-on-the-journey-of-hope.

Ebaugh, Helen Rose, and Janet Saltzman Chafetz. 2000. "Structural Adaptations in Immigrant Congregations." *Sociology of Religion* 61 (2): 135–153.

Ecklund, Elaine Howard. 2005. "'Us' and 'Them': The Role of Religion in Mediating and Challenging the 'Model Minority' and Other Civic Boundaries." *Ethnic and Racial Studies* 28 (1): 132–150.

———. 2006. *Korean American Evangelicals New Models for Civic Life*. Oxford University Press.

Gonzales, Roberto G., Carola Suárez-Orozco, and Maria Cecilia Dedios-Sanguineti. 2013. "No Place to Belong: Contextualizing Concepts of Mental Health among Undocumented Immigrant Youth in the United States." *American Behavioral Scientist* 57 (8): 1174–1199.

Gonzales, Roberto G., Veronica Terriquez, and Stephen P. Ruszczyk. 2014. "Becoming DACAmented Assessing the Short-Term Benefits of Deferred Action for Childhood Arrivals (DACA)." *American Behavioral Scientist* 58 (14): 1852–1872.

Hacker, Karen, Maria Anies, Barbara L. Folb, and Leah Zallman. 2015. "Barriers to Health Care for Undocumented Immigrants: A Literature Review." *Risk Management and Healthcare Policy* 8: 175.

Heredia, Luisa. 2011. "From Prayer to Protest: The Immigrant Rights Movement and the Catholic Church." In *Rallying for Immigrant Rights: The Fight for Inclusion in 21st Century America*, edited by Kim Voss and Irene Bloemraad. University of California Press.

Hirschman, Charles. 2004. "The Role of Religion in the Origins and Adaptation of Immigrant Groups in the United States." *International Migration Review* 38 (3): 1206–1233.

Jang, Yeol. 2018. "There Are 4454 Korean Churches Across the US." *Korea Daily*, January 24. https://www.koreadailyus.com/4454-korean-churches-across-us/.

Kim, Kwang Chung, R. Stephen Warner, and Ho-Youn Kwon. 2001. "Korean American Religion in International Perspective." In *Korean Americans and Their Religions: Pilgrims and Missionaries from a Different Shore*, edited by Ho-Youn Kwon et al. Pennsylvania State University Press.

Kwon, Victoria Hyonchu. 2014. *Entrepreneurship and Religion: Korean Immigrants in Houston.* Routledge.

Lee, Jennifer, and Min Zhou. 2015. *The Asian American Achievement Paradox.* Russell Sage Foundation.

Lee, Zuk-Nae. 1999. "Korean Culture and Sense of Shame." *Transcultural Psychiatry* 36 (2): 181–194.

Levitt, Peggy. 2003. "You Know, Abraham Was Really the First Immigrant: Religion and Transnational Migration." *International Migration Review* 37 (3): 847–873.

Manangan, Camille Bianca. 2018. "Korean-American Sanctuary Movement." *Church & Society*, October 3. https://www.umcjustice.org/news-and-stories/korean-american-sanctuary-church-movement-736.

McConville, Shannon, Laura Hill, Iwunze Ugo, and Joseph Hayes. 2015. "Health Coverage and Care for Undocumented Immigrants." Public Policy Institute of California.

Menjívar, Cecilia. 2000. *Fragmented Ties: Salvadoran Immigrant Networks in America.* University of California Press.

Menjívar, Cecilia. 2006. "Liminal Legality: Salvadoran and Guatemalan Immigrants' Lives in the United States." *American Journal of Sociology* 111, no. 4: 999–1037.

Min, Pyong Gap. 1991. *Koreans in America.* Yoo Lim Moon Hwa Sa.

Min, Pyong Gap. 1992. "The Structure and Social Functions of Korean Immigrant Churches in the United States." *International Migration Review* 26 (4): 1370–1394.

Min, Pyong Gap, and Jung Ha Kim. 2002. *Religions in Asian America: Building Faith Communities.* AltaMira.

Mora, G. Cristina. 2013. "Religion and the Organizational Context of Immigrant Civic Engagement: Mexican Catholicism in the USA." *Ethnic and Racial Studies* 36 (11): 1647–1665.

Nicholls, Walter J., 2013. *The DREAMers: How the Undocumented Youth Movement Transformed the Immigrant Rights Debate.* Stanford University Press.

Patler, Caitlin. 2014. "Racialized Illegality: The Convergence of Race and Legal Status Among Black, Latino, and Asian American Undocumented Young Adults." In *Scholars and Southern California Immigrants in Dialogue*, edited by Victoria Carty, Tekle Woldemikael, and Rafael Luévano. Lexington Press.

———. 2018. "To Reveal or Conceal: How Diverse Undocumented Youth Navigate Legal Status Disclosure." *Sociological Perspectives* 61 (6): 857–873.

Pitkin Derose, Kathryn P., Jose Escarce, and Nicole Lurie. 2007. "Immigrants and Health Care: Sources of Vulnerability." *Health Affairs* 26 (5): 158–1268.

Portes, Alejandro, and Ruben Rumbaut. 2006. *Immigrant America.* University of California Press.

Prentice, Julia, Anne Pebley, and Narayan Sastry. 2005. "Immigration Status and Health Insurance Coverage: Who Gains? Who Loses?" *American Journal of Public Health* 95: 109–116.

Ramakrishnan, S. Karthick, and Irene Bloemraad, eds. 2008. *Civic Hopes and Political Realities: Immigrants, Community Organizations, and Political Engagement.* Russell Sage Foundation.

Suárez-Orozco, Carola, Hirokazu Yoshikawa, Robert Teranishi, and Marcelo Suárez-Orozco. 2011. "Growing Up in the Shadows: The Developmental Implications of Unauthorized Status." *Harvard Educational Review* 81 (3): 438–473.

Sudhinaraset, May, Irving Ling, Tu My To, Jason Melo, and Thu Quach. 2017. "Dreams Deferred: Contextualizing the Health and Psychosocial Needs of Undocumented Asian and Pacific Islander Young Adults in Northern California." *Social Science & Medicine* 184: 144–152.

Vaquera, Elizabeth, Elizabeth Aranda, and Isabel Sousa-Rodriguez. 2017. "Emotional Challenges of Undocumented Young Adults: Ontological Security, Emotional Capital, and Well-being." *Social Problems* 64 (2): 298–314.

Warner, R. Stephen, and Judith G. Wittner, eds. 1998. *Gatherings in Diaspora: Religious Communities and the New Immigration.* Temple University Press.

Wong, Janelle, Kathy Rim, and Haven Perez. 2008. "Protestant Churches and Conservative Politics: Latinos and Asians in the United States." In *Civic Hopes and Political Realities: Immigrants, Community Organizations, and Political Engagement*, edited by Ramakrishnan, S. Karthick, and Irene Bloemraad. Russell Sage Foundation.

Wong, Janelle S. 2018. *Immigrants, Evangelicals, and Politics in an Era of Demographic Change.* Russell Sage Foundation.

Zong, Jie, and Jeanne Batalova. 2017. *Korean Immigrants in the United States.* Migration Policy Institute.

NOTES

1. Throughout the chapter I use pseudonyms and keep details vague to protect the identities of respondents.

2. In the pre-interview survey, nearly half of Mexican respondents indicated "Catholic" for their religious affiliation (the others wrote "N/A"), but religion surprisingly emerged in only two of my interviews with them.

3. Five Korean respondents indicated that they were "Agnostic" for their religious affiliation, and one indicated "Buddhist."

4. After coding transcripts into broad categories, Korean respondents' transcripts were further coded inductively based on emergent themes around coethnic organizational resources and the role of the Korean church.

5. The Bishops of the United States and the Bishops of Mexico collaboratively wrote a statement called "Strangers No Longer: Together on the Journey of Hope" / "Juntos en el Camino de la Esperanza Ya no Somos Extranjeros" on the pressing need for immigration reform in 2003.

6. This represents the number of followers on November 27, 2023. https://www.facebook.com/SanctuaryChurchNetwork/.

8

Chardi Kala

Resilience and Perseverance Through Adversity

PRATISHTHA KHANNA

I remember in 1994 my papa visited the United States for the first time, and he returned with a wealth of pictures from Disneyland in Anaheim, California, and his travels to Las Vegas, Nevada. The spinning Mad Tea Cups and the towering Excalibur Hotel and Casino were the extent of my understanding of America. When I arrived at Dulles International Airport on April 25, 2002, I was mesmerized by the neatly parked cars and endless clean highways.

However, as I later learned, all "pursuits of life, liberty, and happiness" in the "land of opportunities" are not attuned to the narrative that attract families from across oceans to this stolen land that does not even belong to the self-proclaimed gatekeepers today. In this chapter, I share my family's struggle to survive an outdated immigration system that does not acknowledge the stressors it places on the very fundamentals of democracy as well as my quiet yet ensuing protest to attain higher education.

As student doctors, we are trained to make educated guesses to reach a definitive diagnosis when presented with a patient case otherwise called "differential diagnosis." The process of brainstorming a potential diagnosis, though challenging, is what makes us better physicians. This process highlights the importance of partnering with patients and colleagues to provide informed and adequate care. My pursuits within the U.S. higher education system while an undocumented immigrant and later a "DACAmented" immigrant required a similar approach.

In 2007, I was sixteen years old and a sophomore in high school when I unearthed the truth about papa's immigration case. We could not proceed with changing our residency status; doing so could have led to our deportation. Within days, I saw the eagerness and wit in my parents' eyes about building the American Dream turn into despair, confusion, and heartbreak. Papa arrived to the United States on April 18, 2001, with a passport and visa, months before the attacks on the Twin Towers. His tourist visa expired in mid-October 2001, and although he filed a change of status application within the valid window, his immigration attorney filed the application with U.S. Citizenship and Immigration Services a week after his visa had expired. Though mamma, Waris (my younger brother), and I entered the United States in 2002 with a valid entry, our fates were already decided because we were included as "dependents" on papa's immigration application.

This lapse in the immigration attorney's professional judgment meant that my family was at the mercy of an archaic "system" that predates the advent of modern means and reasons for migration. It is a *system* that repeatedly hits snooze on alarming statistics about the abuse of migrant children, labor, and lost potential across many industries. While a layperson may tell those individuals struggling to navigate the maze of immigration to simply "get in a line," given the state of the current U.S. immigration system, that *line* does not even have a definite beginning or end. I have yet to see a larger tragedy in the Western world, in a first-world nation with a large sector of society that refuses to educate itself about or acknowledge the underbelly that provides the foundation to its economy.

As a high school student, the challenges that I had to face became personal and tangible. Unlike my friends, I could not get a driver's permit or apply for work authorization and obtain a job because I did not have a Social Security number or valid residency status in the country. Those aspirations ended abruptly. The following year, while my friends took advantage of the Common Application to apply to colleges and scholarships in bulk, I struggled with the first page of the online application because I did not have a Social Security number. While being bombarded with information about the Free Application for Federal Student Aid (FAFSA) through career services and guidance counselors at my high school, no one could answer my questions on how to navigate the specific challenges that I was facing.

I remember feeling disheartened and exhausted every day. With my friends, I could not articulate the sentences needed to communicate the magnitude of desperation that I was facing. Moreover, none of them could relate to what I was going through. The constant rigmarole with counselors at school became less and less encouraging. After months of asking for help and being referred to the same resources, I was disheartened. I kept quiet about my challenges at school. Internally, I struggled with questions to which I had no answers. I had never felt so isolated.

As I began my senior year of high school, amid swinging emotions and after exhausting all my resources, I decided to tell my parents. Unlike softer tales of parents encouraging their children through times of adversity, my parents' approach had always been one of setting an example. Contrary to what I had imagined, the dead ends in my pursuits were their new challenges. With tears in my eyes, I remember sitting across the table from my father and staring at his solemn, tired eyes, hunched back, shrinking stature, and withering laugh lines. He said, "We are not going to compromise on this. Your education and a better future are why we came here." I hadn't seen that confidence and "can-do" attitude in over a year.

Within the next week, on a school day, mamma took off from work, picked me up from school, and drove me to a local community college. She worked at a fast-food restaurant in a nearby mall that one of the community college academic counselors often frequented. Over the years, through small talk, mamma learned about his work, and he often asked her about us: Waris and me. He had once mentioned, "Well if you need any help with your kids when they go to college, let me know, I will guide them." Without an appointment, we landed in the guidance office and requested to speak to Mr. Robbins. We waited for some time as he attended to scheduled student appointments, and then he came to the waiting area and escorted us back to his office.

I looked around the office dressed in the Washington football memorabilia and sat quietly as my mother told him about my dilemma in broken English. I clenched a copy of my unofficial high school transcript in case I was asked to prove my potential. As I gazed around, while listening to my mother, he reached back in a pile of papers and placed a fat stack of an application in front of me. I looked through the application—for the Rouse Scholars Program. He interrupted mamma and said, "While I speak to your mother, please fill out the application."

We left his office after an hour and twenty-seven minutes. During that visit, I submitted my application for admission and a handwritten essay to the college. He looked over my unofficial high school transcripts and stapled them onto the application. While walking us out to the lobby, he said, "Expect an official decision in the mail within the next week." I remember being quiet during the ride back home. I felt that mamma had placed too much hope on this opportunity. She was gleaming thinking this was it; I had been accepted. I was not ready to celebrate yet. What if I got rejected? What if my exceptional grades in gifted and talented and Advanced Placement classes and my extracurricular pursuits in student government, peer mentorship, and marching band were not enough? What if they also asked for a Social Security number?

To my surprise, a few days later a package arrived in the mail. I was accepted to the Rouse Scholars Program at Howard Community College! Mamma rejoiced. I continued reading through the acceptance conditions. There was a caveat. I had to pay international tuition for the course work. Looking further into the financial breakdown of every credit hour, my excitement dampened.

That night, mamma joyously placed the packet in front of papa. The fatigue in his eyes was briefly replaced with relief and excitement. Throughout the following months, I discussed the tuition burden with my parents. They raised me with a perfect balance of naïveté and practicality.

Though my parents would never entertain the thought of me not pursuing higher education, their aging bodies could not sustain the burdens of survival. However, papa's standard reply to my apprehension was, "You don't worry about the money, just focus on your studies." Little did he understand that I carried an immense burden of guilt that my aspirations came at the cost of their comfort and health, and I continue to carry that burden today.

I graduated high school and started the long road of higher education pursuits in the fall of 2009. Aware of the sacrifices my parents were making to send me to college, my priority list was short: academic success. I enjoyed interacting with peers and faculty mentors. As the first year of college began, I was fortunate to find an academic mentor and a fearless ally: Mrs. Dunnigan. She consistently checked in with me, valuing my mental health and emotional well-being as an integral part to my academic success. I was positively taken aback!

Privately, I was not so kind to myself. I questioned my worth against the tremendous sacrifices that my parents were making every day. My days started early. Since I was not able to drive, my parents adjusted their work schedules around my classes. I remember conversations with papa during those years mostly occurred in the car because he returned home long after I had gone to bed. Mamma worked tirelessly to support papa, or she was in the kitchen preparing for the next day. While my classmates were vocal about the challenges of physics lab and organic chemistry, I remained silent, aware that my qualms with organic chemistry came at an unimaginable cost—my parents' simple pleasures and health.

During one of the check-ins with Mrs. Dunnigan, I confided in her about the challenges of financing my education and the struggles my parents were facing. She encouraged me to apply to merit-based scholarships. Regardless of the internal battles that gripped my consciousness and made it hard to fall asleep at night, I continued to work hard. Academically, it was rewarding.

After the first semester, I qualified for merit-based scholarships. With ample guidance from Mrs. Dunnigan and senior program alumni on how to secure continued private, merit-based scholarships, I excelled. I wrote thank-you notes and attended donor luncheons and "meet and greets" to talk about what I was able to achieve with the scholarships. Along with focusing on my education and augmenting the tuition burden with scholarships, without telling my parents I started working. I cleaned homes on Saturdays and earned fifty dollars per day of work.

Culturally and socially, I was out of place, yet my parents always enforced the value of an honorable work ethic. They completed higher education in India; however, in the United States papa worked the graveyard shift at a gas station where he stocked shelves and scrubbed public toilets and later drove a cab while mamma worked in the fast-food industry. My parents always instilled the value of honest *Karm* (Karma, meaning one's duty) and that no job was too small.

I did not let "what people would say" bother me. My goal was to cover miscellaneous school expenses and to be able to buy myself coffee. After a few weeks, I told my parents that I was cleaning homes on the weekends. They asked about my intentions to take up work while enrolled in a heavy course load. I assured them that I was prioritizing my education. Without hesitation, they championed my efforts to make the most of what I was able to do.

Throughout my time in community college, I was strategic with my time and course load. At the time, all students graduating with an associate's degree in Maryland were allowed to bring sixty credit hours when transferring to a state public university. I saw this as an opportunity to further alleviate the financial burden of paying international student tuition at a four-year university. I was balancing a full course load each semester with work and academic networking with alumni and mentors.

I realized that my routine was far removed from the frivolous pleasures enjoyed by other twenty-year-olds. While it was natural to envy the ease that my peers were afforded simply by the privilege of birth or residency, I took pride in being the first in my family to pursue higher education in America. I applied and was accepted to the University of Maryland, Baltimore County (UMBC) for the spring 2012 semester. In December 2011, I graduated with an associate's degree in biology (premedicine) from Howard Community College.

The excitement was short-lived. Scholarship opportunities for undocumented students at four-year institutions during this time were limited, if not nonexistent, in Maryland. I moved to California in early 2012 with the hopes of establishing residency there so that I could eventually finish my undergraduate education with greater financial support. At that time, California was one of the few states that acknowledged the plight of undocumented college students and offered tangible solutions to students' financial hardships. My parents' support did not waver, and they upended their lives and network of family friends in Maryland and moved to California with me. However, like many other undocumented immigrant families, that year was pivotal for us. On June 15, 2012, from the Rose Garden at the White House, the Deferred Action for Childhood Arrivals (DACA) program was announced.

I immediately deferred my admission to UMBC for the fall 2012 semester, and we moved back to Maryland. I was excited to use the basic scraps of dignity and livelihood given to me—a Social Security number and work authorization. These scraps that derailed simple aspirations a few years prior became a lesson in gratitude. It became second nature to me to push open doors that were closed to others like myself. The authenticity of my limitations taught me the value in professional networking, articulating words and sentences that were sensitive yet firm, and the merit of hard work.

I began working part time as an exam proctor for the Student Support Services Office at UMBC. Back in 2009, while struggling to attend college, I could not have imagined working and receiving documented pay, filing taxes, and financially helping my parents while being a full-time student. DACA paved the way for this to happen, and I remain grateful for this miniscule step toward the change that President Obama had originally promised on the campaign trail.

Though there was positive change and growth academically, my internal battles were ongoing. To distract myself, I spent the majority of my energy on my education. Papa dropped me off at UMBC on his way to work early in the mornings, and I used to spend long hours in the library when not in class or at work. There was a sense of renewed energy and relief. In summer 2013, mamma suffered a hemorrhagic stroke. She had suffered from debilitating headaches and high blood pressure her entire adult life. Without medical care because of a lack of health insurance, she took over-the-counter painkillers, masking her headaches. Due to the worsening nature of the disease, she suffered a hemorrhagic stroke. I was aware of the physical and psychological toll my parents were putting themselves through, but the stroke emboldened my concerns and anxiety about their health.

We rushed her to a local emergency room. She could barely open her eyes and even vomited the water she attempted to drink. While being transferred to Medstar Washington Hospital Center in Washington, D.C., we were relieved that she was conscious, alert, and communicating. She was admitted to the neurological intensive care unit and placed under observation while the doctors contemplated if she needed surgical intervention.

Once in a room, she called me closer and whispered, "Pratishtha, how are we going to pay for this?" I stared blankly at mamma, heartbroken. While holding back tears, I kissed her forehead and said, "I will find the answer but right now, I want to focus on taking you back home, healthy." In just a few hours, the roles had reversed. Now, I was reassuring my parents. That moment taught me love; fierce, protective, and ready to work so that I could bring her back home. This was the kind of love my parents had poured in me to ensure my wins and successes.

I stayed with her overnight and was relieved when she insisted on using the bathroom and not the bedpan, a sign that the stroke had not disabled her. The following morning, an MRI confirmed that the bleed was sustained and did not require surgery. We brought her home after three days. Mamma was upset that she could not work and support papa. Along with remaining committed to finishing school and working part-time, I took mamma to her physical therapy and rehabilitation sessions.

As my college graduation neared and most of my friends either were admitted to medical school or succeeded at securing jobs with the National Institutes of Health or other credible organizations as part of their gap year(s), I remained in limbo. I did not fit the picture of a traditional medical school aspirant. While my parents and I worked endlessly so that I could complete my undergraduate studies, how could they afford medical school while driving a cab and working in the fast-food industry on minimum wage?

I brainstormed and narrowed my focus: financial stability, family, and eventually returning to academia. In February 2014, I started working as a medical scribe in the emergency room at Baltimore Washington Medical Center in Glen Burnie, Maryland. The experience provided me the environment I needed to continue my career pursuits. I was surrounded by medical professionals who became mentors, which allowed me to observe provider-patient interactions in acute care settings while I built up my medical vocabulary. These experiences were transformative and pivotal to my growth as a future physician. In May 2014, I graduated with a bachelor's degree in biology, and in June, a year after the stroke, mamma returned to work.

A few weeks prior to college graduation at UMBC, I returned to Howard Community College. This time it was for work training. I explored short-term careers to gain bedside experience and decided to train as a certified nursing assistant. Though bedside experience is not a requirement for medical school applicants, I wanted to maximize the two years of surety afforded to me by DACA. Also, as a student of human sciences, I wanted to be at the patients' bedside because I was not interested in research. Going to neighboring nursing homes to practice patient care skills excited me. However, after being exposed to the fast-paced, acute care setting of the emergency room, I wanted to practice in a hospital. My clinical instructor suggested an advance certification as a patient care technician (PCT) that would place me in the hospital setting.

Accordingly, I became a Maryland state certified PCT in November 2014 and started a paid clinical internship to specialize in skills specific to the medical ICU (MICU) at Johns Hopkins Hospital in January 2015. Monday through Friday, my days began at 5 a.m. and ended at 8 p.m. The satisfaction and relief felt by my parents were evident; they were vocal about how proud and happy they were that I was relentless and intentional in my pursuits. Though there was a sense of growth through the opportunities now available to me, I never took a break to reflect on my achievements.

I remained frugal with praise and appreciation for myself because I knew that I was guaranteed certainty only in two-years increments through DACA. Gradually, I began to consistently contribute to expenses, alleviating some of the burdens my parents had carried for so long. I allowed myself to celebrate small successes by asking papa to come home at a reasonable time because I now had a steady income and he did not have to work such long hours. I felt a sense of satisfied indulgence when my family of four sat together to eat dinner most nights of the week. Until that time, birthdays and anniversaries were cel-ebrated in passing because my parents worked endlessly to make ends meet.

As I finished training and commenced a full-time position in the MICU as a PCT, I continued to work part-time in the emergency room. In May 2015, papa suffered an embolic stroke that affected his speech. He had diabetes, over the years, and due to being undocumented without health insurance, he had mini-mal medical oversight on the worsening disease progression. That morning, papa was at work driving the cab.

One of his friends, whom I call Harry Uncle, noticed that his cab had been parked for many hours. Harry Uncle drove to the spot and saw that the car was parked and papa was sitting inside. He asked papa why he was not picking up his phone. Papa looked at him and smiled. Harry Uncle asked if he was alright. Papa again looked at him and smiled. Harry Uncle was alarmed and drove papa to the hospital, where mamma and I joined him. A CT scan confirmed that he had a stroke, particularly affecting an important speech center of his brain.

Papa was discharged from the hospital after a week. During that visit, he was placed on insulin and started speech therapy. I continued working two jobs and became papa's at-home therapist. Between work shifts, I hurried home and took him out for walks. On those walks, I talked to him and sometimes waited for half an hour for him to articulate and speak the words he intended in response to me. It was the first time I had seen papa become frazzled by the challenges he was facing. With medical approval, he returned to work within a month while continuing speech therapy.

To support my family and build a professional resume, I continued work-ing. During that time, I enjoyed the friendships I was building while observing and learning from opportunities that surrounded me. Many of my friends who worked alongside me as nurses, advanced care nurse practitioners, physician assistants, and physicians became the community and allies who applauded and supported my aspirations to return to academia. Some volunteered their time to peer edit my personal statements, while others discussed Medical Col-lege Admissions Test (MCAT) concepts in the context of advanced medical practice when I struggled with the material.

In late August 2015, I rushed papa to the emergency room. He was on a morning walk when he started to experience chest pain. By the time I picked him up a few yards away from our apartment, he was drenched in sweat as if he had stepped out of the shower with his clothes on. I returned to work for a night shift in the MICU after papa was admitted at a local hospital. I called his nurse every two hours to check on him. Papa suffered from recurrent heart attacks overnight and had developed aspiration pneumonia. Due to worsening heart damage that led to decreased levels of consciousness, he was placed on a venti-lator and airlifted to Johns Hopkins Hospital, Coronary Care Unit (CCU), five floors beneath where I was ending my night shift.

I shivered as I signed the waiver forms for an emergency coronary stent placement. Papa was invincible. He was always in *Chardi Kala*, a state of being adapted from the Sikh belief that despite the circumstances, always remain in rising spirits. I stood by his bedside, while he was transferred from the gurney to his hospital bed only to be hurried to the catheter lab. I cried. The attending physician wrapped his arm around me and allowed a few seconds for me to hug papa. I whispered to him, "I need you. Fight and please come back." By the time mamma and my brother Waris got to the hospital, I had locked my emotions away and channeled the custodian, devoid of weakness and the fright that gripped me when I saw papa on the ventilator.

After eight days in the CCU, papa was discharged home on September 2, 2015. We were thrilled to celebrate his sixty-first birthday on September 10. On November 16, papa collapsed at home. I started CPR and frantically called 911. He was taken to the emergency room, where physicians were not able to revive him after multiple rounds of CPR. That night, I lost a part of myself that lived in constant fear of losing my parents. Within a few seconds, those fears became my reality. More importantly, I lost an irreplaceable friend and confidant.

Since his passing, I realized that I will never be old or successful enough to come to terms about losing papa. However, I somehow had to continue to function. The following Monday, I returned to work with passion fueled from grief and loss. That passion also strengthened my pursuits. I studied for the MCAT and started compiling personal statements for postbaccalaureate programs. Though I worked hard academically throughout my time as an undergraduate student, the fatigue reflected in some of the more rigorous, didactic science and math courses.

As I was writing and editing my personal statements, I realized the value of social and professional alliances. I was selective about sharing my immigration status and the struggles that came with attaining higher education in the professional setting. The select few colleagues who became friends and allies who were aware of these struggles also shared similar aspirations of professional and academic growth. They volunteered to become peer editors. This objective oversight provided me with a deep understanding of what the admissions committees were targeting in resilient applicants, an incredible advantage. It was an audience that I didn't have access to before.

After unsuccessfully applying to postbaccalaureate programs for three years, I applied and was accepted to Western University of Health Sciences' College of Biomedical Sciences in Pomona, California, for the fall 2018 term.

The joy of acceptance was matched with feelings of great uncertainty. How will I afford higher education at an out-of-state, private institution? Switching to being a full-time student meant sacrificing financial security and placing a massive burden of survival on mom and Waris. Leading up to my acceptance of the admissions offer, I remember going up and down the steps of the thirteen stories of Sheikh Zayed North Tower at Johns Hopkins Hospital during my lunch break, contemplating yet again questions to which I did not have any answers. I tried to silence my guilt and anxiety with exercise, but these thoughts would not cease.

Even though I had DACA, I did not qualify for FAFSA. Private loans came with exorbitant interest charges that would exhaust my earnings while repaying the loans. While contemplating long-term financial stability and personal and professional fulfillment, I decided that temporarily sacrificing financial stability was the necessary step toward honoring the sacrifices my parents had made for my future. I opened a GoFundMe account and hesitantly turned to the South Asian community with a plea for donations for my first semester's tuition.

Though in South Asian communities a veil of secrecy about personal matters is tradition, I chose to share the difficulties I faced due to my immigration status. I consciously highlighted my passion for higher education and medicine and openly shared the disabling multigenerational, systemic atrocities imposed by the broken immigration system on undocumented families. I did not want to be glorified as a "good kid" who was going to become a physician because it is the "ideal" pursuit. Rather, I was determined to become a physician although I did not have the ease afforded to my peers by the privilege of birth or residency status. While writing and editing several drafts of my personal statements for graduate and professional programs, I learned that powerful storytelling is essential.

Though it was incredibly unnerving because I was reaching out to a community that was not necessarily immersed in immigration advocacy, the value of allies with diverse social networks was evident. In about two weeks my fund received close to $14,000 in donations, several of them anonymous. As I did with scholarships received during my time at Howard Community College, I commemorated donors with a personal thank-you note detailing how the donation was being utilized. As I learned through my previous experiences, this gesture was crucial.

I also utilized this as an opportunity to educate my allies. Taking the time to address each donor and detailing how their donation had helped me tangibly access education provided donors with a personal insight about hardships I would face if I did not have access to these funds. This made them aware of not only my struggles but also similar hurdles that other undocumented or DACA-mented students who also do not qualify for traditional education loans face. It was necessary to be as transparent as I could be so that the community was informed and vigilant about the stresses faced by all undocumented students.

I can never repay the debt of kindness and humanity that the community that has championed my strides showed me. From monetary donations toward tuition to generously opening their hearts and home for me to stay in California (rent free), I could not have celebrated these successes if not for them.

Though I had decided to take a leap and pursue graduate and professional studies full-time, I intently saved. With my savings I was able to alleviate the burden of rent for my family in Maryland throughout the duration of my graduate school studies from fall 2018 to spring 2020. To account for other expenses such as gas and insurance while I lived in California, I worked part-time as a PCT.

I matriculated into the Master of Sciences in Biomedical Sciences postbaccalaureate program at Western University of Health Sciences in Pomona, where I excelled academically. Focusing on health sciences fed my niche interest in human medicine; I enjoyed physiology. From learning about the Henderson-Hasselbalch equation in applied acid base chemistry to maintain homeostasis to the dynamics of spontaneous respirations, I was previewing my future. As the first semester neared an end, my student account charges totaled above $22,000. The cycle of anxiety and uncertainty returned.

I remember experiencing palpitations in the middle of the night, awakening to thuds echoing in my ears, drenched in sweat. It was not the first time I had experienced bouts of anxiety with fears of survival. In high school, while struggling to attain college admission I experienced severe hair loss and sought to hide patches of thinning hair. Through undergraduate studies, I consistently gained weight and struggled with sleep hygiene. And like many times before, I did not have time to address the underlying trauma that led me to experience excessive anxiety. The deadline for the tuition deposit was nearing, and I did not have the funds to continue in the program.

During one of the research seminars hosted by the College of Biomedical Sciences at Western University of Health Sciences, I had a chance encounter with Ms. Tanisha Hampton, the executive assistant to the dean and director of student affairs. Ms. Tanisha was always engaging with students. We were a class of nineteen students, so we were afforded ample time with faculty and administration. Though Ms. Tanisha was very approachable and always ready to problem-solve, I was very hesitant to open up about the financial limbo I was in for the consecutive semesters.

After pondering options without resolve, I emailed Ms. Tanisha and requested to meet. Leading up to the meeting, I drafted a one-page plea for financial aid from the school. I focused on academic successes during the first semester and barriers to accessing traditional financial aid due to my immigration status. As I walked to her office, I remember trembling with fear. I could only think that the administration would hold me responsible and question my decision to matriculate since I knew funding and completing my education without sizable scholarships would be impossible. They would question my credibility too, I thought.

But I was not ready for what followed that meeting. Two days after the meeting, I was sitting in the dean's office with Ms. Tanisha and the dean. He informed me that Ms. Tanisha spoke to him in detail about my conversation with her and made a personal plea to the dean to help alleviate the tuition burden so that I could continue my education. Paired with my plea and her advocacy on my behalf, he decided to approve merit-based scholarships for each of the remaining three semesters to cover full tuition. The only condition applied was that I would have to uphold academic standards. I remember becoming numb.

Mentors and allies like Mrs. Maura Dunnigan and Ms. Tanisha Hampton helped pave my way forward. They volunteered, with my permission, to share my experiences of living as a DACAmented youth determined to pursue my own happiness, in high-level rooms where critical decisions were being made, with those individuals who held administrative power and ability to provide the resources I needed to live my American Dream. If not for them I could not have been successful in my own journey, and I thank them every morning in my prayer of gratitude, just as I thank my parents for making the sacrifices they made on my behalf. But really, a thank-you will never suffice.

I graduated as a master of science in biomedical sciences in May 2020. In June 2020, I retook the MCAT and applied to medical schools. Through the years, I remained connected to physicians, nurses, and academic allies who had mentored me. I shared short summaries of my accomplishments that year so that they remained informed of my continued efforts of getting into medical school. As I applied, I reached out, and they willingly agreed to write letters of recommendation. In early 2021, I was able to adjust my immigration status to becoming a legal permanent resident. Currently, I am a third-year medical student in the trenches of clinical clerkships.

My journey through higher education up to medical school has been an applied lesson in perseverance. Pushing open doors to opportunities that were otherwise unavailable to me due to my immigration status became imperative. Along the way, if a door was locked, I opened windows. I realized that I could compete academically with my peers, however, despite having competitive transcripts, I had to advocate for myself, and many like me who were being pushed into the shadows without a fair chance to access their American Dream. Taking the onus of my future and self-worth was the most fundamental step of my journey. I did not let a piece of paper or a broken "system" define my potential.

As I built this path, my parents, mentors, and professional colleagues who believed in my abilities and passions laid the foundation. These experiences have taught me the value of discipline, consistency, and intuitiveness. As necessary as it was to recognize the hurdles in my path, it was even more important to be intuitive and steadfast in working to find solutions. Oftentimes, I felt fatigued when I could not readily get answers to my questions from academic counselors. However, I returned to their offices and asked who could provide directions for the next steps in my journey. My persistence was mostly met with admiration.

I feel that the aspects of my personal drive that have shaped my journey are relatable to most children of first-generation immigrants, regardless of career path. We all have missed mom and dad on birthdays and anniversaries. We all have graduation pictures where our parents' physical and psychological fatigue is evident in their withering eyes. While accommodating the fads to "fit in," we all return to homes that smell like spices our ancestors cooked with on Diwali or the steam of pine needles used to make songpyeon during Chuseok. We all are driven by the sacrifice of familiarity, culture, and language made by our parents for us. And so, until I am able to repay this debt, I chose to live in *Chardi Kala*, by continuing to be resilient and persevere through all adversity.

9

Embracing Dreams Against Odds

A DACA Recipient's Reflection on Navigating Higher Education and a Career in STEM

ZHELIN JEFF LI

The Impact of DACA's Rescission

May 10, 2018, was a Thursday during the fourth year of my PhD candidacy at the University of California, Riverside (UCR). I was on my lunch break when I received a text message from my mother: "Your father passed away." I remember vividly that an immense wave of confusion rushed into my head. Unable to comprehend the phrase, I texted back, "What do you mean?" When the whirlwind of texts and phone calls settled, I had come to the realization that my father had suddenly passed away from a heart attack in China. The very next thing I recall was running to UCR's Undocumented Student Office. The only objective on my mind was to get to the program director and explore my options of traveling back to China. The director saw the frantic look on my face and sat me down. She closed the door, and I told her what had happened. Was there a way for me to attend my father's funeral overseas as an undocumented individual? I probably already knew the answer, but I didn't want to acknowledge it.

At the time, the Trump administration had rescinded the Obama administration's Deferred Action for Childhood Arrivals (DACA) program (U.S. Department of Homeland Security 2017). While several lawsuits were filed challenging the rescission, the sole mechanism for DACA recipients (aka DREAMers) like myself to travel outside of the United States was through advance parole, and such applications were no longer being approved (U.S. Department of Homeland Security 2017). In the following days, I wrote to my local congressmen and even my California senator's office, begging for authorization to attend my father's funeral in China. Their responses were along the lines of condolences, prayers, and "we stand with you." Yet there was no viable option to go see my father before his cremation without giving up the entire life I had built here in America. It was the most disheartening moment of my life. Freedom of movement is a human right, and no one should have to choose between seeing their loved ones and their own livelihoods.

Arriving to the United States

My DACA journey began when I was fourteen years old. My mother brought me to the United States when she married an American citizen. However, her new marriage fell apart shortly after my controlling American stepfather tried to annul the marriage. Her entire world was turned upside down. By the time I was sixteen, my mother and I had left the abusive household to stay at multiple domestic violence shelters throughout Inglewood, West Covina, and Lancaster in California. I recall that we escaped the house by telling my stepfather we were going to a restaurant while my mother's friend drove us to a shelter at an undisclosed location. At one of the shelters, we shared a room with four others and slept on a bunk bed. In the morning, my mother woke up at six o'clock and performed chores and attended women's classes focused on supporting abused spouses/partners in coping with trauma and becoming independent. I, on the other hand, missed school days and was completely disconnected from the outside world for months.

Fortunately, we were able to rent a section of a living room in an Indonesian couple's house after months of moving around shelters and motels. It was a makeshift room with wooden boards as walls. It was almost primitive, but it felt cozy and safe. My mother found a job at a local Nissan dealership near the San Gabriel Valley. Since she can speak Mandarin and has a sales background, she was able to cater to their Asian customers. I enrolled at Arcadia High School as a sophomore. This was the first time I had consistent schooling for over a year. I was also lucky to have entered the United States with a K-2 visa. A valid visa meant that I could obtain a Social Security number (SSN). This powerful document allowed me to find a job at the local McDonald's restaurant at the corner of Rosemead Boulevard and Duarte Drive to earn some money during high school. Nowadays, I often joke about how my first job was with a *Fortune* 500 company, and I was not exaggerating. The year 2006 was just the beginning of my mother's immigration case, which was riddled by domestic abuse, bureaucracy, and annulment; it was the beginning of a decade-long legal battle. When I turned twenty-one in 2009, I officially "aged out" of legal status and claimed my undocumented DREAMer identity. I use the term "undocumented" in this chapter because I sincerely believe that no human being is "illegal."

Navigating Community College and University as a DACA Student

Due to the lack of resources and guidance on how to navigate the U.S. higher education system, community college was the only option for me. At Pasadena

City College (PCC), I faced the harsh reality that there was no federal financial aid or loans available to undocumented students despite being raised in a low-income, single-parent household. It was not feasible to attend college full-time before the passing of the California DREAM Act, which allowed undocumented students to gain access to certain state-based financial aid and loans (Raza et al. 2019). To fund my education, I had to get creative, and my entrepreneurial spirit took flight in 2009, two years before the act's passage. My mother and I started a small importing and exporting business by leveraging the booming e-commerce scene. The business generated a stable income to support me through PCC and, more importantly, made me realize that there was a way to persevere through hard work regardless of my immigration status.

Like many who had to balance work and school, it took me more than four years to transfer to a four-year university. I took the time and additional courses at PCC to find what I was truly passionate about. I accumulated enough credits and obtained two associate's degrees. By the time I got to California State University, Los Angeles (CSULA) in 2012, DACA was announced during Obama's FORWARD reelection campaign (U.S. Citizenship and Immigration Services 2015). It was an exciting time for DREAMers like myself because we all thought that coming out of the shadows and being undocumented and unafraid would encourage lawmakers to help us forge a pathway to citizenship. In hindsight, the political capital was there, but the political will was spent on the passage of Obamacare, which might have been a determining factor that led to the loss of the Democratic supermajority in Congress. It was a pivotal moment in which those decisions might have foreshadowed the knee-jerk reaction that gave rise to the modern conservative movement, polarizing today's political spectrum. For me, the extra time at PCC meant that I was an "older" community college student at twenty-four years old. I matured, made lifelong friendships, and was laser focused on my future goals.

CSULA was where I worked at my first lab with Dr. Craig Barrett from the Biology Department. Call it a family legacy, since my father and grandfather were both biochemists in China; I knew I wanted to pursue a career in science and graduate school. I also knew I needed more lab experience. Volunteering at a research lab did not and still does not require legal status in the United States. I helped Dr. Barrett set up his lab and dove into the studies of California native plants through the Council on Ocean Affairs, Science, and Technology program. Dr. Barrett loved his coastal shrubs and his palm tree species belonging to the family Arecaceae. We published two peer-reviewed journal articles highlighting the importance of ecological conservancy. I was awarded a university-funded scholarship based on our collaboration regardless of my immigration status. Being an older undergraduate student also gave me a sense of urgency and focus; I graduated within a year and half with a bachelor's in biology cum laude and was in the top 5 percent of my class. Coincidentally, my DACA application was approved in 2014, and I became a member of the first cohort of DACA recipients. This status directly enabled me to pursue a doctorate at UCR.

A Dream of Pursuing a PhD in STEM

Here's how DACA literally saved my higher education dream. When I was accepted into the Genetics Genomics and Bioinformatics (GGB) PhD program at UCR, the administration office inquired about my immigration status. Graduate students are often considered as employees (teaching assistants and lab researchers) of the university. PhD students under this work-study model receive benefits including having their tuition covered and are compensated with a living wage while they teach and perform research for the university using mostly federal funds. DACA provided employment authorization to address all the uncertainties through my admission process. In fact, the I-765 portion of DACA (employment authorization) and SSN are sufficient for any graduate school onboarding paperwork.

DACA also brought me psychological relief. Under its protection, I was able to dive into the intricate world of RNA biology and neuroscience at Dr. Sika Zheng's lab. We worked on multiple disease modalities such as amyotrophic lateral sclerosis (ALS), Duchenne muscular dystrophy (DMD), and cystic fibrosis (CF). I published my first research paper as the first author in the *RNA Journal* in December 2016. The joy of academic success was further magnified when I presented my research at the Eleventh Annual Salk Institute, Foundation ISPEN, and Science Symposium and the Tenth Annual SoCal Glial-Neuronal Interactions in Health and Disease Symposium. Yet the proudest moment during my graduate school career came when I represented the University of California Regents at the 2017 AAAS Annual Meeting in Austin, Texas, to speak about the challenges facing undocumented students in higher education, bringing greater awareness to our small university population. Interestingly, Joe Biden, then former vice president and now former president, was the keynote speaker at the same meeting.

The truth is, DACA made my PhD dream possible by legally providing employment authorization, a driver's license, and an SSN. However, it did not guarantee a future in academia. For example, it did not grant access to federally funded programs such as the prestigious National Science Foundation (NSF) or National Institutes of Health (NIH) fellowships. DACA graduates were not allowed to apply for the fellowships, not because of academic merits but simply due to their residency status. Further, there is still no pathway for DACAmented PhD graduates to pursue a tenured professorship in most STEM disciplines due to our inability to apply for federal funding. Federal funding is a lifeline for running a research lab, which is often required at top-tier R1 research institutions. It is virtually impossible for any DACA scientists to build their own academic research labs without this funding mechanism, thus eliminating the tenure potential for DREAMers. I can only pray the positive impact of the DACA policy over the past decade will eventually overcome the stigma where all academics, with or without DACA, can be evaluated on a level ground for the betterment of our nation and science.

On a brighter note, for the first time I was "qualified" to compete with my peers for a few private fellowships. I was a 2016 honorable mention (top 10 percent of 2,300 applicants nationwide) of the ultracompetitive Ford Fellowship at the National Academies. The Soros Fellowships for New Americans was another great opportunity for graduate students regardless of their immigration status. Though I am saddened that the Ford Fellowships will be winding down by 2028, more organizations are stepping up and being more DACA/undocumented student friendly. For example, TheDream.US National Scholarships present some of the most lucrative scholarships for undergraduate and graduate undocumented students. Immigrants Rising also brings a lot of resources under one roof for students to explore. In addition, I was awarded the Chancellor's Distinguished Fellowship and the Dissertation Year Fellowship specific to University of California PhD candidates. The rule of thumb, I have found, is that university, state, and private foundation scholarships are usually status agnostic about a student's immigration status or at the least these scholarships are "status negotiable." Federal grants, however, remain inaccessible to DACA recipients in general. With the support of fellowships and working as a graduate student researcher / teaching assistant, like many DACAmented graduate students, I was able to earn a livable wage and receive health care benefits while dedicating myself to my research. If finances are ever a concern stopping you from pursuing knowledge or continuing your journey in higher education, then know that there is a way to overcome those financial burdens even as the future of the DACA program remains highly precarious.

On the other hand, imagine the difficulties facing undocumented graduate students without DACA. The bureaucratic red tape around getting employed, filing taxes, commuting to school without a driver's license, and even opening a bank account has deterred so many talented individuals from reaching their fullest potential and obtaining higher degrees in the undocumented community, not to mention the psychological trauma of living without legal protection where they have to constantly worry about deportation instead of focusing on their education.

Professional Career in Biotech

Despite the bumpy road, I successfully defended my dissertation and joined the biotech private sector in December 2019. I wanted to use my business and science hybrid background to help accelerate drug discovery in the biotech industry. DACA truly simplified the entire job-hunting process and enabled me to pursue more career-oriented opportunities. DACA recipients can gain more experiences by applying for part-time jobs and/or volunteering and by studying abroad through advance parole, an opportunity which up until now many undocumented students have been deprived of. I was able to apply for jobs without any hesitation concerning background checks. The I-9, Employment Eligibility Verification, from employers was no longer an obstacle for full-time DACA employees like myself. I ended up at a San Diego–based biotechnology company called Illumina. It was the major technology provider in human genetic sequencing. We worked with organizations such as 23andMe, the University of California, San Francisco, and other major research organizations to provide personalized care for patients. At Illumina, I continued my education to strengthen my business acumen by enrolling in Johns Hopkins University's MBA program. Illumina also helped fund a portion of the business schooling through internal career development stipends.

Now I work as a business development manager at Thermo Fisher Scientific, one of the largest life science companies in the world. In this role, I support Southern California biotech innovators in bringing more cell gene therapies (CGT) to patients. CGT is a relatively new modality for cancer and autoimmune and other rare diseases. Considering lymphoma, for example, the cell therapy approach is to take the patient's own white blood cells and genetically modify them to kill invasive cancerous cells. Or in the case of a rare genetic disorder, the specific gene therapy will help correct or deliver the necessary functional gene copies to a patient to treat the illness. These new CGT drugs are more potent, are less harmful, and target previously untreatable diseases. They are literally "living" drugs that save lives. Knowing that every conversation I have could potentially lead to lifesaving cures is such a rewarding experience. I am proud to have gone through this journey from an undocumented immigrant kid to a scientist and a businessman, but most importantly as a DACA recipient and a DREAMer. This does not erase the fact that I lost my grandfather in 2014 and my father in 2018 without a chance to say goodbye. All I can do is hope that they can be proud of who I have become and know their legacy will never be forgotten.

The Many Challenges and Road Ahead

We, DACAmented/undocumented immigrants, must find strength within ourselves and each other as the road ahead may be even more treacherous. First, I foresee additional challenges as DACA recipients start approaching the prime of our careers in our mid-thirties and forties. The potential requirement of frequent international travel can seriously hinder our ability to reach our career goals. What if a DREAMer gets an opportunity to work overseas? What if a

DREAMer gets to lead an international organization that requires working across countries and borders? Without concrete reentry permission, DACA-mented individuals will again need to fight for their values. Moreover, the new-est college DREAMer entrants can no longer apply for DACA protections due to ongoing litigation. This means these young people are once again without an SSN and employment authorization. I find it ironic that we are now facing the same obstacles we overcame almost twenty years ago. We have come full circle, but not in a positive way. Almost two decades ago, when I worked at McDon-ald's, the employer did not ask specifically about your residency status as long as you were able to provide an SSN, especially when you were a high school kid looking for your first part-time job. Imagine the DREAMers who were not able to secure an SSN; how can they even fill out the most basic job application with-out being interrogated about their immigration status?

This is the third time that DACA has come under scrutiny since its incep-tion in 2012. Many people may have forgotten the Obama administration's 2014 attempt to expand the DACA program to include parents of U.S. citizen and law-ful permanent resident children and provide a three-year renewal period instead of a two-year one. This resulted in litigation and the subsequent defeat of the Obama administration's efforts to expand the program in the Texas I case (Olivas 2020). In 2017, the Trump administration's cancellation of DACA once again pushed DREAMers briefly into the spotlight (Smith 2023). The upholding of the DACA program, however, was the result of a technicality in the case, *DHS v. Regents of the University of California*. Yet at the time of writing, this positive ruling has been slightly diminished by the 2017 Texas II ongoing law-suit, which challenges the jurisdiction of the Department of Homeland Security to implement DACA under the Immigration and Nationality Act of 1952 (Smith 2023). Since the Fifth Circuit Court of Appeals issued a recent ruling holding that the DACA program is unlawful, young DREAMers who are coming of age can apply for employment authorization cards or obtain a temporary protection status for SSN, but their applications are not currently being processed (Smith 2023). At this moment, it can be understood that this lower court ruling will likely be upheld by the now conservative supermajority on the U.S. Supreme Court. Many are now realizing that DACA is built on a house of cards and lacks legal safeguards. The Obama administration's executive action is not a perma-nent solution for the more than 825,000 undocumented youth living in the United States today (Bruno 2021). These uncertainties are not only traumatizing for DREAMers but also nonconstructive to the United States since DACA recipi-ents have brought an undeniably positive impact on a socioeconomic level.

In a 2023 national study, Wong et al. surveyed 817 DACA recipients and found that 83.1 percent of respondents were employed with a median annual income of $60,000. The Demographic and Economic Impacts of the DACA Recipients survey also highlighted that nearly 600,000 DACA recipients pay

$9.4 billion in taxes each year to the U.S. and state governments (Truong 2021). Moreover, these households hold $25.3 billion in spending power after taxes in their local economies (Truong 2021). The report also notes that 343,000 DACA recipients work in jobs deemed essential by the Department of Homeland Security, including as health care workers, educators, and food supply chain workers (Truong 2021). Further, the nonprofit organization FWD.us recently conducted a study looking into the future contributions of DACA recipients over the next ten years. They report that DACA-eligible individuals will contribute at least $390 billion in wages and $117 billion in combined taxes over the next decade, in addition to the estimated $33 billion taxes from the past decade (FWD.us 2022a). These objective truths about the DACA program and its recipients overwhelmingly support the numerous positive contributions of the DACA community and contradicts the outdated stereotypes of undocumented population as overutilizing public benefits and resources, proving that DACA recipients are a critical part of the fabric of American society.

In fact, ending DACA could bring catastrophic consequences to local communities. FWD.us indicates a potential loss of a thousand jobs per day for two years if DACA is rescinded, scarring the economy and essential infrastructure/services (FWD.us 2022b). The Institute on Taxation and Economic Policy (2018) similarly warned that repealing the working status of DACA recipients would reduce estimated state tax revenue by nearly $700 million per year. Moreover, according to the most recent Congressional Survey on DACA, nearly 1.3 million people live with DACA recipients, including 300,000 U.S.-born children with at least one DACA parent (Bruno 2021). The end of DACA could mean the systematic breakdown of families and abandonment of 300,000 children from at least one of their parents. This kind of inhumanity is against the founding principles of America as the world leader for human rights.

Undocumented and Unafraid: Final Advice from a DREAMer to Fellow DREAMers

At this point, I hope my personal experiences combined with all the evidence shared above have shed some light on not only our struggles but also our potentials. At the end of the day, history will tell our DACA narrative. In the meantime, we will continue to exemplify DACA excellence with each and every single one of us. After spending more than a decade in academia and the private sector, I would like to share six pieces of advice with my fellow DREAMers and anyone who is looking to pursue a future career in STEM:

1. Be bold, curious, and open-minded. Explore new technologies, methods, and opportunities whenever there's a chance. Doing so will hardwire your thought process to keep innovating and solving problems.

2. Go to professional conferences, whether you are a scientist, an entrepreneur, a graphic designer, or a software engineer. I've learned much from attending different conferences and discussing new ideas with fellow scientists and professionals. It is the most potent medium to get inspired.

3. Network, network, and network. It is essential to start building a professional network of like-minded people; these peers will often share resources together. Start by simply creating a LinkedIn page.

4. Practice when you are preparing for interviews. The tenth interview presentation will always be better than the first one. Seek out feedback after each interview and use them to refine your personal story.

5. Start building a résumé or CV. In industry, you will start by creating a résumé that is roughly two pages. There is rarely a scenario where you will need a résumé longer than that in the first five years of your career. A CV is more relevant if you decide to work in academia.

6. Confidence is key. Being undocumented and/or DACAmented can diminish your self-esteem. However, confidence can also be built. It comes from the mastery of a skillset, a success story, or a personal triumph. Confidence is often a key trait professionals look for. If you don't believe in yourself, how do you expect others to believe in you?

All undocumented people, including DACA recipients like myself, should embrace and be proud of our heritage. Regardless of whether you came from China, Korea, Vietnam, Mexico, El Salvador, Guatemala, or anywhere else in the world, the United States is a place we all can call home. We are all waiting for that day when we can proudly, and legally, call ourselves Americans.

REFERENCES

American Immigration Council. 2021. "Deferred Action for Childhood Arrivals (DACA): An Overview." September 30. https://www.americanimmigrationcouncil.org/research/deferred-action-childhood-arrivals-daca-overview.

Bruno, Andorra. 2021. "Deferred Action for Childhood Arrivals (DACA): An Overview." American Immigration Council, February 5. https://www.americanimmigration council.org/research/deferred-action-childhood-arrivals-daca-overview.

FWD.us. 2022a. "DACA Fix." December 5. https://www.fwd.us/news/daca-fix/.

———. 2022b. "What Happens If DACA Ends?" August 22. https://www.fwd.us/news/what-if-daca-ends/.

Institute on Taxation and Economic Policy. 2018. "State and Local Tax Contributions of Young Undocumented Immigrants." April 30. https://itep.org/state-local-tax-contributions-of-young-undocumented-immigrants/.

Olivas, Michael A. 2020. *A Legal and Political History of the DREAM Act and DACA.* New York University Press.

Raza, Syeda S., Zyshia Williams, Dalal Katsiaficas, and Lydia A. Saravia. 2019. "Interrupting the Cycle of Worrying: Financial Implications of the California DREAM Act in the Lives of Undocumented College Students." *Review of Higher Education* 43 (1): 335–370.

Smith, Hillel R. 2023. "The Legality of DACA: Recent Litigation Developments." CRS Legal Sidebar, LSB10625. Congressional Research Service, September 20. https://crsreports .congress.gov/product/pdf/LSB/LSB10625.

Truong, Trinh Q. 2021. "The Demographic and Economic Impacts of DACA Recipients: Fall 2021 Edition." https://www.americanprogress.org/article/the-demographic-and-econo mic-impacts-of-daca-recipients-fall-2021-edition/.

U.S. Citizenship and Immigration Services. 2015. "2014 Executive Actions on Immigration." April 15. https://www.uscis.gov/archive/2014-executive-actions-on-immigration.

U.S. Department of Homeland Security. 2017. "Memorandum: Rescission of DACA." September 5. https://www.dhs.gov/archive/news/2017/09/05/memorandum-rescission-daca.

Wong, Tom K., Ignacia Rodriguez Kmec, Diana Pliego, Karen Fierro Ruiz, Debu Gandhi, and Trinh Q. Truong. 2023. "National DACA Study." https://www.americanprogress .org/article/daca-boosts-recipients-well-being-and-economic-contributions-2022 -survey-results/.

PART FOUR

Mental Health, Activism, and Community Healing

10

The Intersection of Identity

Navigating My Undocumented Asian Experience and Becoming an UndocuAsian Mental Health Professional

HUYEN "KIKI" VO

"Why me?"

I wanted so badly for someone, just anyone to help me make sense of my chaotic world; just someone to explain why tragic and negative events kept happening to me.

I wanted answers for my pain.

My name is Huyen "Kiki" Vo and I'm an undocumented Vietnamese immigrant, a burn/trauma survivor, and a licensed mental health therapist.

This is my story.

I was born in a rural village in South Vietnam. Growing up, all I knew was playing in the street with my sisters, helping my mom with chores, and picking coffee beans with my dad. We were a family of seven. My father was a farmer, and my mother was a stay-at-home mom helping to take care of the kids. We didn't have much money, but we had each other and that was more than enough.

Life was simple, calm, and peaceful. I was very happy.

Everything changed in the flash of a second on November 12, 2000. I was nine years old. It was a dark evening around seven o'clock and there was no electricity in the village yet. Like many families, my family used kerosene lamps as sources of light. My younger sister (eight years old) and I were studying in the living room. I remember persuading her to stop studying to go with me to get some candy from my mother's small shop; my mother had a shop next to the house where she sold sweets and goods to boys and girls in the village. As my younger sister and I walked to the shop, we ran into our second youngest sister who was only three years old at the time; the two of them also followed. Unexpectedly, we ran into our mother. She was busy pouring gasoline into a small bottle so she could take that bottle and pour it into my father's motorcycle. Then, the next day, he could drive to the local shop to get a portable electric bin for us to study.

The next second happened so fast that my mother couldn't react fast enough.

My younger sister was holding a kerosene lamp, and with the intention of helping, she leaned in to where my mother was pouring the gas. Suddenly, a flame ignited. My sisters and I panicked at the sight of the fire.

The fire was small at first, but because we were so frightened by it, all three of us sisters ran back inside the shop. Seeing her children go toward the shop, my mother could not bear leaving us behind. She ran back inside with us, trying to tell us to get out. Unfortunately, in less than a few minutes, the flame got so big that my sisters and I became too scared and just froze. Panicked, my courageous mother stood right in front of us, with her arms spread wide. She told us to stand behind her, that we would be okay—dad would come and rescue us. Those few minutes felt like an eternity in hell.

The fire kept blazing and getting hotter. We were stuck, and I could tell that I was getting engulfed in the smoke. It was getting harder for me to breathe. I briefly looked over and next to me; I saw my sisters screaming, also desperately gasping for air. I could feel my clothes and skin melting. I was in and out of consciousness, thinking that I was going to die in that shop. Just when I was about to close my eyes, my father jumped through the fire and saved me. One by one, he ran in and out of that burning store and rescued my mother and sisters.

No words can describe the intolerable pain my sisters and I were going through. I remember hearing the screeching scream from my two sisters. "đau quá, đau quá ba ơi" (It hurts a lot, it hurts a lot, daddy). One of my sisters was rolling on the ground, wailing and begging for the pain to stop.

In the ambulance, I glanced over and saw my mother looking so helpless. My mother sustained the most burns out of all of us since she used her body as a shield to protect us in the house fire. I never saw my mother in such a state of agony. All I could feel was guilt for being the one leading my sisters to the shop. I looked over to my mother and whispered, "Con xin lỗi, mẹ" (I'm sorry, Mom).

Those were my last words to her.

She passed away in the adult hospital while I was in the critical care unit at the children's hospital trying to make it through. I did not get a chance to attend my mother's funeral. Until this day, I have not had the chance to go back and visit her grave. There is this empty hole in my chest whenever I think of her. Even though I was young, losing her felt like losing a part of me. And that feeling of loss forever stays with me, no matter how much time has passed. If it were not for her selfless sacrifice, shielding me from the flames, I might not be alive today.

My father did not have time to properly mourn the loss of the love of his life. After the accident, my father became a widow and had to take care of his daughters' needs. He stayed up around the clock to tend to our wounds and wipe away our tears. He was mentally, physically, and emotionally drained, but he pushed through the pain of losing his wife in order to keep us alive.

I was just a child, too young to fully grasp everything that had happened. The aftermath of being critically burned in the fire was unbearable, both physically and emotionally. I was no longer recognizable from head to toe, with wounds so fresh and sensitive that the slightest breeze would cause me paralyzing pain. The loss of my mother, on top of the burn injury, was so overwhelming for my nine-year-old heart to handle. I instinctively entered survival mode, with my mind and body shutting down as a way to cope with the overwhelming trauma. To this very day, my recollection of the time before the accident remains fragmented.

The fire set a rebirth for my life. I was no longer that happy and carefree child.

United States: The Land of the American Dream(s)?

Because of the fire, we also lost a lot of money. One day while we were on the street begging for money, this Vietnamese American tourist lady spotted us. She wanted to help us apply for a tourist visa to come to the United States for medical treatment since we did not have the money to afford the burn care needed in Vietnam. She knew of a network of nonprofit hospitals that provided treatment to children with burns regardless of the family's ability to pay. On the night of the fire, my other two younger sisters were with extended family members so they did not get hurt. My father had no choice but to leave both of them (one and six years old) behind with his brother and my maternal grandparents in order to accompany my burn-injured sisters and me to the United States. I cannot even fathom the heartache my father was experiencing, having to leave his two young kids behind.

We arrived in Boston on April 20, 2002; I was just two months shy from turning eleven. For two years straight, my burn-injured sisters and I were in and out of the hospital, having reconstructive surgeries and physical therapy that were excruciating on every level. I remember having metal rods stuck in each finger and needing to wear splints and compression garments on both arms. Our visa was going to expire on April 20, 2004, and we were not done with our burn treatment. My father knew that if we were to go back to Vietnam, we would not get the appropriate care we needed or have the money to afford it. Like any parent, my father prioritized our needs and future and took a risk to leave the East Coast before our visas expired. We resettled in Sacramento, California, since there was a burn hospital there similar to the one in Boston.

Nothing could have prepared us for living life as undocumented immigrants. When we moved to Sacramento, we did not know anyone except some distant relatives from my father's side of the family. However, they treated us horribly. They often made comments like, "nobody would ever want to marry you" to my sisters and me. In my culture, being beautiful is a big factor for girls—and to them, we were no longer considered beautiful because of our scars. They also looked down on my entire family since we were undocumented and poor; they were ashamed and embarrassed of us. "Saving face" was more important than supporting us when we needed them.

To this day, I still do not remember all the details that transpired, but two years after we arrived in Sacramento, my father managed to bring my two non-injured younger sisters to the United States from Vietnam. By 2006, we were finally together again as one family under the same roof. The reunion was filled with overwhelming joy and grief. It had been four years since I last saw or spoke to my sisters. I was also grieving my mother, who couldn't be there with us, and simultaneously I knew at the tender age of 14 that I had to step up and help my father take care of my four younger siblings.

Now looking back, I realize that there were also some unexplained lapses in my memory due to growing up in survival mode. Certain life events which were filled with intense emotions ended up becoming foggy and somewhat fragmented in my mind. It was as if my brain was compartmentalizing, shuffling, and blocking certain memories to protect me and keep me alive.

Everything in the environment felt unsafe and scary. On top of not being able to speak English, my scars added another layer of complexity that was overwhelming and challenging for my teenage self to navigate. I did not see or know anyone who looked like me at school or in the community. It was hard to make friends, and I was often stared at, bullied, and called names like "scarface" and "Freddy Krueger." The noise in the world was so loud that I began to internalize it all and I thought I was broken.

Then, there was a moment that has stuck with me until today. I was around fourteen years old and in eighth grade. I ran home upset and in tears. I ran straight to the bedroom and sat on the bottom bunk bed and told my younger sister that I wanted to change my name. Kids at school were starting to make fun of my Vietnamese name, "Huyen." They kept calling me "When" while sneering and laughing. So, I told her that moving forward my nickname would be "Kiki," and she and my other sister would have their own nicknames. I wanted so desperately to fit in and not stand out more than we already were with our broken English and burn scars.

During those six years in Sacramento my family and I were living below the poverty line. We could not apply to local welfare benefits, get a driver's license, or get access to health insurance due to our legal status. My father did not speak English, so he only worked odd jobs (such as cleaning people's restrooms, chopping fish at the market, and mowing lawns) to earn money. Before heading to work at the crack of dawn, he would hand me a ten-dollar bill, instructing me to make sure to go to the market after school to get groceries for my sisters and I to cook dinner. Some nights, he made sure my sisters and I got to eat first before he ate whatever was left over. On some weekends I had to go to the flea market with the neighbor to help sell things to earn extra money. There was no such thing as me just being a kid and doing things for fun. Without knowing so, I also assumed the "social worker" role for my family by the time I was fourteen. I was in charge of finding free community resources (e.g., bus tickets, food, used clothes, etc.) and helping my father with tasks such as filling out legal documents, looking for odd jobs, and translating at doctor's appointments. Whatever I did not know how to do, I just had to figure out somehow—even if that meant using the dictionary and searching word by word to sharpen up my English quickly. My father relied on me as his right hand.

I learned at a young age to be resourceful in order to survive. And that constant survival mode put my whole body in a chronic state of anxiety, stress, fear, and hypervigilance. I was worrying about things that a kid should not have to worry about. I often worried if we would have enough food to eat or clothes to wear. I was worried about going under anesthesia and not being able to wake up from that sleep. I was especially worried about not seeing my father post-surgery. After losing my mother at a young age, I also feared suddenly losing my dad. At the time, my father was working long hours, and as a result my sisters and I hardly got a chance to spend quality time together with him. I knew that he had to work, but as a child, not seeing him around as often as I would have liked still made me feel really sad. Since my mother passed away, my father did not really know how to communicate that he cared about me or my mental well-being. He did not say "I love you" or show affection, and as his daughter, that was all I wanted.

My mental health started to deteriorate at the beginning of my junior year of high school. I started to develop stress-induced seizures and depression. One evening, after an argument with my father, I let my emotions get the best of me and impulsively overdosed on my seizure medications. I wanted to end my life because I thought my father did not love me.

I could not have been more wrong.

I woke up to the sight of my father crying, asking if I was okay, and repeatedly saying how sorry he was. At that moment, I knew that I made a terrible mistake. I had never seen him express his emotions or cry about me, so I made the assumption that he did not care. However, he had always shown his love through actions, and I just did not see it. I also did not process that culturally, as a Vietnamese father, he never got a chance to learn how to express his emotions or affection to his children. It was my mother who took care of me when she was alive. I was so in my own world that I did not see that my dear father was suffering too; he needed someone to see his pain too.

That hospitalization after overdosing on my seizure medication woke me up and opened the door for my father and I to start working on our relationship. However, just as we were making progress, our lives took another unexpected turn. One Saturday, I accompanied my father to a local community health clinic for a free medical checkup. I was his translator, so the doctor broke the news to me first. The doctor told me that my father had liver cancer. At that moment, I just froze. I felt like the air just got knocked out of my chest. I asked the doctor if he was lying or if he had made a mistake. All I could think was, how could my dear father, a selfless and hardworking man, get cancer? How could God punish him and us like that? Why us? Nothing made sense at all; I just felt numb.

His condition quickly escalated, and he needed a liver transplant. Because of his undocumented status, the hospital could not put him on the registry for a liver donation. He could not get outpatient treatments like chemotherapy either. All he could access was the emergency room in times of crisis. There were many days when he was in so much pain but insisted that we did not seek help because he feared that we were going to get deported. On those days, all I could do was watch him suffer. Seeing my father in such a vulnerable state was unbearable. I felt helpless, alone, and so angry with the system. My anxiety, depression, and fear intensified as his conditions worsened.

One evening, I could not bear watching my father in pain anymore, so I called 911 to have an ambulance take him to the emergency room. I did not care about the possibility of being deported; I just wanted the doctor to take care of my sick father. His skin was turning yellow from liver failure, and he was losing weight drastically.

I will never forget that evening. In the emergency room, I watched as doctors and nurses rushed to his bed and stuck a long needle into his bone. My father screamed in horror—an image forever imprinted in my mind. One doctor pulled me aside and gently broke the news to me. He shared that my father's potassium level was dangerously high and that he had about two days left to live.

My fragile heart was not prepared, and all I could do was break down and cry. I felt like someone just punched me in the stomach and knocked the air out of me. I could hardly breathe. Despite being in pain and barely talking, my father put on a brave face and muttered to me, "đi về nhà, khóa cửa và đảm bảo rằng may chị em đi học ngày mai" (Go home, lock the door and make sure you and your sisters go to school the next day).

I obeyed my father's words and went home without knowing that it would be my last time seeing his brave face. He passed away at eleven forty-five the next morning, November 10, 2009.

There are not enough words in the English or Vietnamese language to describe the pain I was in. My father was my world. I felt like my whole world was collapsing; he was the only parent I had left, and he was gone. I was devastated and heartbroken. My worst fear had come true.

My sisters and I became orphans. At the time of his death, I was already eighteen years old, so I was legally an adult. Because my siblings (seventeen, thirteen, twelve, and eight years old) were still minors, they became wards of the court, and there were only a few options I had available to explore: I could have either brought them back to Vietnam, adopted them and become their legal guardian, or placed them in the foster care system. None of these choices were viable options. I refused to go back to Vietnam and let all my father's sacrifices be in vain. I knew that I was not in a position at eighteen years old to provide adequate care for my younger siblings. I certainly did not want my sisters to be separated from each other and enter the system.

Through all the chaos, there was one particular lady who was consistently there since the news of my father's diagnosis. I met her when I was fourteen years old while attending a burn camp. During my father's final days, she made a promise to my dad that she would help take care of us. After his passing, she held my hands and helped me plan my father's funeral. After a few months, she and her partner made a decision that changed the trajectory of our lives forever. They decided to legally adopt my younger sisters and became their guardians. By doing that, they ultimately were able to help my sisters get their documentation and most importantly keep all my sisters together under the same roof. Since I was already eighteen, I did not qualify and fell out of the loop; I became a DREAMer without a pathway to citizenship.

Even though losing my father broke my heart, it was during this turbulent time that I witnessed people from all walks of life (e.g., schools, churches, hospitals, and nonprofit organizations) come together to support my sisters and me. These strangers poured their time, energy, resources, and love onto us like we were their family. They did not judge us because of a piece of paper or how we looked—rather, they saw that we were hurting and in need of love. Seeing people showing up for my sisters and I during the most vulnerable time gave me hope again. Their belief in my light and potential gave me hope to believe that everything was going to be okay.

I can rise up from the unbearable pain. Life is still worthy of living.

Rewriting My Story

And so, I mustered up the courage and pushed forward in honor of my parents' sacrifices and my community's kindness. That senior year, I put all my energy and effort into applying to colleges and scholarships. Even with his last words at the emergency room, my father reiterated the importance of obtaining a higher education as the key to escaping poverty. He also knew the harsh reality of being undocumented and a burn survivor—the world might not be fair.

Thanks to the encouragement and support of mentors in the community, I applied to the University of California, Berkeley (UC Berkeley) and was accepted. The day I received my acceptance letter was a moment of immense relief, as if a heavy weight had been lifted off my shoulders. I never would have imagined that I, an undocumented immigrant from Vietnam, would get a chance to learn at one of the best universities in the nation. I felt like my parents were watching over me, providing me with unyielding strength and determination to keep fighting.

Affording school presented another hurdle. In 2010, as an undocumented immigrant student, I did not qualify for federal financial aid or loans. Fortunately, due to my extensive commitments to volunteering in high school, I was able to apply for scholarships that did not require legal status in the United States. This covered my tuition for one academic year at UC Berkeley. Then, in fall 2021, the California DREAM Act passed, granting me (and students like me) access to in-state financial assistance. To make up the remainder of funding that I needed, I juggled multiple part-time jobs and relied on the generous fundraising efforts of my community. Without their unwavering support, I would not have been able to graduate from UC Berkeley.

It was at UC Berkeley where I encountered fellow undocumented Asian students, mirroring my own journey. For the first time, I found myself amid a community that understood the intricate interplay of fear and uncertainty tied to being undocumented in America, particularly within the context of Asian identity. I immediately felt a sense of connection like I was not alone. I started to realize that the common theme through all my traumas, pain, and loss was my deep desire to be heard and seen and to be accepted for all the layers of my identity. Through the unconditional support, encouragement, and love from various people (friends, professors, and staff) in different spaces across campus, I started to feel safe to exist and be my authentic self. I started to get out of my survival mode and heal; I started to shine.

And I knew in my heart that I wanted to create a safe and brave space like that for others.

I graduated from UC Berkeley with my degree in social welfare in 2014 and went on to pursue my master's in social work with a concentration in community mental health at California State University, East Bay. In February 2022, my dream came true. I remember walking out of the exam room, holding that score report from the California Board of Behavioral Sciences with one simple word that changed my life, "PASS." I immediately ran to the restroom and just wept. I had achieved something that was only in my wildest dreams as an undocumented immigrant. At that moment, I felt my parents' spirit surrounding me, letting me know that they were proud of me.

I knew from that point onward that a new door full of possibilities had just opened up. I was more determined than ever to leverage my professional expertise and knowledge as a licensed clinical social worker (LCSW) to elevate and amplify the voices of my communities.

Being an UndocuAsian Therapist: Supporting UndocuAsians in Mental Health

In 2022, I took the first step toward creating a safe space for individuals like myself by launching my own private practice: VOice Psychotherapy. My goal is to provide a welcoming environment where people can feel affirmed, understood, and embraced for all aspects of their identity, especially those whom society has marginalized—due to our legal status, skin color, or socioeconomic background.

I knew from my own lived experiences and from hearing the stories of other undocumented friends that there are cultural stigmas that make it challenging for undocuAsians (undocumented Asians) to speak up and talk about mental health. We were often told not to cause a scene or talk about taboo topics such as mental health or immigration status in order to "save face" for our families. Many of us undocuAsians grew up suppressing or dismissing our emotions and needs. As a result, our voices have become silent, and consequently we may end up struggling with mental health symptoms such as anxiety and depression. Even when undocumented Asians muster the courage to seek help, it is challenging for them to find Asian mental health providers who can relate and understand the complex immigrant experience.

Since 2022, I have been partnering with organizations nationwide to lead mental wellness support groups for undocumented API (Asian and Pacific Islander) individuals. The purpose of the group is to cultivate a nonjudgmental space that encourages undocuAsian individuals to show up as their authentic selves. Each group has between eight and fifteen participants from all across the United States. Throughout the six weeks, the themes discussed are chosen by participants to prioritize their voices and needs. We delve into various topics, including healing from intergenerational trauma, managing uncertainty, dating while undocumented, self-care tools, navigating work/career, setting boundaries with families, the "good immigrant" narrative, and more. At the end of each support group, participants frequently express feeling less isolated and more hopeful after connecting with others who share similar experiences.

I believe that people heal people. As someone who is also directly impacted by these issues, I can relate to the majority of things that participants share in the group. I can offer compassion, empathy, validation, and concrete resources (if requested). Without a doubt, facilitating these mental wellness support groups has been one of the most rewarding experiences of my life, and I plan to continue doing so. Every week, I leave the group feeling awed by my community's capacity to navigate life's obstacles with such radical joy, softness, and strength. They are determined to center their well-being and continue their healing journey despite living within a system that was not created with their needs in mind.

Rebirth: Rising from Ashes

If I was to go back in time, I would not change a thing—even if it meant never experiencing the pain of being burnt, the challenges of being an undocumented Asian immigrant in this country, and the loss of both my parents.

One of the hardest lessons I learned was that even though I did not have control over my immigration and childhood traumas, I do have a CHOICE over my healing. Nothing can justify the pain, trauma, and injustice I have experienced AND at the same time, being fixated on trying to find the answer to the question "Why me?" just holds me back in time and causes me more suffering. And I do not deserve that.

I can grieve while giving myself permission to let go of things I cannot control in order to move forward. I do not have to approve or like the bad things that have happened in order to radically accept the current reality. There was a chain of events, and there were causes for everything, even if I do not know why. This process is not easy or linear either. It took me over a decade to give myself grace and self-compassion to sit with grief, and some days it ebbs and flows.

I firmly believe that mental wellness does not mean being in a perpetual state of happiness. It is not about avoiding feelings of sadness, anger, or fear. Rather, it revolves around an individual's willingness to sit with and tolerate the discomfort and uncertainty in life. It is about one's decision to choose to coexist with multiple contradicting emotions without taking actions that lead to further suffering. If there is one lesson I have learned so far in this short life is that even when the external world is not conducive to my mental well-being, I still have the power to create my own internal system of safety to reduce the impact of harm or injustices that may come my way.

I take immense pride in the person I have become. I am a manifestation of my deceased parents' wildest dreams and legacy. Through it all, I have risen from the ashes to be my own protector while advocating for others in need. I recognize that the very qualities I once struggled with are the ones that allow my clients to connect with me, reassuring them that they are not alone. I have been there and I stand firmly by their side. By fully embracing my authentic self, I am empowering others to do the same and helping them realize that their voice and needs are valid and important.

No matter what the future holds, I will continue to use my educational and professional privilege as an undocumented Asian licensed therapist in this country to walk side by side with my people and support them in their mental wellness journey. Together, we will not only survive but *heal* and *thrive* in this life.

11

Recollecting Resistance

A Retrospection on UPLIFT's UndocuAsian Community Organizing During the DACA Era and Trump Administration

SIYUE LENA WANG AND MADISON VILLANUEVA

We write this chapter in 2024 as we approach the twelfth anniversary of the Deferred Action for Childhood Arrivals (DACA) program and the upcoming presidential election. The immigrant rights movement has had to adapt to seismic political shifts through different presidential administrations, from the Obama administration's implementation of DACA while simultaneously deporting record numbers of migrants to the Trump administration's openly xenophobic and persistent implementation of anti-immigrant rhetoric and policies. Throughout these periods of upheaval, undocumented Asian (undocuAsian) organizers have taken part in the immigrant rights movement and mobilized in larger numbers than has been portrayed in the media. We dedicate this chapter in honor of UPLIFT and its valiant efforts to organize undocumented Asian and Pacific Islanders (undocuAPIs) from the beginning of the DACA era and through the Trump administration. This grassroots community organization was led by undocuAPI youth in the greater Los Angeles area who mobilized to engage in immigrant rights work through advocacy, community outreach, raising awareness, and leadership development. Drawing on Chicana feminist *pláticas* as a methodology (Fierros and Delgado Bernal 2016), we, coauthors Lena and Madison, engaged in a series of informal conversations to recount our lived experiences as formerly undocumented individuals and as core members of UPLIFT. Through these pláticas, we validate and value our lived experiences and create a space of "reciprocity, vulnerability, and reflexivity" (Fierros and Delgado Bernal 2016, 114). This process allowed us to co-construct knowledge and theorize our interconnected struggles, while examining the structural conditions that continue to tokenize, diminish, and exploit undocumented immigrant youth and their movements.

The term "undocuAPI" is central to UPLIFT's mission—rooted in inclusivity and visibility for all undocumented API immigrants. While the term acknowledges the historical erasure of undocumented API communities, we recognize that the API umbrella can itself obscure the distinct experiences of Pacific Islanders, who navigate unique migration histories, contexts, and systemic challenges. Though "undocuAPI" serves as a political term that envisions inclusivity and solidarity across API communities, we primarily use "undocuAsian" throughout this chapter. This choice reflects our own backgrounds—Lena as Chinese and Madison as Filipino—and our awareness that our experiences differ from those of undocumented Pacific Islanders. We seek to avoid conflating these distinct realities and erasing the struggles of PI immigrants. We use "undocu-API" only in the context of UPLIFT's work to acknowledge the presence of Pacific Islander–identifying members and the organization's commitment to fostering a broad, inclusive coalition. While Pacific Islanders have historically been underrepresented in undocumented advocacy spaces, UPLIFT has taken steps to include meaningful participation and representation of PI undocumented youth within its organizing efforts. We also briefly mention the term in relation to the Dream Summer Fellowship program created by the UCLA Labor Center and which is a national leadership program for immigrant youth and allies to develop as social justice leaders that has organized undocuAPI youth.

This chapter begins by contextualizing UPLIFT's history within the undocumented youth movement, followed by a critical analysis that addresses the invisibility of undocuAsians. We conceptualize care and inclusivity as the foundational pillars and framework for UPLIFT's work to combat and cope with erasure. Last, we reflect on the challenges faced by the movement and highlight promising lessons for future generations who continue to fight for undocumented students and intersectional organizing against multiple forms of oppression.[1] Throughout the narrative, healing and care are emphasized as fundamental to the relationship between coauthors, epitomizing our organizing and ideological approach within UPLIFT to foster community, personhood, and mutual healing.

Our Story of UPLIFT: Intersecting Journeys in UndocuAsian Organizing

Our journeys to finding UPLIFT began years apart, but within higher education institutions that provided a point of connection for individuals seeking resources, community, and support. Madison's exposure to undocumented student advocacy began at the 2010 Immigrant Youth Empowerment Conference (IYEC), an annual event put together by IDEAS, the undocumented student organization at UCLA. This was a key year in immigration policy with the federal DREAM Act gaining traction.[2] The federal bill proposed a convoluted pathway to citizenship for a select group of undocumented youth who met eligibility requirements based on age, criminal background checks, and higher education or military service. Mere weeks prior to the conference, IDEAS experienced the loss of two champions and alumni, Tam Tran and Cinthya Felix, groundbreaking pioneers for the undocumented youth movement, some of the first undocumented students to enter graduate school, and nationally recognized advocates of the federal DREAM Act (UCLA Institute for Research on Labor and Employment n.d.). They spoke openly about their immigration status, despite the risks it posed, and eventually traveled to Washington, D.C., where Tam testified before Congress on behalf of the federal DREAM Act. Part of the IYEC dedicated time to commemorating them and raising funds for their families. Seeing a community of undocumented people coming together to both build power and provide tangible support in times of hardship opened Madison's eyes to a different way of navigating her status.

Madison continued to attend the IYEC in subsequent years, gaining information on resources and policy updates. One such resource was the Dream Summer Fellowship, a nationwide program placing undocumented youth in internship/fellowship opportunities at nonprofit organizations to participate in immigrant rights work. In 2013, Madison was accepted into the program as part of its undocuAPI cohort, which matched undocuAPI interns to API-serving nonprofit organizations to build the capacity for immigrant rights work in API communities. Although her experiences at the IYEC introduced Madison to the immigrant youth movement, Dream Summer gave her the opportunity to participate alongside other undocuAsians. Madison described it as a political awakening that allowed her to build relationships with other undocuAsian youth and led her to many pathways where she advocated for herself and her family. Another such resource was ASPIRE LA, which Madison joined after her Dream Summer internship to continue staying connected with members of the undocuAPI community. The Los Angeles–based grassroots organization was led by undocuAPI youth and would eventually change their name to UPLIFT.

UPLIFT was founded in 2010 as ASPIRE UCLA by an undocumented Asian student on campus who sought a space where he did not feel like a "minority within a minority." The namesake originated from ASPIRE, a pan-Asian undocumented youth organization in the San Francisco Bay Area. IDEAS and ASPIRE provided guidance to ASPIRE UCLA in its nascent stages. By 2012, the desire to reach more undocuAPIs led to the decision to transition out of the UCLA campus and into the greater Los Angeles area. A new name accompanied the change: ASPIRE LA. Asian Americans Advancing Justice Southern California (AAAJ SoCal) housed the budding organization, with one staffer overseeing the activities before hiring a second part-time staff member in 2014. The staff organizer, typically selected from UPLIFT's general membership, was integral in executing the mission as well as facilitating political education for members and coordinating campaigns. The next name change to UPLIFT was formalized in 2016 after members further carved out the identity of the group. The organizational pillars were identified as follows:

1) Uplifting UndocuAPI Narratives
2) Leadership Development
3) Community Engagement
4) Membership Support

Members of the organization played a significant role in amplifying undocuAsian experiences through advocacy. In sharing their lived experiences with AAAJ SoCal, their stories were brought to legislative spaces. As members grew in their leadership and political consciousness throughout the years, they brought their stories to the media and to legislative visits themselves, advocating for policies like Deferred Action for Parents of Americans and Lawful Permanent Residents (DAPA), Health4All, AB 2000, and AB 60.[3] This series of federal and state legislation aimed to extend legal protection for undocumented immigrant parents, ensure health access for all Californians, and provide in-state tuition for undocumented youth. UPLIFT also participated in actions as members of ICE Out of LA, a coalition of grassroots and nonprofit organizations in Los Angeles that worked to combat the deportation and criminalization of immigrants.[4] Members mobilized around these efforts because it reflected their values in increasing inclusivity and protections for those marginalized in the undocumented immigrant community, like their parents (DAPA, Health4All, AB 60), those with nontraditional educational pathways (AB 2000), and those impacted by the criminal justice system (ICE Out of LA).

Beyond advocacy, members connected with other immigrant rights and Asian-serving organizations to highlight the intersections of these communities. Key partnerships with larger nonprofits provided the opportunity to meet with other undocuAsians around the country. In 2014, a historic gathering took place involving forty-five individuals from three undocuAsian organizations—UPLIFT, ASPIRE, and Revolutionizing Asian American Immigrant Stories on the East Coast (RAISE) from New York—along with individuals representing the National AAPI DACA Collaborative. The AAPI DACA Collaborative was composed of nine organizations that have decades-long track records of serving Asian American and Pacific Islander communities, including Asian Americans Advancing Justice affiliate organizations in Washington, D.C., San Francisco, Chicago, and Los Angeles; Asian American Legal Defense and Education Fund; National Korean American Service & Education Consortium (and its affiliates Korean Resource Center in Los Angeles and Korean Resource and Cultural Center in Chicago); and South Asian Americans Leading Together. The gathering in Oakland, California, was the first of its kind that aimed to build a nationwide undocuAsian network. These pioneering groups continued to convene in subsequent years, partnering with preexisting conferences that afforded them their own track. The next gathering took place in 2015 at the Asian Pacific American Labor Alliance (APALA) Convention in San Diego, then in March 2016 at the Asian Americans Advancing Justice Conference in Los Angeles; and in December 2016 at the National Immigration Integration Conference in Nashville, Tennessee. By the time of this final gathering, President Trump had been elected for his first term in office, sparking an urgency among the organizations for federal protections for the vulnerable immigrant population. In 2017, UndocuBlack Network, a nonprofit organization for and led by undocumented Black individuals, and NAKASEC brought together the undocumented Black and Asian communities—including UPLIFT—to advocate for a "clean" Dream Act in Washington, D.C. Another historic gathering, the multiracial front advocated for an updated version of the 2010 policy of the same name that removed the language of criminalizing provisions and instead provided language for inclusive protections, especially for the two often marginalized groups.

With origins in student organizations, UPLIFT members went to universities across California to simultaneously raise awareness of the undocuAsian population and recruit members. Madison returned to UCLA's IYEC several times in hopes of recruiting new members in the same manner that she had been recruited. At the 2019 conference, Madison and Lena's paths intersected. Feeling empowered by the community, Lena became an active member of UPLIFT and soon joined Madison in cofacilitating workshops. An opportune presentation by the two at the 2019 Keeping the Dream Alive Conference at Sacramento State University sparked a yearlong partnership with Immigrants Rising, an immigrant rights organization where another UPLIFT member worked. Envisioning institutional inclusivity for undocuAsian students in higher education, Madison and Lena engaged in community-centered focus groups with undocuAsian students and educators throughout California, which inspired cowriting the practitioner's guide titled "Increasing Inclusivity for Undocumented Asian and Pacific Islanders in Higher Education" that drew national attention and more than a thousand views (Immigrants Rising 2024). This project reinvigorated discussions about serving diverse undocumented students in higher education. Given the urgent need from educators and higher education institutions, this project extended to a series of educators' gatherings in the summer of 2021, which bridged practices, spaces, and practitioners into holistic support for all undocumented students.

In the same year, however, AAAJ SoCal implemented an organizational restructuring that terminated UPLIFT's staff, effectively severing the group's access to funding, meeting spaces, and—most importantly—opportunities to engage in timely policy advocacy with legislators and coalitions. We explore the implications later on in the chapter. Members continued meeting online during the COVID-19 lockdown to host activities on storytelling, art, and movie screenings and to explore recovering the organization by finding a fiscal sponsor. However, the process proved to be too taxing for members as they balanced the demands of full-time jobs and supporting their families.

Dual Marginalization: The Invisibility of
UndocuAsians in the Immigrant Youth Movement

Although the racialization of immigration as a Latinx issue by the public contributes to the invisibility of undocuAsians, the racialization of Asian Americans as a "model minority" plays a hefty role as well (Kim and Yellow Horse 2018). Originating during the civil rights era, this mythical trope has been weaponized to position Asian Americans in opposition to other communities of color and their efforts toward racial justice. Despite polls showing that Asian Americans have increasingly voted progressive (Schaeffer 2023), conservative Asian Americans continue to be a vocal presence. This political positioning invisibilizes Asian Americans in social justice movements, and this phenomenon has translated to undocuAsians in the immigrant rights movement. Both activists and undocumented immigrants are erased within the Asian American community since these contradict the stereotype of the "law-abiding model minority."

On an interpersonal level, we explored the ostracization within our coethnic community due to disparities in immigration and socioeconomic status. In our Asian communities, being undocumented is often perceived as an individual failure rather than a systemic problem. The fault is placed on individuals for failing to go through proper channels to obtain legal status, rather than on convoluted immigration policies that are intentionally designed to allow only a select few to earn permanent residency. UndocuAsians typically respond by practicing nondisclosure of immigration status to avoid exclusion, shame, microaggressions, hostility, and threats (Buenavista 2018). Paradoxically, this feeds into the model minority myth and the erasure of undocuAsians. When individuals do disclose their status, especially within the public arena as part of the immigrant rights movement, undocuAsians face the risk of being shunned from our own communities. Having sacrificed belonging in our communities exacerbates the frustration that comes with being overlooked as a minority in the immigrant rights movement. The dual marginalization from our Asian American and undocumented immigrant communities prompted the creation of politicized spaces like UPLIFT to regain a sense of belonging, community, and power (Dao 2017).

Critical Consciousness, Transformative Resistance,
and Intersectional Organizing

UPLIFT catalyzes the development of critical consciousness among its members enabling them to recognize the structural forces shaping their lives and empowering them to take collective action to transform the unjust conditions immigrants and people of color confront on a regular basis. The organization helps members understand that undocumented status is not an individual failure but a systemic one—a sociopolitical condition constructed by the U.S. government to keep immigrants from living their dreams. This system traps immigrants in a state of marginalization, vulnerability, and demoralization through pervasive border spectacles and criminalization. UPLIFT also promotes political education that links migration, U.S. imperialism, immigration policies, and the livelihoods of undocumented immigrants to make sense of our migration stories within the context of national and global politics. This has helped us to unlearn the shame and stigma, revealing that our migration was a result of globalization, and our legal status was a consequence of racist immigration policies designed to exploit our labor. This shift in perspective, from viewing our situation as an individual failure to recognizing it as a systemic failure, was life-changing, as it highlighted the deliberate roles of white supremacy and capitalism.

This shift in critical consciousness allows UPLIFT members to identify the sociopolitical structures and policies shaping their experiences to reclaim our agency and dignity. This sense of self-efficacy translates into a growing responsibility for collective struggles and collective actions for social change (Solórzano and Delgado Bernal 2001). We are worthy of this country because we are members of this society. Our allegiance is to our people and our undocumented community, and we want to build a better world because we deserve it. UPLIFT solidifies this critique of oppression and desire for social justice through direct actions, advocacy, and narrative shifts within the immigrant youth movement. This transformative resistance is fostered by key role models, who share unique undocuAsian identities and a commitment to social justice. Madison, for instance, became a transformational mentor for Lena by using her experiences to guide Lena's political identity development and empower her to create social and institutional changes through teaching, researching, and community building. The seeds of critical consciousness and transformative resistance are further nourished by engaging with Black feminist scholars like Kimberlé Crenshaw and Angela Davis to underscore the interconnectedness of immigrant struggles with other communities of color. Being radical means addressing the root causes of all forms of oppression; being politically radical means we envision something better for everyone—not only beyond the confines of citizenship, but toward the creation of more just and inclusive communities. From this relational understanding of immigration, surveillance, and policing UPLIFT participated in actions like "Not One More Deportation," "ICE Out of LA," and collaborations with the Undocu-Black Network including legislative visits, rallies, and community gatherings. This intersectional analysis of shared and nuanced struggles translates into concrete acts of support for broader communities facing multiple layers of social marginalization, thus fostering an intersectional organizing framework that motivates UPLIFT to build coalitions and solidarity across racial, ethnic, and citizenship boundaries (Terriquez, Brenes, and Lopez 2018).

Organizing in the Nonprofit-Industrial Complex:
Tokenization and Activist Burnout

Despite UPLIFT's radical intersectional approach and commitment to transformative justice, it is nonetheless embedded within a nonprofit-industrial complex that operates under neoliberal ideologies and organizational structures. This complex, as described by Claire Dunning (2024), is structurally dependent on government and private funding, making it far from independent and often serving to maintain the status quo and control social justice movements. As Audre Lorde said, "The master's tools will never dismantle the master's house" (1984). This funding structure inherently undermines the radical movements sponsored by nonprofit organizations, as they operate within and are influenced by the unjust socioeconomic structures and ideologies that create inequalities in the first place. UPLIFT, as a grassroots youth organization, is not immune to the influence of business-oriented nonprofit organizations. It was housed under AAAJ SoCal and the project of one of their staffers, who was also a member of UPLIFT, and it consequently functioned as an informal program of the nonprofit organization. Activities were limited by the rules of AAAJ SoCal, and the burden of navigating this bureaucracy fell on core organizers of UPLIFT. Having no formal relationship with AAAJ SoCal led to having no protections for UPLIFT. This loose, contingent relationship eventually collapsed when AAAJ SoCal faced a financial crisis and disbanded its immigration advocacy team, simultaneously severing ties with UPLIFT. This decision reflected a lack of investment by one of the most influential national Asian American civil rights organizations, bolstering the feeling that immigrant rights was not a priority issue area, thus stranding UPLIFT and undermining seven years of advocacy work. This devaluation of UPLIFT and its members' well-being speaks to the tokenization of undocuAsian youth leaders.

All UPLIFT members, except for one full-time and one part-time staffer, were volunteers. The physical and emotional labor was valued by larger Asian / Asian American organizations only because many UPLIFT members were organizing for free. Immigrant rights work is personal but oftentimes underappreciated and rarely paid. Our lived experiences become our labor, then our labor becomes personal. When our work is not supported by institutions, it feels like an attack on our personhood and our community. UPLIFT's leaders dedicated their lives to advocacy, while AAAJ SoCal simply "let go" of the liaison team and the programs that UPLIFT members had invested their college and professional lives into. This tokenization of undocumented young adults for institutional and policy changes, without sustainable investment and genuine care, left many UPLIFT organizers burnt out and hurt. Meanwhile, the stall of comprehensive immigration reform, the rise of anti-immigrant sentiment, and the use of immigration as a political pawn in elections continued to accumulate anger, disappointment, and burnout among generations of youth leaders.

"We Need to Take Care of Each Other and Ourselves": Collective Care and Healing Toward Liberatory Praxis

Throughout our conversations in writing this piece, Madison emphasized the importance of "taking care of the community," a pillar of the UPLIFT model of organizing that includes membership support. As we begin to theorize the meanings of being an undocumented and Asian organizer and as we contemplate lessons for future generations, we realize this plática reignites the need to share our history and lessons. We cannot allow the undocumented youth movement to be reduced to simply obtaining college resources. Our identities and experiences stay with us, demonstrating that this is a political issue involving politicized identities. Our struggle does not end when we attain individual success in higher education. If undocumented people do not have the foresight to organize for what comes after college, the movement is going to die.

Although this conversation and chapter are seminal in reclaiming UPLIFT's legacy, the burnout and trauma from the movement and nonprofit organizing prevent great leaders like Madison and other members from proactively sharing UPLIFT stories. Madison explained that if she was more healed, she would feel more ready to share these experiences. She wants to get to a point where she can tell the story of UPLIFT more publicly and strategically, but there is still so much trauma to process. Many others feel the same, which is why they are no longer part of the movement. But that's why we have to care for each other. The condition of possibility for this chapter is because we are doing this together, with each other. The practice of collective care and healing begins by recognizing that self-care is self-preservation and an act of resistance. Despite all circumstances, we find joy in life, in our body-mind-soul, and in our relationships with one another. It is through these radical acts of collective care and healing that transformation happens within us as individuals and through us as UPLIFT.

Conclusion

The story of UPLIFT that we have recounted in this chapter is a testament to both the power and the perils of organizing within the nonprofit-industrial complex. It reveals how radical immigrant youth movements, despite their vision for justice, are often constrained by bureaucratic structures that prioritize institutional survival over grassroots transformation. The dismantling of UPLIFT by a larger nonprofit organization reflects a broader pattern in which undocumented organizers, particularly undocuAsian activists, are tokenized for their labor but denied the long-term investment necessary for sustainable movement building. These structural vulnerabilities were further exacerbated by the first Trump administration, which openly sought to dismantle immigrant protections and expand the criminalization of undocumented communities. In this hostile landscape, the labor of undocumented organizers remains both essential and undervalued, leading to systemic exploitation and burnout.

Yet, even within these oppressive conditions, transformation remains possible. UPLIFT's legacy reminds us that true resistance is not only about legislative victories or policy changes but also about how we reconfigure ourselves in moments of crisis. If we are to continue the fight for immigrant justice, we must critically engage with the structures that limit us while simultaneously cultivating new ways of organizing that prioritize sustainability, healing, and collective care. The exhaustion and burnout experienced by many UPLIFT members underscore the need for movements that nourish the spirit as much as they challenge oppressive systems. In a world that seeks to dehumanize immigrants, healing becomes a revolutionary act—a way to reclaim our dignity, honor our experiences, and sustain our spirits as we fight for justice. Healing and collective care are not separate from organizing; they are the foundation of it. Our collective resistance is rooted in the radical love and care we show for one another, the relationships we build, and the ways we humanize each other in the face of systemic dehumanization. By centering collective care as a form of resistance, UPLIFT modeled a movement that prioritized the well-being of its members alongside policy advocacy, offering a powerful counternarrative to mainstream immigrant rights frameworks.

At the same time, we must confront the daunting realities we face. The nonprofit-industrial complex and first Trump-era policies continue to create significant obstacles, from funding constraints to intensified criminalization. The dual marginalization of undocuAsians—within both the immigrant rights movement and their own communities—further complicates the fight for justice. The question now is not just how we resist but how we do so without reproducing the very systems that exhaust and exploit us. How do we build movements that are both sustainable and radical? How do we organize beyond the limits of nonprofit dependency while recognizing the material realities that make alternatives difficult to sustain?

This is a crucial moment to organize and learn from UPLIFT's example as we enter a new phase of resistance. The previous and current Trump administration's attacks on immigrants are part of a broader system of fascism, imperialism, and racist anti-immigrant campaigns that seek to divide and control us. But UPLIFT reminds us that transformation is possible. By embracing intersectional organizing, critical consciousness, and transformative resistance, we can challenge the systems that seek to erase us. As we navigate this moment of crisis and possibility, we must commit to resisting not only policies that oppress but also the frameworks that limit our liberation. UPLIFT's legacy demands that we continue building movements that are as sustainable as they are transformative. This is not just about fighting for a place in this country—it is about envisioning and creating a world where we are all free.

Acknowledgments

We extend our deepest gratitude to the community members and mentors who believed in our work, investing their time, wisdom, and care. Your support and feedback have strengthened this chapter and deepened our commitment to uplifting the voices at its core. We recognize all UPLIFT members, especially leaders Anthony Ng, Madeleine Villanueva, RJ Ronquillo, and Set Ronquillo, whose contributions are central to the undocuAsian movement and the fruition of this chapter. Their labor, vision, and resilience have paved the way for meaningful change through their lifelong dedication to organizing, immigrant rights advocacy, and radical transformation. We also honor Dr. Tracy Lachica Buenavista, whose tireless support of the undocuAPI movement since its inception has been instrumental. Her advocacy made this chapter possible. A special thanks to Dr. Kevin Escudero and Dr. Rachel Freeman-Wong, the editors of this volume, for their thoughtful engagement, critical insight, and patience in working with us during challenging times. This book marks a historic milestone as the first to honor and visualize undocuAsian resistance, and we are deeply honored to be part of it. We are grateful for their dedication and efforts in making this work possible. This chapter reflects the collective knowledge, resilience, and vision shared with us by mentors, peers, and community members. May it be the beginning of a broader recognition of undocuAsian youth organizers, with more to come as the fight continues. United, we believe the fight endures, and together, we are one.

REFERENCES

American Immigration Council. 2024. "The Dream Act: An Overview." Last modified May 8, 2024. https://www.americanimmigrationcouncil.org/research/dream-act-overview.

Buenavista, Tracy L. 2018. "Model (Undocumented) Minorities and 'Illegal' Immigrants: Centering Asian Americans and US Carcerality in Undocumented Student Discourse." *Race Ethnicity and Education* 21 (1): 78–91. https://doi.org/10.1080/13613324.2016.1248823.

California Department of Motor Vehicles. 2025. "AB60 Driver's Licenses." https://www.dmv.ca.gov/portal/driver-licenses-identification-cards/assembly-bill-ab-60-driver-licenses/.

California State University. 2015. "AB540 and AB2000 California Nonresident Tuition Exemption." https://www.calstate.edu/attend/student-services/resources-for-undocumented-students/Documents/AB540_AB2000_Form.pdf.

Collins, Patricia Hill. 2000. *Black Feminist Thought: Knowledge, Consciousness, and the Politics of Empowerment*. 2nd ed. Routledge.

Crenshaw, Kimberlé W. 1990. "Mapping the Margins: Intersectionality, Identity Politics, and Violence Against Women of Color." *Stanford Law Review* 43: 1241–1299.

Dao, Loan Thi. 2017. "Out and Asian: How Undocu/DACAmented Asian Americans and Pacific Islander Youth Navigate Dual Liminality in the Immigrant Rights Movement." *Societies* 7 (3): 17. https://doi.org/10.3390/soc7030017.

Dunning, Claire. 2024. "The Origins of the Nonprofit Industrial Complex." Law and Political Economy Project, May 29. https://lpeproject.org/blog/the-origins-of-the-non profit-industrial-complex/.

Fierros, Cindy, and Dolores Delgado Bernal. 2016. "Vamos a Platicar: The Contours of Pláticas as Chicana/Latina Feminist Methodology." *Chicana/Latina Studies* 15 (2): 98–121.

Health Access. 2023. "Who We Are." Last accessed June 15, 2024. https://health-access.org

ICE Out of LA Coalition. n.d. "About ICE Out of LA Coalition." http://iceoutofla.org/en /about-us/.

Immigrants Rising. 2024. "Increasing Inclusivity for UndocuAPI Students on Your Campus." January. https://immigrantsrising.org/wp-content/uploads/Immigrants-Rising _Increasing-Inclusivity-for-UndocuAPI-Students-on-Your-Campus.pdf.

Kim, Soo Mee, and Aggie J. Yellow Horse. 2018. "Undocumented Asians, Left in the Shadows." *Contexts* 17 (4): 80–85. https://doi.org/10.1177/1536504211881287.

Kunreuther, Frances, and Sean Thomas-Breitfeld. 2015. *The New Now: Working Together for Social Change.* https://buildingmovement.org/wp-content/uploads/2019/08/The-New -Now-Working-Together-for-Social-Change.pdf.

Lorde, Audre. 1984. "The Master's Tools Will Never Dismantle the Master's House." In *Sister Outsider: Essays and Speeches.* Crossing Press.

Schaeffer, Katherine. 2023. "Asian Voters in the U.S. Tend to Be Democratic, but Vietnamese American Voters Are an Exception." Pew Research Center, May 25. https://www.pewresearch.org/short-reads/2023/05/25/asian-voters-in-the-u-s-tend-to -be-democratic-but-vietnamese-american-voters-are-an-exception/.

Solórzano, Daniel G., and Dolores Delgado Bernal. 2001. "Examining Transformational Resistance Through a Critical Race and Latcrit Theory Framework: Chicana and Chicano Students in an Urban Context." *Urban Education* 36 (3): 308–343.

Terriquez, Veronica. 2015. "Intersectional Mobilization, Social Movement Spillover, and Queer Youth Leadership in the Immigrant Rights Movement." *Social Problems* 62: 343–362.

Terriquez, Veronica, Tizoc Brenes, and Abdiel Lopez. 2018. "Intersectionality as a Multipurpose Collective Action Frame: The Case of the Undocumented Youth Movement." *Ethnicities* 18 (2): 260–276. https://doi.org/10.1177/1468796817752558.

UCLA Institute for Research on Labor and Employment. n.d. "Tam Tran '06 and Cinthya Felix '07." Our Stories, Our Impact. Accessed June 30, 2024. https://ourstoriesourimpact .irle.ucla.edu/tam-tran-and-cinthya-felix/.

U.S. Department of Homeland Security. 2017. "Deferred Action for Parents of Americans and Lawful Permanent Residents Recession Memo ('DAPA')." June 15. https://www.dhs .gov/publication/deferred-action-parents-americans-and-lawful-permanent -residents-recession-memo-dapa.

NOTES

1. Intersectional organizing is rooted in Black feminist theory of intersectionality, as explained by Crenshaw (1990) and Collins (2000). This theory describes how multiple forms of oppression and power intersect and interlock to shape the unique experiences of individuals at the intersections of these identities. Intersectional organizing

is a strategy that centers the experiences and leadership of people affected by these multiple systems of oppression (Kunreuther and Thomas-Breitfeld 2015). An intersectional approach to social movement has also been theorized by Terriquez to serve multiple functions: diagnosing issues, motivating action, and bridging different social movements.

2. The Development, Relief, and Education for Alien Minors (DREAM) Act proposes to grant U.S. citizenship to undocumented students or those who entered the country while still children. It was introduced in Congress in 2001. Dreamers like Tam Tran and Cinthya Felix were the first groups of students advocating for this bill (American Immigration Council 2024).

3. Following DACA, the Obama administration announced the DAPA program in November 2014 to extend deferred action status to unauthorized immigrants who have lived in the United States since January 2010 and whose children were either American citizens or lawful permanent residents. This executive action was immediately challenged in court and rescinded by the secretary of the Department of Homeland Security, John F. Kelly, on June 15, 2017 (U.S. Department of Homeland Security 2017).

   The Health4All campaign is aimed at expanding access to health care for all Californians, regardless of immigration status. Through a decade-long coalition with the California Immigrant Policy Center and over 150 organizations, several milestones have been achieved under this initiative. In 2016, California provided full-scope Medi-Cal benefits to all low-income children, regardless of immigration status. This was extended in 2020 to young adults ages nineteen to twenty-five and in 2022 to adults fifty and older. The most recent expansion, starting in 2024, allows all income-eligible individuals to access Medi-Cal, making California the first state to offer such comprehensive benefits to undocumented older adults (Health Access 2023).

   AB 2000, signed into law in California in 2014, expands the eligibility criteria for in-state tuition to more students under AB 540. AB 2000 amended the eligibility criteria to the attainment of three years' worth of high school credits from a California high school and a total of three or more years of attendance in California elementary or secondary schools, or a combination of those schools (California State University 2015).

   AB 60, signed into law in 2013 by Governor Brown, directs the Department of Motor Vehicles (DMV) to issue driver's licenses to any eligible California residents, regardless of immigration status. AB 60 represents an enormous victory for immigrant communities as it allows undocumented adults to obtain a valid driver's license and state ID (California Department of Motor Vehicles 2025).

4. The ICE Out of LA Coalition (n.d.) consists of diverse community members from Los Angeles County, united against deportations and the criminalization of migrants. They aim to promote full civil and human rights through an open-source campaign using various innovative tactics.

Epilogue

RACHEL FREEMAN-WONG
KEVIN ESCUDERO

As the contributors to this edited volume, *UndocuAsians: Lived Experiences and Social Movement Activism Across the Diaspora*, discuss in their chapters, the everyday experiences of Asian undocumented communities are multifaceted and consist of myriad strategies for navigating and resisting racist and xenophobic systems. While public narratives often focus on the experiences of Latinx undocumented immigrant communities, Asian undocumented immigrant community experiences warrant further attention (Alcantar et al. 2024; Chavez 2008). Further still, the heterogeneity within the Asian undocumented immigrant community has often been underexamined. Researchers have estimated that approximately 11 percent of the 11.2 million undocumented immigrants residing in the United States today (~1,204,000 people) were born in countries across Asia, with the largest populations hailing from India, the Philippines, and China (Van Hook, Gelatt, and Soto 2023).

While undocumented immigrants face many similar institutionalized forms of discrimination, it is important to examine the nexus of race/ethnicity and immigration status. In particular, scholarship has shown that undocumented immigrants from certain racial and/or ethnic groups face particular forms of oppression including Black and Latinx communities being deported at higher rates than their immigrant peers (Farrell-Bryan and Peacock 2022). Some researchers attribute these disparate rates to anti-Black and anti-Latinx bias in policing practices and immigration enforcement ideologies (Golash-Boza 2018). Related, while a great deal of research on this topic has explored the experiences of Latinx undocumented immigrant communities, a growing body of scholarship has begun to explore Asian undocumented immigrant communities' navigation of everyday life and resistance to oppressive systems (Bjorklund 2018; Buenavista 2012, 2018; Chan 2010; Escudero 2020; Kim and Yellow Horse 2018). In doing so, this research has built upon previous work on the racialization of illegality by considering the impact of this approach when examining the lives of immigrants from different racial/ethnic groups. In line with this emerging area of scholarship, *UndocuAsians* sheds much needed light on the particular intersections of being Asian and an undocumented immigrant in the United States. For example, describing the nuances of this particular experience, contributor Tracy Lachica Buenavista explored how research frequently explains the underrepresentation of Asian undocumented immigrant voices as a reflection of Asian undocumented community members' cultural sense of shame. Complicating this view, however, Buenavista argues that institutional systems of oppression should be seen as a source of this phenomenon rather than relying solely on the use of deficit models that blame these instances on communities' own cultural values and beliefs.

As increased research has focused on the activism of Asian undocumented immigrant communities, this work has also detailed the emergence of community-based organizations across the nation leading efforts to advocate for members of this community. Empowering API, an organization led by Asian undocumented immigrant students and professionals and sponsored by the UCLA Labor Center and the Asian Pacific American Labor Alliance, created a Zine called *Did You Eat Yet?*, featuring stories, poems, and artwork by Asian undocumented immigrants. Moreover, organizations such as the National Korean American Service & Education Consortium (NAKASEC) continue to lead important advocacy and community-building work, including hosting nationwide calls for Asian undocumented immigrant youth to build connections with each other. In the appendix, we have included a list of some key organizations that work specifically with Asian undocumented immigrant communities today.

As discussed in the introduction, this edited volume has sought to showcase some of the latest research, theory, and advocacy work regarding undocumented immigrant communities across the United States. Given that research is often conducted in silos and is not always in conversation with the critical advocacy work that directly impacted activists and their allies are undertaking, *UndocuAsians* seeks to place academic research and community-based work led by undocumented professionals and students in conversation. Therefore, half of the chapters in this edited volume are testimonials by Asian undocumented and/or formerly individuals discussing their personal stories immigrating to the United States, navigating everyday life, making sense of their experiences and their identities, and pursuing their careers. These testimonials are written by academics, artists, filmmakers, an aspiring doctor, and a licensed therapist. These essays are then placed in conversation with the other half of the edited volume's chapters, which are research-based essays analyzing multifaceted aspects of Asian undocumented immigrant community experiences including the history of U.S. immigration policy, the racialization of Asian immigrant communities, and Asian undocumented individuals' daily lives. Many of the contributors who authored research chapters identify as Asian / Asian American and as first- or second-generation immigrants. This was a key choice on our part as editors given that we aimed to support writing about this topic that not only centered but also meaningfully engaged the lived experiences of directly impacted community members.

As this edited volume highlights testimonials by Asian undocumented individuals alongside some of the latest research about the lives of these community members, it is understandably not meant to be representative of the entire Asian undocumented immigrant community. We proactively recruited authors whose racial/ethnic backgrounds included Vietnamese, Thai, South Korean, Chinese, Filipino, and Punjabi. It is also important to note that the narratives of Asian undocumented community members in this edited volume, many of whom have earned graduate degrees and are pursuing careers in a variety of professional fields, represent a unique subset of the broader undocumented immigrant community. For instance, in his study of Mexican and Central American undocumented immigrant youths' lives in Southern California, sociologist Roberto G. Gonzales (2015) developed the framework of "early exiters" and "college-goers": "College-goers' ongoing presence in the academic world allowed and encouraged them to continue to dream and to plan bright futures. In contrast, early exiters had trouble looking past immediate needs of survival and making ends meet" (33). Greater examination of both Asian undocumented immigrant "college goers" and "early exiters" is indeed highly important and necessary. At the same time, as the chapters in *UndocuAsians* demonstrate, legal liminality can even become uniquely pronounced during the graduate education process and upon entry into the U.S. workforce.

Future research might explore some of the topics that have been covered in *UndocuAsians* in more depth such as intersecting identities of oppression and coalition building between undocumented immigrant groups from different racial and ethnic groups. Several authors in this book discuss the role of intersecting identities in relation to being both Asian and undocumented. Legal scholar Kimberlé Crenshaw, building on the work of generations of Black feminist scholars, theorized a legal approach to the concept of intersectionality as it specifically related to Black women being marginalized by white women and Black men, in both feminist and Black empowerment spaces (Crenshaw 1991). This concept of intersectionality can be explored further as it relates to other marginalized identities including Asian American experience and being LGBTQ+ and/or having a disability.

Such work might also explore in greater detail the role of racial and ethnic solidarity as part of coalition building efforts in support of rights for all undocumented community members. For example, research could examine the dynamics of Asian and Black undocumented immigrant communities who have been building coalitions, such as the efforts to develop partnerships between UPLIFT, an Asian undocumented led organization, and the UndocuBlack Network, a Black undocumented-led organization, which Siyue Lena Wang and Madison Villanueva explore in chapter 12. It could also be interesting for researchers to explore the role of coalition building across different Asian ethnicities. For instance, as shown in *UndocuAsians*, Asian undocumented immigrant communities consist of a broad range of histories (including histories of immigration to the United States), languages, cultures, and religions.

This edited volume sheds light on the particular experiences of Asian undocumented immigrant communities. As the fight for immigrant rights continues, the authors in this edited volume have outlined a series of potential ways to look forward, especially as more research is being developed and a new generation of undocumented immigrant youth leads the next wave of community-led activism. Instead of suggesting a particular set of policy recommendations to implement, *UndocuAsians* leaves readers with a focus on the humanity and strength of this community that is too often left out of dominant political discussions.

REFERENCES

Alcantar, Cynthia Maribel, Rachel E. Freeman, Victoria Kim, and Martha Ortega Mendoza. 2024. "(Un)Deserving Mexican Activists: How Online News Media During the Trump Era (Un)Justly Represents Undocumented Students in Higher Education Across Differing State Contexts." *Journal of Diversity in Higher Education* 17 (5): 692–705.

Bjorklund, Peter, Jr. 2018. "Undocumented Students in Higher Education: A Review of the Literature, 2001 to 2016." *Review of Educational Research* 88 (5): 631–670.

Buenavista, Tracy Lachica. 2012. "Citizenship at a Cost: Undocumented Asian Youth Perceptions and the Militarization of Immigration." *AAPI Nexus: Policy, Practice and Community* 10 (1): 101–124.

———. 2018. "Model (Undocumented) Minorities and 'Illegal' Immigrants: Centering Asian Americans and US Carcerality in Undocumented Student Discourse." *Race Ethnicity and Education* 21 (1): 78–91.

Chan, Beleza. 2010. "Not Just a Latino Issue: Undocumented Students in Higher Education." *Journal of College Admission* 206: 29–31.

Chavez, Leo. 2008. *The Latino Threat: Constructing Immigrants, Citizens, and the Nation.* Stanford University Press.

Crenshaw, Kimberlé. 1991. "Mapping the Margins: Intersectionality, Identity Politics, and Violence Against Women of Color." *Stanford Law Review* 43 (6): 1241–1299.

Escudero, Kevin. 2020. *Organizing While Undocumented: Immigrant Youth's Political Activism under the Law.* NYU Press.

Farrell-Bryan, Dylan, and Ian Peacock. 2022. "Who Gets Deported? Immigrant Removal Rates by National Origin and Period, 1998 to 2021." *Socius* 8. https://doi.org/10.1177/23780231221091224.

Golash-Boza, Tanya. 2018. "Raced and Gendered Logics of Immigration Law Enforcement in the United States." In *Race, Criminal Justice, and Migration Control: Enforcing the Boundaries of Belonging*, edited by Mary Bosworth, Alpa Parmar, and Yolanda Vázquez. Oxford University Press.

Gonzales, Roberto G. 2015. *Lives in Limbo: Undocumented and Coming of Age in America.* University of California Press.

Kim, Soo Mee, and Aggie J. Yellow Horse. 2018. "Undocumented Asians, Left in the Shadows." *Contexts* 17 (4): 70–71.

Van Hook, Jennifer, Julia Gelatt, and Ariel G. Ruiz Soto. 2023. "A Turning Point for the Unauthorized Immigrant Population in the United States." Migration Policy Institute, September. https://www.migrationpolicy.org/news/turning-point-us-unauthorized-immigrant-population.

APPENDIX

In this appendix, please find a list of some of the organizations that work with undocumented immigrant communities at large, as well as a list of those that work specifically with Asian undocumented immigrant communities.

National Organizations

Immigrants Rising
Informed Immigrant
National Immigration Law Center
Presidents' Alliance on Higher Education and Immigration
TheDream.US
UndocuBlack Network
UndocuProfessionals
United We Dream

Organizations with a Focus on Asian Undocumented Immigrant Communities

Asian Americans Advancing Justice (AAJC)
Empowering API
National Korean American Service and Education Consortium (NAKASEC)
Revolutionizing Asian American Immigrant Stories on the East Coast (RAISE)
UPLIFT

ACKNOWLEDGMENTS

Kevin and Rachel would like to begin by thanking all the contributors to the *UndocuAsians* edited volume: Cynthia Maribel Alcantar, Tracy Lachica Buenavista, Esther Yoona Cho, 'Inoke Hafoka, Set Hernandez, Ju Hong, Amandeep Kaur, Amritpal Kaur, Jaspreet Kaur, Pratishtha Khanna, Victoria Kim, Jessica Law, Zhelin Jeff Li, Sara P. Lopez Amezquita, Trisha Mazumder, Bo Thai, Rikka De Joya Venturanza, Madison Villanueva, Huyen "Kiki" Vo, and Siyue Lena Wang. Without your openness to writing about and sharing these stories, this project would not have been possible; we are truly indebted to the critical work that you all do each and every day for members of the Asian undocumented and broader immigrant community. We would also like to thank Dr. Daniela Pila, co-organizer of the "Liminally Legal Asians: Consciousness Raising, Political Activism, and (Re)Articulations of Belonging in the United States" Conference at Brown University, for all her efforts in bringing together the initial set of authors for this volume as part of a two-day convening in the fall of 2018. Thank you to Kris Cho, a Brown undergraduate alumna, who assisted with the initial copyediting of the chapters and Lauren Meraz, a recent Brown undergraduate alumna, who undertook the task of copyediting the complete volume. We would like to express our appreciation to Brown University's Swearer Center for Public Service, Department of American Studies, and Division of Research for funding this project.

We are very appreciative for our editor at Rutgers University Press, Carah Naseem, who has provided invaluable guidance in putting together this edited volume throughout each step of the process. It was also a pleasure working with Lisa Banning, the project's initial acquisition editor at the press. Thank you to the peer reviewers for their very helpful feedback on the chapters and manuscript overall.

Kevin would like to thank Dr. Zelideth María Rivas and Dr. Robert G. Lee for the generous advice they provided to him upon embarking on such a project. He is also grateful to Brown University's Department of American Studies for their encouragement in undertaking a project that is inspired by the work of undocuAsian activist and former department PhD student, Tam Ngoc Tran.

Rachel would like to thank the Population Studies and Training Center at Brown University, where she was a postdoctoral research associate. She would also like to thank her wife, Jess Freeman-Wong, for reading several of the chapters and providing helpful suggestions.

NOTES ON
CONTRIBUTORS

CYNTHIA MARIBEL ALCANTAR is the youngest daughter of Rosario and Javier Alcantar, both Mexican immigrants from Jalisco, Mexico. Her experiences growing up poor and in an underserved, predominantly Mexican immigrant community in the Inland Empire significantly shaped the way she views and experiences the world and led her to want to pursue college to create social change. These experiences coupled with her professional, doctoral, and research experiences in higher education informed her passion for serving multilingual immigrant students and families. Her research focuses on the social structures that impact the social mobility and integration of racial/ethnic minoritized and immigrant populations in the United States. Cynthia is currently an associate professor in the School of Education at Loyola Marymount University. She received her bachelor's degree from the University of California, Riverside, master's degree from Claremont Graduate University, and PhD from the University of California, Los Angeles.

TRACY LACHICA BUENAVISTA (she/her) is the daughter of immigrants from the Philippines and a mothering scholar. She works as a professor of Asian American studies and core faculty member of the Doctoral Program in Educational Leadership at California State University, Northridge (CSUN). At CSUN, Dr. Buenavista was the co–principal investigator and cofounder of the CSUN DREAM Center, Asian American Studies Pathways Project, Ethnic Studies Education Pathways Project, and the Faculty of Color Wellness Collective; and serves as a member of the Project Rebound Community Advisory Committee. In her research she utilizes critical race theory to examine how race, (im)migration, militarism, and carcerality shape the educational access, retention, and experiences of People of Color. She is coeditor of *"White" Washing American Education: The New Culture Wars in Ethnic Studies*, *Education at War: The Fight for Students of Color in America's Public Schools*, and *First-Generation Faculty of Color Narratives: Reflections on Research, Teaching, and Service*.

Growing up as a child of Korean immigrants in Los Angeles, **ESTHER YOONA CHO** witnessed the beauty and the pain of what it means to be an immigrant in the United States. Motivated to examine and address the inequalities within our vast and vibrant immigrant community, Esther completed a PhD in sociology at the University of California, Berkeley, where her research explored the ways in which the lived experiences of undocumented Asian and Latinx young adults are racialized in the United States. Her work has been published in various outlets including *Social Forces*, the *Asian American Law Journal*, and the *Russell Sage Foundation Journal of the Social Sciences*. This work would not have been possible without each individual who entrusted their story with her, and she will always be grateful. Currently, Esther is the research programs director of undergraduate research at Stanford University, where she endeavors to tackle systemic barriers that persist for historically excluded student communities.

KEVIN ESCUDERO is the son of a Vietnamese/Cambodian refugee mother and Bolivian immigrant father. He is also an associate professor of American studies and ethnic studies and affiliated faculty member in the Sociology Department and Population Studies and Training Center at Brown University. His research and teaching focus on comparative studies of race, ethnicity, and Indigeneity; U.S. imperialism and settler colonialism; immigration and citizenship; social movements; and law. His book *Organizing While Undocumented* examined Asian and Latinx undocumented immigrant youths' use of an intersectional movement identity to build coalitions with members of similarly situated groups. He is the director and principal investigator of the Immigrant Student Research Project Lab, which is in the process of fielding a national survey of immigrant graduate and professional degree students across legal statuses to better understand student experiences and develop policy recommendations to increase support for members of this student population. Previously, he served as Brown's special advisor to the provost for undocumented and DACAmented students and as a faculty fellow for the university's Undocumented, First-Generation, and Low-Income Student Center.

RACHEL FREEMAN-WONG is a scholar whose research analyzes the dynamics between student activists and higher education leaders, institutional change, and educational equity for immigrant and other marginalized students. Her community and professional work, research, and teaching have explored and advocated for educational equity for marginalized student populations including immigrant, undocumented, and LGBTQ students. Rachel's research has been recognized by the Ford Foundation and has been published in Harvard Education Press, the *Journal of Diversity in Higher Education*, the *Journal of College Student Development*, *Community College Review*, and the *Journal of College Access*. She has worked with many Asian communities: she supported Bhutanese communities' neighborhood organizing efforts for two years in Oakland, California; taught in two public high schools in Okinawa, Japan, for two years; and collaborated with numerous undocumented Asian and Latinx professionals and community organizers on advocacy projects for undocumented students. Rachel was formerly a postdoctoral research associate in population studies at Brown University and the director of programming for My Undocumented Life. She earned her PhD in education, with a specialty in race and ethnicity, from UCLA's School of Education, a master's degree in higher education administration from Harvard's Graduate School of Education, and a bachelor's degree in philosophy from the University of Chicago.

ʻINOKE HAFOKA is a child of immigrants who came from the islands of Tonga. Hafoka earned his doctorate degree in education, with a focus on race and ethnic studies from the University of California, Los Angeles. He has had opportunities to research, write, and publish together with his colleagues on the experiences of undocumented students. Currently, he is an assistant professor in Pacific studies at Brigham Young University–Hawaii, an institution that serves many students from Oceania and Asia and supports them in navigating their schooling within U.S. tertiary institutions.

SET HERNANDEZ is a filmmaker and community organizer whose roots come from Bicol, Philippines. As a queer, undocumented immigrant, their filmmaking dwells in the intersection of the poetic and the political. Their feature debut "unseen" received an Independent Spirit Award and was shortlisted for Best Feature at the IDA Documentary Awards. Set's past documentary work includes the short "COVER/AGE" and impact producing for "Call Her Ganda." An alumnus of the Disruptors Fellowship, Set is also developing both a TV comedy pilot and a feature-length screenplay. Since 2010, Set has been organizing around migrant justice issues, from deportation defense to health care access. They cofounded the Undocumented Filmmakers Collective, which promotes equity for undocumented immigrants in the film industry. Set's work has been supported by Firelight Media, Sundance Institute, NBCUniversal, and the Ford Foundation, among others. In their past life, Set was a published linguistics researcher, focusing on the area of bilingualism. Above all, Set is the fruit of their family's love and their community's generosity.

JU HONG is the director of the UCLA Dream Resource Center, an organization that empowers immigrant youth and allies to be at the forefront of social justice movements. In 2013, Ju challenged former President Obama on his administration's record number of deportations during a presidential speech at the Betty Ong Center in San Francisco, California. His courageous action appeared in national and international media. Ju often shares his immigrant story at conferences and universities to educate and inspire people to take action on immigration issues. The 2016 documentary *Halmoni* uplifts Ju's experience as an undocumented immigrant from South Korea and his bold advocacy in the pursuit of justice for immigrants. Ju currently serves as the board chair of the National Korean American Service & Education Consortium (NAKASEC), a nonprofit that organizes Korean and Asian Americans for social, economic, and racial justice. He is also a member of the Leadership Council of Immigrants Rising, an organization that transforms the lives of immigrants through education. Ju graduated from the University of California, Berkeley with a bachelor's degree in political science and from San Francisco State University with a master's degree in public administration.

AMANDEEP "AMAN" KAUR is a Punjabi Sikh actress and filmmaker from Los Angeles, California. She cofounded Brown Girl Joy (BGJ) Productions in 2018 with her two elder sisters. Through acting, Aman hopes to bring authentic South Asian representation to the big screen and inspire young Brown girls like herself to pursue careers in the film industry. BGJ Productions latest film, *Zindagi Dobara*, won the Tasveer Film Fund for Best LGBT Screenplay and premiered at film festivals like Outfest Fusion, Tasveer, BAFTA qualifying Cambridge Film Festival, Los Angeles Asian Pacific Film Festival, and many more. She received the Dream in Color Grant from Women Who Create in 2022. Aman completed her BA in Asian American studies and gender women studies with a minor in queer studies from California State University, Northridge in 2023 and received the Wong Sayaman Equality Award for her efforts to champion LGBTQIA+ South Asians. In 2025, Aman hopes to begin her journey to pursue a juris doctor degree.

AMRITPAL KAUR (AMRIT) is a queer Punjabi Sikh artist and educator whose work spans storytelling, immigration advocacy, and systems building. Rooted in California's Punjabi Sikh diaspora, they co-founded Brown Girl Joy Productions with their sisters, creating a collective home where queer, immigrant, and Sikh stories are not softened or simplified but told on their own terms. Through film, writing, teaching, and organizing, Amrit builds cultural work that disrupts tokenizing narratives and insists undocumented, queer, and diasporic lives set the blueprint for liberation. They hold a master of fine arts in social documentation from UC Santa Cruz, with concentrations in critical race and ethnic studies and feminist studies. Amrit is directing *Sacred Silhouettes*, a feature documentary tracing Punjabi Sikh migration and intergenerational memory. Currently, they teach as an adjunct lecturer in the University of California system and remain engaged in movement organizing. Their leadership has been recognized with the national 2025 SUCCESS Higher Education Leadership Award and over fifteen international film awards, including the Netflix-supported Tasveer Film Fund.

JASPREET KAUR is a queer Sikh filmmaker and community advocate who hails from Punjab, India. After witnessing the xenophobia following 9/11, she began using film as a transformative tool to challenge stereotypes and create community-led change. As one of the only undocumented Sikhs at Harvard

College, she studied human perseverance and oral storytelling through folk-lore and theater. She wrote feature film and TV screenplays during her A24 x Made in Her Image mentorship and Artist Disruptors Fellowship. In 2024, without access to federal aid, she fundraised to graduate debt free with an MFA in screenwriting from the University of Southern California. She is the first ever screenwriting Paul and Daisy Soros fellow and an NBCUniversal Point Foundation scholar. Through her company, Brown Girl Joy Productions, she is committed to creating innovative and inclusive mentorship and production practices to ensure filmmaking is a ccessible and sustainable for underrepresented communities. She is an adjunct lecturer in the Los Angeles Community College District and a writer on the Netflix and Warner Bros television drama, *Unaccustomed Earth*.

PRATISHTHA KHANNA is currently a fourth-year medical student. Born in New Delhi, India, she grew up in Howard County, Maryland. In 2010, she became involved in grassroots organizing by participating in sit-ins and protests to advocate for undocumented youth. Hailing from the largest southeast Asian subcontinent, she was at odds with stereotypes, expectations of excelling academically without a fair opportunity to attain higher education due to her undocumented status. In 2014, she voiced the plight of high-skilled, undocumented labor and the tremendous loss of potential such as the case of her father and many others like him to then–U.S. Secretary of Labor Tom Perez. Through the years, she continued her ultimate protest against the broken immigration system: attaining higher education. In 2014, she graduated with a bachelor of arts in biology from the University of Maryland, Baltimore County and in 2020 a master of science in biomedical sciences from Western University of Health Sciences.

VICTORIA KIM is a child of immigrants who came from South Korea. Growing up, she had intermittent moves between South Korea and the United States, experiencing both the United States' and South Korea's K–12 education systems. Her upbringings and educational experiences have led her to be interested in understanding racially/ethnically minoritized student populations, particularly Asian American student experiences, and institutions that serve them, including Asian American and Native American Pacific Islander–serving institutions. Victoria earned her doctorate degree in social sciences and comparative education with a specialization in race/ethnic studies from the University of California, Los Angeles. Currently, she is an assistant professor of higher education in the Department of Educational Leadership and Policy Studies at the University of Texas at San Antonio.

JESSICA LAW is a PhD candidate in the Department of Sociology at the University of California, Berkeley. As the daughter of Hong Kong immigrants, she is committed to building global solidarity and working toward liberation. In her time as an organizer, she has worked on campaigns for ethnic studies, economic justice, and police abolition. She now spends time building worker power as a steward in her union. Her academic research is derived from an interest in coalitional politics that grew out of these experiences. She broadly studies issues related to racial formation, the state, identity politics, and social movements. Her dissertation project explores the development, use, and political consequences of the "racial equity" framework in municipal government. She holds a master's degree in sociology from UC Berkeley and a bachelor's degree in sociology and race studies from the University of Chicago.

ZHELIN JEFF LI was born in China and came to the United States with his mother in 2003 at the age of fourteen. Dr. Li holds a PhD in genetics and bioinformatics from University of California, Riverside, and an MBA from Johns Hopkins University. He has published peer-reviewed research articles and book chapters in the field of RNA biology and rare genetic disease/gene therapy. His tenure in the biotech industry has included positions at Illumina and Benchling, most recently as cell gene therapy business development manager at Thermo Fisher Scientific. Dr. Li has been advocating for the Deferred Action for Childhood Arrivals program in higher education since 2014, speaking at conferences such as the American Association for the Advancement of Science annual meetings while bringing more awareness to the undocumented graduate community.

SARA P. LOPEZ AMEZQUITA (Ella, her, hers) is associate professor of English at Queens College, City University of New York (CUNY). Through ethnography-based investigation and community engagement, her research looks to how immigrant and racialized youth negotiate and transform writing practices, languages, and national borders. Sara is also co–principal investigator with CUNY's first of its kind Initiative on Immigration and Education (CUNY-IIE). Sara's works have appeared in *Literacy in Composition Studies* and *Journal of Adolescent & Adult Literacy*, among other journals and peer-refereed edited collections.

TRISHA MAZUMDER is an educator committed to empowering students and fostering inclusive learning environments. Her advocacy within South Asian communities has deepened her belief in the importance of creating spaces where every student can thrive academically and grow personally. Guided by a vision of equitable opportunity and collective empowerment, she continues to champion inclusive education and community building. Trisha earned both undergraduate and graduate degrees from UCLA, making her a Double Bruin.

BO THAI is an undocumented artist/entrepreneur/educator from Thailand. He graduated from the University of California, Irvine with an international studies degree and is passionate about community building and art. Bo currently owns a clothing line that blends advocacy and fashion called Illegal Drip. He is also a tutor at Dynasty's United, tutoring kids in marginalized neighborhoods. In the past, Bo was heavily involved with immigration advocacy fighting for rights for himself and others. Without DACA, Bo pursued entrepreneurship and contract work to make ends work and now is doing workshops with different colleges to teach other undocumented students ways to navigate life without a work permit. Occasionally, he organizes shows and marketplaces for People of Color and immigrants. He also loves nature, hiking, fitness, and different forms of art. He is currently based in Los Angeles.

RIKKA DE JOYA VENTURANZA is a mother scholar and proud daughter of Filipino immigrants. Her lived experiences within a mixed-status family have profoundly shaped her understanding of race, identity, and belonging. Alongside friends, colleagues, and students impacted by U.S. immigration policy, these relationships have also provided a critical perspective on how race differentiates experiences of illegality across communities of color throughout the educational pipeline. With her expertise in developing equity programs and teaching ethnic studies courses at Asian American, Native American, and Pacific Islander–serving institutions in California, Rikka has engaged in culturally responsive pedagogy and intersectional action research while publishing scholarship that seeks to advance equity agendas in serving immigrant-origin college student populations. Currently, Rikka teaches Asian American centered courses at The City College of New York. She earned her PhD in education at UCLA's School of Education, specializing in race, ethnic, and cultural studies within the Division of Social Sciences and Comparative Education. She received her MS in education and BA in communications at California State University, Fullerton, and her associate's degree in liberal arts at Cypress College.

MADISON VILLANUEVA was born in the Philippines and immigrated to California at the age of seven. Growing up undocumented in Los Angeles's San Fernando Valley fueled her dedication to improving the lives of low-income immigrant communities of color. While seeking resources, Madison found the undocumented youth movement and joined to create impact that would allow for her and her community to thrive. As one of the leaders of UPLIFT (an undocumented Asian and Pacific Islander [undocuAPI] youth-led organization based in Los Angeles), she advocated for immigrants on the local, state, and national levels while building a network of undocuAPI changemakers. Madison received her BA in Asian American studies from the University of California, Santa Barbara. She continued championing undocumented students by promoting educational equity, eventually helping to establish the Undocumented Student Services department on campus. She brought this experience to California

State University, Northridge as the DREAM Center supervisor, where she served over a thousand undocumented students during her three-year tenure.

HUYEN "KIKI" VO, LCSW, is a licensed therapist, burn survivor, and DACA recipient based in the Bay Area, California. Born in Vietnam, she was brought to the United States at the age of ten for medical treatment for her burn trauma. She became the eldest sister among four siblings to attend college. Huyen received her bachelor's degree in social welfare from the University of California, Berkeley and her master's in social work with a concentration in community mental health from California State University, East Bay. Growing up as an undocumented Vietnamese immigrant, she carried the weight of mental health challenges along with systemic barriers that often felt invisible to others. These early lived experiences fuel her passion to create radical spaces where individuals are honored, seen, and valued in their wholeness. She is the founder of her private practice, VOice Psychotherapy, where she provides culturally responsive and anti-oppressive therapy and consultation services to BIPOC clients and mission-driven organizations. In the pursuit of contributing to the healing and empowerment of her community, she serves as a wellness support group facilitator for two Bay Area nonprofit organizations: Immigrants Rising and the Legalization Project. She finds ease and healing in dancing, cooking, working out, and being outdoors.

SIYUE LENA WANG is a first-generation immigrant from Northeastern China whose transformative journey—from migrant worker to educator and scholar-activist—fuels her commitment to uplifting the often-overlooked challenges and joys of immigrant communities. Her coming of age in the underserved Asian and Latino communities of the San Gabriel Valley, alongside her experiences navigating legal limbo, shaped her firsthand understanding and critical insights on race, immigration, and belonging. Recognizing the unique struggles of undocumented Chinese immigrants—many of whom are asylum seekers—Lena has committed her life to amplifying these overlooked narratives and channeling her creative energy into advocacy, action, and solutions that directly improve the livelihoods of immigrant communities. As a nontraditional student, English learner, systemically vulnerable immigrant, and beneficiary of higher education, she is dedicated to mentoring community college students through the Center for Community College Partnerships and empowering undocumented youth through her leadership in Improving Dreams, Equality, Access, and Success (IDEAS) at UCLA. Through IDEAS, Lena found UPLIFT—an undocumented Asian American and Pacific Islander (undocuAPI) youth organization based in Los Angeles—and, most importantly, a chosen family. Since joining UPLIFT in 2019, she has been actively involved in increasing the visibility of undocuAPI narratives through collaboration and conference presentations. Bridging scholarship and community advocacy, Lena's dissertation examines how racialization and illegality shape the educational aspirations of young undocumented adults. She has led community-centered research on undocumented Asian women's reproductive health and language access, facilitated prison education programs for incarcerated students, and investigated college affordability for undocumented and first-generation, low-income transfer students. To translate research into tangible action, she collaborates with Immigrants Rising and UPLIFT to develop practitioner training resources that foster greater inclusivity for undocuAPI students in higher education. Lena is a PhD candidate at UCLA's School of Education and Information Studies. She holds a master's in education and a bachelor's in linguistics and psychology with a minor in labor studies, both from UCLA.

INDEX